ONE BUGLE NO DRUMS

"No other operation in the American book of war quite compares with this show by the 1st Marine Division."
    S.L.A. Marshall, Army Historian

"Every now and then, the American public needs a reminder that no matter how difficult and trying situations can be, there are Americans who can cope and even be victorious with style."
    The Atlanta Constitution

"Comes alive with vivid action and astute political and leadership observations."
    Robin Moore, author of
    The Green Berets and
    The French Connection

"Exciting and authoritative...an important contribution to the history of the Korean conflict...Ought to be read by anyone who is a serious military historian or who just takes pride in the achievements of our armed forces."
    Charles Robb, ex-Marine
    and former governor of Virginia

ONE BUGLE NO DRUMS

THE MARINES AT CHOSIN RESERVOIR

WILLIAM B. HOPKINS

AVON BOOKS  NEW YORK

Dedicated to Ginny

The author gratefully acknowledges permission to quote from "John Brown's Body" by Stephen Vincent Benét, contained in *Selected Works of Stephen Vincent Benét*, Holt, Rinehart and Winston, Inc., © renewed 1955, 1956 by Rosemary Carr Benét. Reprinted by permission of Brandt and Brandt Literary Agents, Inc.
Unless otherwise indicated, all photos of Marines in combat are used through the courtesy of the U.S. Department of Defense.

AVON BOOKS
A division of
The Hearst Corporation
105 Madison Avenue
New York, New York 10016

Copyright © 1986 by William B. Hopkins
Front cover photograph: AP/Wide World Photos
Published by arrangement with Algonquin Books of Chapel Hill
Library of Congress Catalog Card Number: 86-3490
ISBN: 0-380-70455-2

First Avon Books Printing: June 1988

AVON TRADEMARK REG. U.S. PAT. OFF. AND IN OTHER COUNTRIES MARCA REGISTRADA, HECHO EN CANADA.

Printed in Canada

UNV 10 9 8 7 6 5 4 3

Contents

List of Maps
and Photographs

MAPS

PHOTOGRAPHS

Marines drawing supplies before move south from Yudam-ni

Outpost at Koto-ri
Air drop of supplies
Captured prisoners
Marines inspect Chinese dead
Marine dead being loaded onto truck
Return of Marine sniper patrol
At northern end of blown-out bridge
Chinese prisoners captured near bridge
Moving column nears blown-out bridge
Army 92nd Armored Field Artillery Battalion supporting
   attack
Marines walk to safety after bridge repair,
   alongside Hill 1081
Marines pause for rest on move south
Dead Marines strapped on hoods of jeeps
Supplies awaiting shipment south
Destruction of remaining supplies before evacuation of
   Hungnam

Preface

December 10, 1950, was a very sad day. Yet as I stood on the mountainside and watched the men of the 1st Marine Division move downhill to safety after being surrounded by Chinese Communist soldiers for the better part of two weeks, it was a day of relief. The Chosin Reservoir Campaign was over. Many years have passed since then, and in the minds of the American public it is all but forgotten. But what I saw there is no less vivid to me today than the actual event was. And when I reflect on what happened, my emotions are substantially the same.

Later in the 1950s, I visited my regimental commander, Lieutenant General Lewis K. "Chesty" Puller, by then retired. He insisted that the 1st Marine Division at the frozen Chosin Reservoir was the finest fighting force ever. This view from America's most decorated soldier had support from S. L. A. Marshall, noted United States Army historian who, in an in-depth study of that campaign said, "No other operation in the American book of war quite compares with this show by the 1st Marine Division in the perfection of factual concepts precisely executed, in accuracy of estimate of situation by leadership at all levels and in promptness of utilization of all supporting forces."

Outside the U.S. Marine Corps few will know why one of our nation's finest military historians would proclaim the 1st Marine Division's performance in northeast Korea as probably the greatest ever. Under the harshest conditions ever encountered by American troops—any place, any time—Marines faced an enemy force of twelve Chinese Communist divisions, or approximately 100,000 men, twice the size of the British Army at its peak strength during the American Revolutionary War. They inflicted greater casualties on the enemy than did the Continental Army in its eight-year fight for our independence. Why such a difference? America's superior technical know-how was placed in the hands of properly trained, disciplined soldiers. These soldiers were made to appreciate the dignity of the civilian population, the most important factor in a limited war.

The poorly equipped Chinese Army relied primarily on World War I–vintage arms, but time-honored fighting methods. Its ill-provided soldiers routed our U.S. 8th Army, which enjoyed superior firepower and was far better supplied. The victory marked a changing tide in the political affairs in Asia. Communist China emerged as the major military power among Asian states.

The Chosin Reservoir Campaign stands out as a model military action. In contrast with the performance of the 8th Army, the 1st Marine Division successfully fended off an enemy force many times its size. The reasons for its success were not fully examined by our nation's leaders at the time; neither was the defeat of the 8th Army. Today, thirty-six years later, this story of success and failure is still not comprehended by the great majority of literate Americans. To understand better the art and science of modern war and its inseparable relationship to the political structure, our political and military leaders should address themselves to the unfinished business of Korea.

During most of the campaign, the Marines fought an orderly retreat from the mountains of north-central Korea to the sea. I witnessed the fighting from the vantage point of Company Commander, H&S Company, 1st Battalion, 1st Marines—which we called, "the 1st of the 1st of the 1st." From our division commander, Major General O. P. Smith, down through the ranks, leadership excelled at every level. But the solution to coping with the Chinese mass can be found in the often-times overlooked fighting man's performance.

Historians write about wars, battles, and generals who lead.

In a ground war, most of the fighting is done at the company level and below, by privates, corporals, sergeants, lieutenants, and captains. When an officer is promoted to major, he becomes less the fighter and more the executive. The general in charge is the chief executive officer—the chief decision maker. He may once have been a fighter—or he may not have been. Historians refer to generals as fighters, while with the passage of time the real fighters become mere statistics in the history books. Nonetheless, it is the strength and character of these "statistics" that shoulder the heaviest burden for success in battle.

The fighting men of the 1st Marine Division were almost evenly divided between Regulars and Reserves, the Reserves coming from 124 selected cities across the nation—Roanoke, Virginia, being one. As the commanding officer of the Roanoke Unit, I had supervised its training prior to its dispersion from the West Coast to Korea.

This story is one of fact. There are no fictional events. All persons are real, although the names of some minor characters have been omitted. The dialogue is based on fact.

Acknowledgments

I wish to thank my friend the late Perry F. Kendig, a former president of Roanoke College, who encouraged me to write this book. In the early stages he helped me develop a style of writing. He warned, nobody will read a book that reads like it was written by a lawyer.

I thank those who read one or more revisions of my manuscript and gave critical comments, namely: Harold Sugg, Robert Fishburn, Cy Bunting, Bill Bagbey, and Cecil Edmunds. Cecil was also instrumental in selecting the book's title.

Thanks are due Frank Kerr, the founder and first president of *The Chosin Few*, for his help in securing the many pictures displayed in this book.

Special thanks are due Gen. Robert H. Barrow, USMC (Ret.), who graciously allowed me to use his unpublished version of the Battle of the Big Hill, and who, together with Col. Wesley Noren, USMC (Ret.), Lt. Col. Don Jones, USMC (Ret.), and Major James C. Adair, USMC (Ret.), contributed to the narrative. Col. David W. Bridges, USMC, now deceased, was also a major contributor.

I wish to thank the personnel at the History Division, Headquarters, Marine Corps; General Douglas A. MacArthur Memorial Archives; Center of Military History, U.S. Army; George C. Marshall Memorial Library; Institute of Military History, U.S. Army; and History Division, Bolling Air Force Base. All were very courteous and most helpful.

I wish to thank Professor Harold Hill, head of Chinese Studies, Washington and Lee University, for his assistance in translating the *Great Resist America and Aid Korea Movement*, composed by the People's Republic Congress, which was checked out of the Asian Division of the Library of Congress. However, the contents of this book proved to be disappointing in that the book seemed to be a compilation of Communist China propaganda broadcasts, most of which could be found in the *Foreign Broadcast Information Service Daily Reports*.

Thanks are due Steven Rhodes, who assisted in revising my original manuscript; Virginia Ann Fowler and Sarah Christensen Cox, for their assistance in the preparation and typing of my first rough draft; and Belle Wyatt.

Special thanks are due Janet Holt Johnstone, my editor.

1

Return to War

The powdery falling snow was the driest I had ever seen, the temperature of five degrees below zero Fahrenheit made almost unbearable by icy winds. At 0500 on December 8, 1950, it was dark, very dark, in the Chosin Reservoir country of North Korea. Snow usually brightens the landscape, even at night, but there was no light here to reflect against its white surface. Even so the piercing, bone-chilling cold failed to prevent us from moving up the mountainside. The 1st Battalion, 1st Marines, walked and climbed in silence. Snow muffled the sound of footsteps. Occasionally a cough or a man's fall broke the quiet, but not often.

Three miles ahead, the 178th Regiment of the Chinese People's Liberation Army (PLA) occupied the high ground immediately south of a blown-out bridge that had spanned a 1,000-foot-deep chasm on the only road that could provide an escape for the entrapped 1st Marine Division and its attachments. For two weeks, twelve enemy divisions had surrounded Marine and Army forces. Four days earlier, the Communist Radio at Peking announced that annihilation of these United Nations soldiers was a mere matter of time—an accurate assessment unless the blown-out bridge span could be replaced.

Unfortunately for the Marines and the other American units, the span over the deep chasm could not be rebuilt as long as Chinese machine guns were kept trained on the approaches to the bridge site. Our mission was to clear the Chinese from the high ground, even though there were more of them than us, so that the span might be rebuilt and the escape effected. In snow, darkness, bitter cold, and against adverse odds, each Marine trudged forward, in full knowledge that a massive blood bath lay ahead.

Fewer than four months ago I had been a civilian, a 28-year-old World War II veteran with a wife and newly born daughter, halfway across the world from this mountain road with its subzero weather and pitch-black darkness, practicing law in the city of Roanoke, Virginia. On August 18, 1950, the officers and men of the 16th Marine Reserve Engineer Company had boarded a westbound train at the Norfolk and Western Station in downtown Roanoke and set off for active duty at Camp Pendleton, California. Swiftly its personnel had been incorporated into various Marine units and most of them sent to Korea.

I had arrived in Korea too late for the Inchon landing, but as commanding officer of Headquarters and Service Company, 1st Battalion, 1st Marine Division, I was part of the 10th Corps expedition sent up the east coast of the Korean peninsula north of the 38th Parallel to Wonsan, and then into the mountains toward the Yalu River. Now, encircled by the Chinese Communist divisions that had come pouring down from Manchuria after United Nations commander Douglas MacArthur had ignored the threat of intervention, the 1st Marines faced the fight of their lives if they were to extricate themselves and make it back to safety.

The history of my own involvement in the Korean War began in 1940, when I enlisted in the U.S. Marine Platoon Leaders Class. I was a student at Washington and Lee University at the time. In April 1942, my senior year, I was called to active duty, and saw combat in the South Pacific before returning to the States in the summer of 1944. After the war I was honorably discharged as a captain in the inactive Marine Reserves.

I had been raised in Franklin County, Virginia. My father was a circuit judge, serving Franklin and Bedford counties. Until I was 12 years old, we lived in Rocky Mount, the county seat; then we moved to a farm six miles out of town. At an early age

I decided to become a lawyer. So, after receiving my discharge from the Marine Corps in 1946, I entered the University of Virginia Law School at Charlottesville, Virginia. The law is a jealous mistress, and law school even more so. Although I read the daily newspapers, I gave little thought to what our country was doing, either right or wrong, in the field of foreign affairs.

During my stay in Charlottesville, I had met Ginny George, a recent graduate of Hollins College, near Roanoke. We became engaged. It had taken only a brief discussion for us to decide that Roanoke was the place where we wanted to live and practice law. So in January 1948, I hung out my shingle in Roanoke, sharing office space with two older lawyers. Office expenses were paid by searching titles for them. Although spending money was hard to come by, Ginny and I decided to get married in June. Afterwards we rented a three-room apartment about two miles from my office. Neither of us owned an automobile, and on most occasions I walked to and from work to save the 20 cents bus fare.

In late November 1948, Colonel Luther Brown, USMC, called at my office. He offered me the command of the 16th Marine Reserve Engineer Company of Roanoke beginning January 1, 1949. At first I refused, saying I knew little about engineering, for I had been an infantry officer during World War II.

"Much of the training is on infantry and weapons subjects," he persisted. I continued to resist.

"You're paid a full day's pay for each two-hour drill, plus a quarterly supplement as company commander," he continued.

"Now you've placed the right bait on the hook," I replied. Soon I was shaking his hand in token of agreement.

I joined the Marine Corps Reserves primarily because I needed the extra money—but having done so I was determined to do the best I could with the company. Initially, after I took command, many members resigned because of the strict discipline demanded. I liked living in a democratic society, but in a military unit there was no place for democracy—fairness, yes; democracy, no. Those who stayed on had pride in the unit.

By the fall of 1949 the company had again reached full strength, where it would remain. Our training classes and attendance at drill were taken quite seriously by the membership, even though no one believed that we would be called to active duty in the foreseeable future. We were totally unaware of how our nation's leaders were dealing with the problem of a little-known country called Korea.

In May 1950 my company received orders to attend two weeks' summer camp at Little Creek, Virginia. Everyone was especially pleased that we would receive training in the Marine Corps' specialty, amphibious warfare. We left Roanoke early in the morning on June 24. When we arrived at Little Creek in midafternoon, the men were told that an inspection of quarters would be held at 0500. Everyone who passed inspection could go on liberty immediately thereafter. By 0500 the bunks, lockers, rifles, and equipment were in tip-top shape.

Sunday, June 25, was a bright, sunny day at Little Creek. After breakfast most officers deserted the barracks to spend the day at Virginia Beach. I read the Sunday newspaper, wrote a long letter to Ginny, and then went swimming in the Officers' Club pool in the afternoon.

That evening I ate dinner alone at the Officers' Club. While sipping a drink, I watched the 6 o'clock news on the brand-new medium of television—still two years away for Roanoke. The announcer reported: "North Korean forces invaded Republic of Korea territory at several points this morning. It would appear from the nature of the attack and the manner in which it was launched that it constitutes an all-out offensive against the Republic of Korea. The United Nations Security Council met this morning at Lake Placid, New York, and is still in progress." What could this mean? No one knew; Korea was a long way off.

At Little Creek we spent two days on the rifle range, then concentrated on amphibious warfare. The noncoms, mostly World War II vets, joked about the attitude of recruits going aboard ship. "I never thought they carried men across the ocean cooped up like this," many said. The consistent front-page war headlines, however, caused our training to take on added significance.

The company officers celebrated the last night of summer encampment by dining at the Officers' Club. We were chatting when it was announced I had a long-distance phone call. Upon my return, I announced laughingly: "This you won't believe! That call came from Roanoke. A mother wanted to know if we were coming back tomorrow. She said there was a rumor back home that we were staying at Little Creek, maybe going to Korea!" All around the table broke out laughing at what we thought to be such a far-fetched idea.

Back in Roanoke, things settled back into routine. Yet there was uneasiness as the North Korean army drove deeply into South Korea, and American forces stationed in Japan joined the fray. On Monday, July 22, I came home early from work at my law office, took a shower, had a bite to eat, put on my uniform, and then drove hurriedly to the Marine Armory on Naval Reserve Avenue. When I reported for duty at 7 P.M., Captain James Einum, the inspector-instructor for the Roanoke Marines, met me at the door. "Bill, you've just received a telegram from the Commandant of the Marine Corps." He smiled as he handed it to me.

Our company was ordered to active duty on August 10. We would travel by train to Camp Pendleton, Oceanside, California. At about this time Ginny would be going to the hospital; we expected our first child between August 5 and 10.

Having served in World War II, I knew what the telegram meant. Oceanside, California, was the jumping-off place to the Pacific. I read the message to Captain Ford Carmack, the company executive officer, Captain Leon Garber, the training officer, and First Lieutenant James Bear, platoon leader of the 1st Platoon, who were right behind me, then to the other officers as they arrived for duty that evening. All the officers had served with Marine units in the Pacific during World War II, and each showed deep concern.

I announced we would go ahead with drill and classes as usual. The telegram would not be read to the troops until everyone was ready to leave. After drill the company assembled in the auditorium. Jim Einum and the members of his staff were present. At 9:30, Ford Carmack reported that the men were waiting. Ford called them to attention when I appeared. I read the telegram:

"The 16th Marine Engineer Company is hereby called to active duty on the 10th day of August, 1950. Captain William B. Hopkins, Commanding Officer, with all the men of the 16th Marine Engineer Company, will forthwith report to duty at the Marine Barracks, Camp Pendleton, Oceanside, California."

The words were no sooner out of my mouth than the men cheered, jumped up and down, beat their rifle butts into the floor, and threw their hats into the air. I thought to myself, What a damn bunch of fools! Great fools, but fools nonetheless.

Their reaction buoyed my spirits for the moment. After the company had been dismissed, everyone left for home; usually some of them stayed to chat or to gather at the beer joint down the street. I headed home to Ginny.

The war news continued bad from day to day. After the July 29 drill, I received another telegram from the Commandant, modifying the original order. Now the company would activate for duty on August 18, leave Roanoke on the 20th, and arrive at Camp Pendleton on the 24th. I welcomed this news, because Ginny would have been discharged from the hospital before we left for California.

There were numerous applications for discharges or deferments, but for each man discharged or deferred, a Marine veteran enlisted in his place. Physical examinations had to be given for each new enlistment. If a man had been honorably discharged as a platoon sergeant, and had a clean police record in the interim, he could re-enlist in the company at the same rank, provided that a vacancy existed. If there were none, he could accept a lower rank. The top NCO positions were quickly filled.

One World War II ex–platoon sergeant, from the adjoining County of Craig, when told that the highest rank available was corporal, decided to enlist anyhow. I told him I regretted that corporal was the best the company could do, and reminded him we might be getting orders for Korea soon after our arrival in California.

"That's fine with me if we go," he replied. "That's what I came here for. There ain't a damn thing over there as bad as living on a farm with a bitchy wife in Craig County!"

I took Ginny to the hospital on August 4. Our first child, a little girl, came on the morning of the 5th. We named her Catherine Dabney Hopkins, after my mother. Ginny's good old-fashioned doctor insisted she stay in the hospital for a full ten days. August 15, three days before our call to active duty, Ginny and Catherine Dabney left the hospital.

The last week was very busy with concerned parents, wives, or friends calling at my law office to discuss deferments. Some were justified, some not. In some instances we were able to do something about them, but in most we could not. Also, I had to close out my law office, after two and a half years of practice. I had obligations to my clients. In addition to being busy, I was worried about Ginny. Her parents were both dead, so my greatest problem was finding a place for her and the baby to stay. We decided on Rocky Mount, Virginia, where her sister, Nannie Saunders, lived. I lay awake every night, thinking about how I would say goodbye.

When the Sunday morning came, I arose early, had breakfast, and then went into the bathroom to wash up. Ginny followed close by. I kissed her goodbye, and closed my bag. Just as I did, she spotted one of her guest towels. "Don't you dare take that guest towel with you! You don't need it where you're going!" she exclaimed without shedding a tear. I gave her back the towel, got into my car, and drove to Roanoke.

The troops, except for one officer, Captain Bernard Schutt, assembled in front of the Marine Armory at 9 A.M. Schutt had received special orders which allowed him to drive his car to California. At roll call, two men were missing. Later we learned that one had been seriously injured in an automobile accident en route to the armory. The other had shot himself through the foot, and was admitted to a local hospital. The skies were overcast when we took our report. After roll call, the men loaded equipment on trucks to take the train.

At 10 A.M., we began our two-mile march. One block from the Marine Armory, Naval Reserve Avenue runs into Jefferson Street, a main thoroughfare. The skies were still overcast. There were no bugles, drums, or music of any kind as we marched in silence down Jefferson Street. Gunnery Sergeant Paul Gibson, the type of Marine seen on recruit posters, and First Lieutenant Roy Kinsey, an excellent drill instructor, counted cadence when someone appeared out of step. A sprinkling of people gathered on either side. No one cheered, no one waved. Two-thirds of the way down Jefferson Street, at St. John's Episcopal Church, a crowd of Sunday churchgoers watched in silence as we passed.

The silence was broken three blocks from the Norfolk and Western Station. Kurt Fleming, a dapper, good-looking Roanoke College summer school student, stood in front of The Sportsman, a news and cigar store. An inactive Naval Reservist himself and a friend of some in the unit, Kurt shouted, "Have fun in Korea, fellows! Have fun! Don't worry about your women—I'll take care of them while you're gone!"

A few smiled, but gave no answer as we marched by at attention. When the column cleared The Sportsman, Kurt repeated, "Remember, don't worry about your women! I'll take care of them. Those I can't take care of myself, I have friends who can. Don't worry about your women while you're gone!"

At the station, a large crowd of relatives, friends, well-wishers, and others had gathered. My younger brother and father had come to see me off. R. H. Smith, president of the N&W, was in the crowd. The overcast skies cleared while we exchanged pleasantries.

An old-time *Roanoke Times* reporter planted himself nearby. His story in the morning paper had read: "No flags will wave and no bands will play this morning as the Marine Reserves of Roanoke, its rank of rookies strengthened by veterans of Guadalcanal and Iwo Jima, leave for active duty." The reporter had his photographer take a picture of my father and me shaking hands. The caption in the next day's paper read, "Goodbye, and good luck, son!"

Many NCOs and officers, with their wives and children,

formed a line to introduce family members, or just to shake hands before the train left. Corporal Paul Martin said proudly, "Cap'n, take a look at my baby boy; he's six weeks old tomorrow!"

"He looks like he's going to make a good football player like you, Paul!" I replied.

"I hope so," he smiled, as he passed with his pretty wife beside him.

"Good luck," she said in a soft voice.

By 11 o'clock it had turned into a bright day, with everyone looking happy, until the train actually began to move out of the station. Then many of the wives, mothers, and relatives broke into tears. The troops aboard were affected by the crowd showing such concern, although most of them felt we were going off on a lark.

The train headed for East St. Louis, Illinois, our first destination on the trip west. The men showed excitement; some had never taken a trip this far away from home, and had never had Pullman accommodations anywhere. Many of the older ones, primarily sergeants and officers, were not so carefree. They sat in their seats and meditated. The officers were berthed in the front car; James Bear, an ex–football star at the University of Virginia, was assigned to the duties of mess officer and chief contact, with Gunnery Sergeant Paul Gibson the NCO in charge of troops.

On the third day of the trip we reached San Antonio, Texas. The conductor announced we would have a 30-minute layover. All men were ordered to take exercise beside the train. It did not take long for someone to discover a whiskey store across the street from the station. First a sergeant or two bought a bottle. Then someone found ice available nearby. Soft drinks were purchased for chasers. The runs on the liquor store gathered momentum.

As we left San Antonio, Jim Bear warned, "Captain, this train is loaded with whiskey. Frankly, I think it's dangerous for these men to have all this booze. There's enough on board to float this thing to California. You know it's against orders to have whiskey aboard a troop train."

"Yes, but I never rode one any distance that the noncoms didn't sneak a drink or two. We won't spoil the fun—we'll control it."

"I'm glad you're in command, not me," he said dubiously.

Each car had a sergeant in charge. "Call the sergeants into this car," I ordered.

"I know there's whiskey aboard this train," I told them, "and this is against orders on a troop train. Now, I'm no prude, and I don't object to drinking in moderation. But I'm holding each of you responsible in the event anybody gets out of line. Understand?"

"Yes, sir!" the group answered in unison.

"Do you contemplate any problem?"

"No, sir, Cap'n, we can handle any problem."

Each sergeant returned thereupon to his car and opened his bottle. In many instances he was the first one of his group to drink too much.

At 5 o'clock in the afternoon, we reached a small town. It was South Texas hot; the men were ordered outside for close order drill on an asphalt apron alongside the train. I never saw orders more botched up, or men look so sloppy. A sergeant would call out, "To the rear march! To the rear march!" and the men would bump into each other coming and going, giggling the whole time. The drill embarrassed me to the point that I ordered everybody back into the train. A number of bystanders wanted to know what was going on. I thought to myself, these men look like recruits, certainly not like seasoned Marine Regulars and Reserves.

Later that evening I was called to the dining car to investigate a report that our men were misbehaving. By that time only the officers had not yet been fed, and I assured the indignant dining car steward that the officers were sober and would give him no trouble.

On the way back to our car I heard a piercing scream coming from farther back in the train. A moment later someone yelled, "Cap'n! Cap'n Hopkins, come fast!" I found a pair of sergeants struggling with a bleeding buck sergeant. He had been beating his fists against the walls, and had run his right fist through the window of the car's back door. His arm had gone com-

pletely through the window, but somehow remained un
scratched to the elbow. But there, about an inch from the elbow
joint, the glass cut deeply, piercing an artery. His was the first
blood I'd ever seen hit the ceiling.

Realizing what he had done, he began yelling. Edsel Via and
Jim Carper, both salty World War II veterans, had thrown him
down and were applying a tourniquet when I arrived. During
the process, he passed out cold. When we pulled into Sander-
son, Texas, his pulse was weak.

We were told there was only one doctor in town. We found a
cardboard clock-notice posted on his door that announced he
was out on a call. The hands of the clock indicated he would
not return for an hour and a half. As luck would have it, however, he had to come back for some instruments. We immediately brought the sergeant into his office.

After tying off the artery to prevent further bleeding, he
shook his head, "My gosh, his pulse is weak! He needs blood,
Captain, and he needs it badly."

"Doc, I have a trainload of blood! You can have all you want.
Most of the damn stuff is saturated with alcohol, though!" My
own blood pressure was rising.

"Sorry, I don't have the tools to extract blood, then give it.
Maybe my friend at Alpine can give blood; that's about 98
miles up the track. I don't think this man can make it to El
Paso. There's no problem getting blood there on instant notice,
but that's 380 miles away. I'll call ahead to Alpine. Maybe he'll
have blood available. If anything can be done, he'll do it. Let's
just hope and pray this man gets there alive!"

At Alpine, the sergeant looked like his veins carried em-
balming fluid. World War II had taught me how quickly a man
could die by going into shock from loss of blood. The doctor
met us at the train. "His pulse certainly is weak," he said worriedly. "I'm sorry, but I have no way of giving him a transfu-
sion."

Again the track was cleared and we sped to El Paso. I stayed
awake in uniform. Midway, I realized the officers had never
been served dinner.

When we arrived early the next morning, an ambulance from
Fort Beaumont General Hospital was at the station. I rode with

the patient to the hospital. Doctors and nurses were ready in the emergency room. I returned wondering if he would live. As soon as I got back on board, I gave orders to throw out all whiskey.

From El Paso to Camp Pendleton it was a dry, dull trip. No scenery, no conversation, and no whiskey. I sat in a seat by myself. I knew I had been too permissive in allowing all that whiskey aboard. Because half of the men had served during World War II, I had rationalized they should have kept everyone in line, but conversion from civilian to soldier doesn't automatically take place upon reporting back to active duty.

We reached Camp Pendleton at 11 A.M. on Thursday, August 24. Bernard Schutt had arrived the previous day. He came to greet us with a contingent of Regular Marine officers, headed by a lieutenant colonel.

The troops disembarked and formed ranks about 50 yards in front of the train. Company health and personnel records were delivered to the officer contingent. After completion of the transfer of command, the lieutenant colonel spoke: "Captain, I've been meeting this train every day for three weeks, and this is one of the finest, if not the finest looking group of Marines I've seen come out here!"

I thanked him, but I thought to myself, I'm glad you didn't see us come across Texas.

2

Retreat to Pusan

The plight of the 1st Marine Division in North Korea during late November and early December of 1950 was not of its own making. The division commander had opposed the advance into this frozen mountainous area only 45 miles south of the Manchurian border. But General Douglas MacArthur had ordered Marine and Army troops forward toward the Yalu River border between Korea and China, in what he perceived to be the final stage of the Korean War, even though Communist China had repeatedly declared its intention to intervene if he did. No military commander in American history had received more warnings of impending disaster, yet failed to heed those warnings, than had MacArthur in North Korea.

However, our grim predicament rested on broader shoulders than those of MacArthur. The United States had not been prepared either militarily or politically to deal with the problem of Korea. The war had its genesis in World War II. First at Cairo in 1943 and again at Potsdam in 1945, Allied leaders had agreed that at war's end Japanese-occupied Korea would become free and independent. With Japan's defeat, the United States and the Soviet Union arbitrarily selected the 38th Parallel as a convenient boundary to accept the surrender of Japanese troops stationed in Korea. The Americans were to take command of the area below the parallel, the Soviets above it. By agreement, a joint commission from the two occupying powers was to develop a four-power trusteeship (the United States, the Soviet

Union, the United Kingdom, and China) which would guide a provisional Korean government until the peoples of Korea could govern themselves.

Little progress was made, due to the demands of the Soviet Union. Meanwhile, it sponsored a Communist regime in North Korea under Kim Il Sung. Years before, Kim had left his homeland, ostensibly to fight the Japanese. He had been trained by the Soviets as a military officer, and is said to have participated in the battle of Stalingrad.

The United States referred the Korean problem to the United Nations. In 1947 a UN commission entered the country to supervise free elections, but Soviet authorities refused to allow the commission into North Korea. The elected government of the Republic of Korea, with Syngman Rhee as president, was for the southern half of the peninsula only. By the end of 1947, Soviet troops had withdrawn from North Korea. The United States completed its withdrawal by June 1949, leaving only an advisory group of 500 officers and men.

The military capability of the United States of America in 1950 was at a low ebb from what it had been barely four years earlier. Immediately after the surrender of Japan in 1945, the American public clamored for dismantlement of the world's greatest military force. Daily the newspapers carried stories about the demand to reduce the high cost of our military establishment. Angry mothers marched on Washington, demanding that their sons be returned home. Congress responded, and by mid-1946 the U.S. Army had been effectively emasculated. The majestic American fleet went into mothballs. Our military and political figures regarded Soviet Russia as the only threat to world peace, but we had the atomic bomb and they didn't. The notion that there might be limited, localized warfare did not seem likely. Our leaders reasoned that if the United States had the strength required for all-out atomic war with Russia, any threat of lesser magnitude could certainly be handled. In the new atomic age the foot soldier, backbone of every military victory since the beginning of time, would no longer be needed.

The Marine Corps, small in comparison with the Army and Navy, soon found itself in danger of being erased altogether from the military picture. Unification became the key word in reorganizing our armed services while also drastically shrinking them. In July 1947, the Armed Forces Unification Act became law. With its implementation General Dwight D. Eisenhower recommended that the Marine Corps be maintained solely as an adjunct of the fleet. According to Eisenhower, no unit should be larger than a regiment. Its size should be limited to some 50,000 to 60,000 men, approximately one-tenth of its peak strength during World War II. General Carl Spaatz, the Air Force Commander, agreed with Eisenhower.

In seeking to maintain its tradition as a superior fighting force, the U.S. Marine Corps found itself clearly on the defensive. In the autumn of 1946, Marine Generals Lemuel Shepherd, Field Harris, and Oliver P. Smith formed a committee of three to orient the effort of the Marine Corps away from preparing for the last war and toward the next. The resulting recommendations led to experiments with helicopters as a means of tactical dispersion against an enemy deploying atomic weapons. The committee laid the groundwork for greatly improved, close tactical air support of ground forces. These generals became strong advocates of the "force in readiness" concept as the basic mission of the U.S. Marine Corps.

In keeping with Washington's military retrenchment, the Marine Corps had shrunk so in size by mid-1947 that its "force in readiness" mission could not be sustained in a division-size operation without a well-trained Reserve. This caused Marine Corps planners to allot a major portion of its defense budget for training active Reserve units. When the Corps embarked on its strong Reserve program, Roanoke, Virginia, was among the first of the 124 cities across the nation selected. It had a history of Marine Reserve training dating back to 1926. Living up to its tradition, the Roanoke unit achieved the distinction of becoming the first company in the United States to reach full enlistment of officers and men. This was shortly after Labor Day, 1947, one month before my graduation from law school.

In 1947, with Eisenhower as chairman, the Joint Chiefs of Staff counseled that "from the standpoint of security, the United States had little interest in maintaining the present troops and bases in Korea—[U.S. forces in Korea] were a liability as any offensive the U.S. might undertake in Asia would by-pass that peninsula. Enemy occupation in Korea could be neutralized by air action." This decision was later announced publicly by General Douglas MacArthur. When interviewed by a correspondent of the *London Daily Mail* in early March, 1949, MacArthur said, "Now the Pacific has become an Anglo-Saxon lake, and our line of defense runs through the chain of islands fringing the coast of Asia. It starts with the Philippines and continues through the Ryukyu Archipelago, which includes its main bastion, Okinawa. Then it bends back through Japan and the Aleutian Island chain to Alaska." This defense line, excluding both Korea and Formosa, was published in the *New York Times* on March 2, 1949.

Ten months later, on January 12, 1950, Secretary of State Dean Acheson, in a speech before the National Press Club, adopted the Pacific defense perimeter previously described by MacArthur. In late January House Republicans vigorously opposed an administration bill that granted $60,000,000 for aid to South Korea for the remaining months of fiscal year 1950. Representative John Vorys, Republican, Ohio, argued that economic aid to Korea was "money down the rat hole." Robert Chiperfield, Republican, Illinois, claimed that "the loss of China rendered South Korea indefensible." Donald Jackson, Republican, California, contended: "South Korea is a Bataan without a Corregidor, a Dunkirk without a flotilla, a dead-end street without an escape—Formosa is a tenable position." With the Republicans voting six to one against it, along with one of four Democrats, the Korean Aid Bill went down to defeat by a margin of one vote. It was reconsidered and passed into law on February 9, but only after substantial aid to Chiang Kai-shek was also included.

The crowning blow came with publication of an interview with Senator Tom Connally, Democrat, Texas, chairman of the Senate Foreign Relations Committee, in the May 5, 1950, issue of *U.S. News and World Report.* When asked if the abandonment of South Korea was going to be considered, he answered, "I am afraid it is going to be seriously considered because I'm afraid it's going to happen, whether we want it to or not. I'm for Korea. We're trying to help her—we're appropriating money now to help her. But South Korea is cut right across by this line—north of it are the Communists with access to the mainland—and Russia is over there on the mainland. So that whenever she takes a notion she can just overrun Korea just like she probably will overrun Formosa when she gets ready to do it. I hope not, of course."

President Syngman Rhee, at long last, made a deeply bitter protest to the State Department. He regarded Senator Connally's remarks, he said, as an open invitation to the Communists to come down and take over South Korea. Rhee also complained about the failure of the United States to provide Korea with air support adequate to meet the North Korean menace.

When the military forces of North Korea unleashed their attack on Sunday, June 25, 1950, an emergency meeting of the United Nations Security Council was assembled. Representatives of ten of the eleven member nations were present at the meeting. Soviet Russia was still boycotting the United Nations, protesting the membership of Nationalist China. By staying away the Soviet Union could not exercise its veto to nullify the Council's action. The Security Council called for a cease fire and directed the North Koreans to withdraw north of the 38th Parallel. By a nine to zero vote, with Communist Yugoslavia abstaining, copies of this action were in the hands of the world press that evening.

President Truman immediately sent a message to General MacArthur: "Assist in evacuating United States dependents and noncombatants. MacArthur authorized to take action by air and navy to prevent the Inchon-Kimpo-Seoul area from falling into unfriendly hands." The next day the President issued instructions for the United States 7th Fleet to move north from the Philippines to the strait between Formosa and mainland China. This action was taken to forestall an attack in either direction, and prevent the war from spreading. Made upon the joint recommendation of the State Department and the Department of Defense, it reversed Truman's previous hands-off policy in the Chinese civil war. The sudden reversal of American policy increased Communist China's distrust of the United States.

The Thursday morning newspapers reported the capture of Seoul. By the weekend, it appeared the Republic of Korea (ROK) Army was disorganized to the point of being ineffective. The government of Syngman Rhee was operating from its provisional capital at Taegu. With the fall of Seoul the Communist "Fifth Column" came out of hiding to help the invaders round up trapped soldiers, police, and governmental officials. Firing squads executed most of the officials on the spot.

On June 29, 1950, the United Nations Security Council passed the momentous resolution that put the United Nations into war against the Communists. The next day MacArthur made a reconnaissance of the Korean battlefield. He reported that South Korea could not be defended adequately without U.S. foot soldiers. President Truman, after conferring with Secretaries Dean Acheson and Louis Johnson and the Joint Chiefs of Staff, readily authorized the use of ground troops. The 24th Army Division, doing occupation duty in Japan, was immediately sent to Korea, but did little at first to stem the tide of North Korean advances.

On July 8, General MacArthur told the commander of the 8th Army in Japan, Lieutenant General Walton Walker, that his troops would control the campaign in Korea. Ten days later Walker arrived on the scene to join General William Dean, commander of the 24th Division.

The war news from the front was not censored. Although the press told of many acts of individual heroics in reporting the retreat of U.S. troops, the newspaper accounts also told of the softness of the American soldier. The Army historian Colonel Roy E. Appleman, an observer in Korea, had this to say about U.S. troops in the early stages of war:

"There were many heroic actions by American soldiers of the 24th Division in these first weeks of Korea. But there were also many uncomplimentary and unsoldierly ones. Leadership among the officers had to be exceptional to get the men to fight, and several gave their lives in this effort. Others failed to meet the standard expected of American officers. There is no reason to suppose that any of the other occupation divisions in Japan would have done better in Korea than did the U.S. 24th

Division in July, 1950. When committed to action they showed the same weaknesses. A basic fact is that the occupation divisions were not trained, equipped or ready for battle. The great majority of the enlisted men were young and not really interested in being soldiers. The recruiting posters that had induced most of these men to enter the Army mentioned all conceivable advantages and promised many good things, but never suggested that the principal business of an Army is to fight."

While Generals Walker and Dean strove to coordinate the defense against the Communist invasion, General MacArthur engaged daily in a top-secret dialogue with the Joint Chiefs of Staff. On July 9 he sent a message that read:

"The situation in Korea is critical. . . . [The enemy's] armored equipment is of the best and the service thereof, as reported by qualified veteran observers, as good as any seen at any time in the last war. They further state that the enemy's infantry is of thoroughly first class quality.

"I strongly urge that in addition to those forces already requisitioned, an army of at least four divisions, with all its component services, be dispatched to this area without delay and by every means of transportation available.

"The situation has developed into a major operation."

On July 10 MacArthur requested a full-strength Marine division. The Joint Chiefs turned him down. Earlier, he had asked for Marines and was given the 1st Provisional Marine Brigade, which was then embarking for Korea. It was thought this force of shock troops would be used to spearhead an early counter-offensive with just two United States divisions.

Five days after the refusal, MacArthur sent another message to the Joint Chiefs: "I strongly request reconsideration of my need for a Marine division. Its availability is absolutely essential to achieve a decisive stroke. If not made available, a much longer and more expensive effort, both in blood and money, will result. I must have the Marine Division by September 10. I cannot too strongly emphasize the complete urgency of my request." The Joint Chiefs honored his second plea.

General Cates, the Marine Corps Commandant, told the Joint Chiefs it was impossible to get the 1st Marine Division up to strength without calling up the Reserves. President Truman authorized and Congress approved the call-up on July 19. The executive order, signed by the President, also froze all persons in the Marine Corps Reserve, so that a discharge could no longer be given upon request.

On July 21 the city of Taejon, the largest city in central South Korea, fell to the Reds. General Dean, commander of the 24th Division, was reported missing in action. The Marine Brigade was on its way, but I had doubts that our troops could hold out long enough for it to arrive. South Korean and U.S. forces were being backed into a 200-square-mile area around the southeastern port of Pusan, called "the Pusan Perimeter."

At first it seemed problematic whether Pusan could hold out, but gradually the situation stabilized. Superior American firepower, air support from Japan, and needed reinforcements halted further advances by the North Koreans. By September 1 the situation was well in hand there, and it was now only a matter of time before we would take the initiative. Each day Reserve units from all over the country arrived at Camp Pendleton in California. Optimism began to soar.

Upon our arrival at Pendleton we learned of plans for classification of the Reserve units. Marines who had served in World War II or who had been in the Reserve for four years would be placed in the first category, for immediate shipment to Korea. Those with previous experience but special specification numbers would be held for further instructions. Those with no previous regular experience or less than four years in the Reserves would be placed in cadres for further training.

Obviously I fell into the first category, even though I did not get orders to ship out immediately. Forty-eight Marines, all enlisted men, received orders to go aboard ship at San Diego on August 28. Platoon Sergeant Charlie Old was the senior noncommissioned officer in this group.

"Charlie," I said, "I'm sorry you're moving out so fast."

"Cap'n Hopkins, isn't that what we came here for?" he answered, smiling.

Not everyone shared Charlie's feelings. In fact, a few felt just the opposite, grudgingly enduring the required physical exams. However, the regular Navy doctors and dentists cooperated fully with the Commandant's urgent request for more Marines in Korea, a need made worse by the President's executive order precluding 17-year-olds from serving in a combat unit. One World War II veteran had second thoughts about leaving so soon after arrival. He worriedly walked through the inspection line. When he got to the dentist's chair, he pulled out his upper and lower plates and placed them on the nearby circular bracket table. The Navy doctor, a lieutenant commander, gave the teeth a thorough examination, not once looking into the veteran's mouth.

"Now, that's what I call a damn good set of teeth if I ever saw one!" he loudly announced. "Next!"

The following morning I learned that I had been classified as an infantry officer and assigned to the first replacement draft, which put me on immediate call for Korea. Perceiving I had little time left in the States, I phoned Ginny and asked her to come out as soon as the doctor would permit.

The 48 Roanoke Marines under Charlie Old were pooled with other Reservists to be assigned to the 1st Battalion, 7th Marine Regiment, then at only half strength. This battalion was commanded by Lieutenant Colonel Ray Davis, an outstanding combat officer. Sergeant Major Sal Campalongo, formerly on the regular staff at Roanoke, was in charge of making placements. The Roanokers asked him to put all in the same company. "We want to be together," they insisted.

"Cain't do that!" Campalongo protested. "I'm going strictly by the book."

A few men with engineer's specifications were placed in the engineer platoon attached to the battalion. The rest were divided between "A," "B," "C," and Weapons Companies. Seeing that every fourth man would be placed in the same company, the remaining Roanokers lined up accordingly. Midway through the assigning process, a Roanoke sergeant asked to be put in Weapons Company. He had been a forward observer for mortars in World War II. This broke the chain. Half of the

Roanokers wound up in "A" Company; the others, with the exception of the sergeant, were in "B" and "C" Companies. They would sail to Kobe, Japan, aboard the *U.S.S. Okanogan*.

When they reported alongside, the first person they met was Kurt Fleming.

"Hey, Kurt!" someone called out. "What the hell are you doing here? You're supposed to be home in Roanoke looking after our women!"

Fleming had had a radar spec number in the Navy in World War II. Radar men were in short supply. The Department of the Navy had issued orders to Kurt three days after we left, flown him to San Diego, and assigned him to the *U.S.S. Okanogan*.

Before he could explain what had taken place, they questioned, "Kurt, did you bring our women with you?" Roanoke Marines joshed Kurt all the way across the Pacific. The *U.S.S. Okanogan* sailed for Kobe on August 31.

Life at Camp Pendleton reminded me of a college reunion. Officers I knew but hadn't seen for five to seven years appeared on the scene daily. Among them was Logan Bowman, from Omaha, Nebraska. Though he came with the Nebraska contingent, I had known him in Salem, Virginia; his people were friends of my family. Logan was tall, handsome, a gentleman of the first order. His father experienced financial difficulties when Logan was ready for college in the late '30s. In lieu of college, he joined the Marine Corps as a private and was awarded a field promotion to second lieutenant after Guadalcanal. He earned an engineering degree on the G.I. Bill after the war.

The training program at Camp Pendleton was excellent, the work day long and hard. At night, most of the officers gathered to talk about World War II experiences, mostly nonbattle. An officer might ask, "Whatever happened to Herr Himmler, the Gestapo agent who was house detective at the U. S. Grant Hotel in San Diego? I wonder if he's still there!" Another told about his unusual experiences at the Grant Hotel in Auckland, New Zealand, and so on.

President Truman accounted for the one sour note during my brief stay at Pendleton. At breakfast on September 6, the local newspaper headlined the story of Truman's blast at the Marines. In answer to an August 29 letter from Congressman Gordon L. McDonough of California, who suggested enlarging the Marine Corps, Truman wrote in part: "I read with a lot of interest your letter in regard to the Marine Corps. For your information, the Marine Corps is the Navy's police force and as long as I am President that is what it will remain. They have a propaganda machine that is almost equal to Stalin's."

I was shocked that any President would say such a thing. Some officer said, "Well, there's your World War I artillery captain showing his pettiness. I didn't vote for the son-of-a-bitch so don't blame me!" I had voted for him, and I was boiling mad. Even after President Truman apologized to General Cates, and later to the president of the Marine Corps League, I could not take his statement with grace. Other Marine officers there felt the same way.

Ginny called to say she had train tickets to California. My mother would keep our baby until she returned to Rocky Mount. She was due to arrive September 15.

3

Inchon–Seoul

Across the Pacific Ocean in Tokyo, plans were nearing completion for the Inchon landing. This amphibious operation, which
involved transporting an attack force by ship around the Korean peninsula and up the western coast, resulted in the capture of Kimpo Airfield and Seoul, the South Korean capital. It
was the stroke that dramatically changed the course of war in
our favor.

General MacArthur conceived the plan as early as July 10.
He planned for the 1st Marine Division to land at Inchon and
capture Seoul. An Army division would follow the Marines,
then travel south to assume a blocking position. MacArthur
felt sure that this daring surprise blow against the enemy's
supply lines would have a devastating effect upon the North
Koreans. As MacArthur later stated: "The history of war proves
that nine out of ten times an army has been destroyed because
its supply lines have been cut off. Everything the Red Army
shoots and all the additional replenishment he needs, comes
through Seoul."

The 10th Corps would be under the command of Lieutenant
General Edward M. Almond, and the Navy attack force under
Rear Admiral James H. Doyle. The short time span left for
planning before the actual event posed tremendous logistical
problems for the Marines and Navy. The 5th Marine Regiment
was withdrawn from the 8th Army defense perimeter, then
outloaded from Pusan. The 1st Regiment, which had been

brought up to strength at Camp Pendleton, was shipped to Japan. The 3rd Battalion, 7th Marines, was serving afloat ships with the 6th Fleet in the Mediterranean. The 1st and 2nd Battalions, 7th Regiment, with 50 percent combat-ready Reserves, sailed from California to Japan in late August and early September. Tokyo, Kobe, and Sasebo were the staging bases for all Marine units except the 5th Regiment. The accelerated activity at these ports caused newsmen in Japan to label the landing "Operation Open Secret."

Roanoke Marines with Lieutenant Colonel Ray Davis's 1st Battalion, 7th, aboard the *U.S.S. Okanogan*, were almost evenly divided between World War II veterans and those with only four years of Reserve training in the 16th Engineer Company. A few of the latter were recent high school graduates. "A" Company's gunnery sergeant made light of Reserves who had never experienced combat or gone through boot camp. "You guys gonna get your training doing the real thing."

On September 15, the day the Marines hit the beach at Wolmi-do, which guarded the Inchon harbor, Ginny arrived in California. We rented a one-room apartment in San Clemente. Logan Bowman and his wife, Peg, occupied another in the same building. Ginny had a check-off list of all the places she wanted to visit, every place I had seen and talked about on my previous trips to California.

While I trained at the base Ginny busied herself as a tourist. We visited a different place each night—the Officers' Club at Camp Pendleton, the Carlsbad Hotel, a Marine favorite, and night clubs at Laguna Beach and La Jolla. An occasional bridge game at someone's apartment served as a respite.

Two days after the landing at Wolmi-do, the Marines climbed the 14-foot sea wall at Inchon harbor in the face of enemy fire. At one time this obstacle was regarded as unscalable. They used ladders in the fashion of medieval warriors attacking a castle. Afterwards cargo nets were placed at strategic spots to make climbing easier for later waves of Marines. By nightfall they neared Kimpo Airfield. By the end of the third day they occupied it. This greatly enhanced our offensive strength; now we had a base that gave our troops close tactical air support for the remainder of the operation. On the fourth day, the Marines headed for Seoul with Colonel Lewis "Chesty" Puller's 1st Regiment leading the way.

In overall command of the 1st Marine Division was Major General Oliver P. Smith, a very fortunate choice. He was not the typical military general. In his library were numerous books on philosophy, politics, and history. He was born on October 26, 1895, in Menard, Texas, the second son of a struggling young lawyer. His father died when Smith was seven years old. His mother moved first to Austin, then a year later to Santa Cruz, California, where she settled. At an early age, Oliver joined his mother and older brother at various menial jobs to make ends meet. Smith was an excellent student in high school, and dreamed of going to college. He hoped to find a career in the consular service. At age 19, with the help of his mother and brother, he acquired enough money to pay his first year's tuition at the University of California at Berkeley. He arrived on campus with only $5.00 in his pocket. He put himself through school by performing odd jobs, mostly gardening. He graduated in the class of 1916.

After graduation, he traveled to New York to join the foreign service of Standard Oil Company. The United States' impending entrance into World War I put a hold on a foreign service career. Smith learned the U.S. Marine Corps was offering ten commissions to graduates of the University of California after completion of an officers' training course. He returned to California, trained at San Diego, and received his commission as second lieutenant on May 14, 1917. He admitted later that he had never heard of the Marine Corps before this offer.

Years later, Smith graduated from the field officers' training school at the Army Infantry School in Fort Benning, Georgia. He taught at the Marine Officers' School in Quantico. He studied at the Ecole Supérieure de Guerre in France. During World War II he served as executive officer for the Marine Corps' Division of Plans and Policies, and participated in battles at New Britain, Peleliu, and Okinawa. Throughout his military career, he embodied the best of the modern general; physically fit, a military student, intellectual, courageous, and a respecter of human dignity.

After Inchon the UN dropped leaflets around Pusan to inform the enemy of the landing. When the North Koreans realized the truth about Inchon, the effect was devastating. MacArthur's prediction of disaster when an army's long supply line becomes severed proved correct. The enemy took flight in every direction.

On September 25 the Marines entered Seoul; its capture was imminent. The progress of the 1st Marine Division made pleasant reading for most, but not all, in California.

Late one afternoon, when I returned to my apartment, I found a note tacked on the door. It had been placed there by my landlord, who asked that I call at his desk. I couldn't imagine what he wanted because my rent was paid in advance. I found him reading a newspaper in his small office.

"Let's walk out on the porch," he said. "These workers make too much noise to do any talking."

We sat on the steps of the front porch, and I saw he was adding rooms to the building.

"They tell me you're a lawyer back east where you come from. That's the reason I want to talk to you."

"I'm a lawyer, but I'm not familiar with California law and I'm not licensed to practice here."

"Well, it's not a legal question that I want to ask you about anyhow," he said. "I've got a big problem, and I'm trying to figure out what to do. You know, two heads are better than one." He looked at me, then paused before continuing.

"How long do you think that war in Korea's going to last?"

"I don't know. Before the Inchon landing it seemed it was going to take a long time. I have my doubts now."

"That's exactly the way I see it," he exclaimed. "That's what worries me! That's my problem. Building those extra rooms is costing me over $1,700, even though I'm doing the wiring. I'll have to borrow $1,200 to get the job finished. The rooms are halfway done, and chances are I won't be able to rent them a couple of months from now."

"I don't see where I come in."

"Well, what would you do if you were me? Would you stop? You have to pay taxes and insurance on empty rooms just like the filled ones."

"I can't answer that."

"I can get my investment back if the war continues, and . . ."

"I can see that," I interrupted. "That $35 a week is pretty steep."

"Steep! You can't get rooms any cheaper unless you get further away from the base. The demand is there," he said raising his voice. "Every day somebody comes by and wants a room I don't have. Rent goes up another $10 at the beginning of the month. The demand is there!" he emphasized.

"Damn! That's a hell of a note," I said, rising to my feet.

"Look, you've got your problems, and I've got mine. I sympathize with you—I'm sorry you've got to go to Korea. But I've got problems, too! Can't you see that it's hard to figure what to do?"

"Yes, I see," I replied as I walked away. "But I can't help you."

"Can't you see what a hell of a shape I'll be in if I'm stuck with a bunch of empty rooms?" As I moved, he raised his voice: "You service guys are all alike! You don't think about anybody but yourselves."

"I'll trade problems with you!" I answered as I entered the front door of the building. Our landlord continued to sit on the steps.

The next day a visitor came to our training camp; it was the buck sergeant who was injured on our cross-country train trip.

"Captain, I've been looking for you everywhere," he said with a broad grin. "I want to thank you for what you did for me, and apologize for all the trouble I caused you aboard the train." He had returned to duty, a small scar on his arm the only evidence of his injury.

"Sergeant, I wasn't thinking about you. I was thinking about me," I joked. "If you'd died, I would've been court-martialed or there would have been a board of inquiry for sure! No way could I have denied knowing there was too much whiskey aboard that train!"

During training on Wednesday, September 27, orders were handed me to fly to Korea at 5:00 the next morning. The post quartermaster issued a carbine packed in Cosmoline for my personal weapon. Ginny was shocked by the abruptness of my leaving. I spent the evening removing the Cosmoline, packing my trunk, and getting ready to leave. Ginny watched in tearful silence as I removed the Cosmoline with hot water and tissue paper. I didn't know what to say or do to brighten the occasion. Once or twice during the night I heard her crying. I couldn't sleep either.

At 4:00 A.M. I got up, took my bags, and again said goodbye to Ginny. This time she was not brave. I made her promise to go to Los Angeles that morning and make arrangements for her immediate train trip back to Rocky Mount.

Logan Bowman and I went to Camp Pendleton to board the plane. It had engine trouble. We waited, waited all day. Finally, at about 4:00 P.M. we were told that the plane could not take off; instead we were to sail to Japan three days later, Sunday, October 1.

In the meantime, Ginny had taken the bus to Los Angeles to make her travel arrangements. That afternoon she rode the bus back to San Clemente. After checking the schedules, I waited at the bus station for her return.

Later she told me about her interesting ride. A young sailor, about 19 or 20 years old, was seated next to her. He appeared to have shaved only a few times, but insisted he had been in the Navy for three years. In fact, he informed her, he was an old salt, a well-traveled man who had been around the world. Seeing Ginny cry, he asked:

"What's wrong, lady?"

"My husband left for Korea this morning," she replied.

"Well, out of sight, out of mind. That's the world of the serviceman's wife. Don't take it so hard, lady. There are lots of good-looking Marine officers, Navy officers, sergeants, and chiefs around here who'll suit you better than him."

"They're not for me!"

"Oh, that's what you say," he persisted. "Look, I've been around, seen the wives kiss the husbands goodbye, cry over them for a day, sometimes as long as a week. But just as sure as night follows day, they get shacked up with the next best thing that comes along."

"Those wives don't have a husband like mine!"

"Oh, come off it!" he said, and then described in detail spe- cific cases where the woman left one officer or chief for another soon after her husband shipped out. "I tell you, you're no different! That's what makes the world go 'round."

When the bus pulled into San Clemente, I was standing in the station lot. I yelled at Ginny from about 75 yards away. She turned, saw me, and came running. We held each other a long time. Suddenly she jerked away.

"Just a minute! Wait! There's something I've got to do." She headed toward the bus, but was too late; it was pulling away. "Oh, my gosh! What will that poor sailor think now?" she said. His head nodded at the window as the bus drove off to San Diego.

We returned to the apartment and spent a quiet, happy evening together. When Ginny left Saturday morning, she said goodbye with no tears. Logan Bowman's wife, Peg, left the same day.

Later in the day, I received word that a lineal list for promotions had been posted at Camp Pendleton headquarters, and that I had been selected for promotion to major. My promotion would become final after orders were received by my commanding officer and I had successfully passed my physical examination. This news was cause for celebration.

Logan and I dined at the Officers' Club, and reviewed the progress of the war. The evening newspaper announced the capture of Seoul. We speculated about the next move. We agreed that the Chinese and Russians would not enter the war.

We decided to continue at the Carlsbad Hotel. Captain Cooke and First Lieutenant McGregor had called a cab and were waiting outside. The four of us rode together. Logan and I had drinks, mingled with the crowd, and watched others dance and cavort. Cooke and McGregor, both fine officers during World War II (Cooke was a Navy Cross winner), sat glumly at the bar and meditated. They were unaccountably despondent when we returned to Camp Pendleton.

Sunday, at 8:00 A.M., the four of us joined a shipload of Marines aboard the *U.S.S. General Walker* and set sail for Japan.

With the favorable progress of the war, the Joint Chiefs anticipated a crossing into North Korea. On September 27 they issued a directive restraining UN ground forces from operating north of a line established from Chongju on the west coast to Hamhung and Hungnam on the east. All major cities in North Korea, those of 50,000 or more, except the east coast port city of Chongjin, were below this line, which ran across the narrowest part of the Korean peninsula.

Although there was no east-west road crossing North Korea above the route from Wonsan to Pyongyang, the line established by the Joint Chiefs gave U.S. troops the smallest front to defend in case of Chinese intervention—only 120 miles. Above this line, the peninsula spread rapidly, reaching 520 miles at the North Korean boundary separating the country from Manchuria and Russia. Only ROK troops could move freely to the border.

On October 1, 1950, Syngman Rhee sent his troops across the 38th Parallel to unify Korea. The North Korean Army was shattered and fled with little semblance of order.

The specter of Chinese Communist intervention was again raised. Premier Chou En-lai first sent a message to the UN on August 20. "Korea is China's neighbor. The Chinese people cannot but be concerned about the solution of the Korean Question." On August 25 and 29 China propagandized two alleged U.S. Air Force invasions of their border. On September 22 the Chinese Foreign Office declared that China would always stand on the side of the Korean people. Then on September 30 Chou En-lai publicly warned, "The Chinese people absolutely will not tolerate foreign aggression, nor will they supinely tolerate seeing their neighbors being savagely invaded by the imperialists."

On October 4, Chou En-lai summoned Indian Ambassador Pannikkar to a dramatic midnight conference. If U.S. troops invaded North Korea, he said, China would enter the war. If only ROK troops crossed the border, China would stay out. This news was relayed to U.S. officials. Both the military and political authorities took it as bluff.

With his subordinates in Tokyo and his cult in the United States, Douglas MacArthur had acquired an omniscience comparable to the gods of ancient Greece. Where Zeus performed feats of weather magic, MacArthur worked exploits of military magic. But MacArthur was human. Humans make mistakes, and there was no Delphic oracle to guide him. At this juncture, things started to go wrong.

The Taebaek Mountain Range begins in South Korea and extends northward to the Yalu River which divides North Korea from Manchuria. What MacArthur determined to do was to reassemble his 10th Corps at Inchon harbor, then move it by ship to the east coast of North Korea. Operating separately, the 10th Corps would proceed up the east coast and the 8th Army up the west coast, with the two always divided by this mountain range.

The Navy disliked this plan because it took numerous troops out of action at a time the enemy was very much on the run. Air Force officers objected to the congestion of the limited port facilities that would result. They made an issue of the fact that the combat capability of both the 8th Army and the 5th Air Force was jeopardized by the outloading of the 10th Corps. General Walker and his staff thought an overland move was best; the 10th Corps should come under the 8th Army and continue its advance toward Pyongyang since it was in such favorable position to attack northward. Walker further objected because the separation of the two forces, the 8th Army and the 10th Corps, violated the U.S. Army unity of command doctrine.

Perhaps the greatest mistake of all was that the field commander-in-chief did not stay in Korea. He occupied quarters hundreds of miles away in Tokyo, in a totally different environment. Information gathered daily at the battlefront was sent to MacArthur's headquarters, where it was viewed through rose-colored glasses before being returned to unit commanders in the form of the nightly situation map and summary.

On October 5, the 1st Marine Division received orders to re-embark at the port of Inchon. By the 7th, all units began withdrawing as the Army relieved them. The next five days were spent loading equipment, weapons, supplies, and personnel aboard the ships in the harbor.

Early in the morning of October 12, the *U.S.S. General Walker*, on which I was sailing from California to Japan, reached Tokyo. As soon as the ship docked, I, together with 46 other officers, all of them captains and lieutenants, received orders to fly immediately to Kimpo Airfield on the outskirts of Seoul.

We arrived late that evening, and were taken to our temporary quarters, a small schoolhouse with low ceilings and unmatted floors that made sleeping uncomfortable even after 12 days at sea. The heads of those over six feet tall touched the ceiling when they stood. The next morning a breakfast chow line was set up for us in the schoolyard. There was plenty of American food—cereal, powdered eggs, hash brown potatoes, bacon, toast, and coffee.

Children came to the schoolyard with their mothers while we ate. The women sent their children to us as we returned our trays. They waited to be given whatever food we didn't eat. They begged in silence, the silence of genuine poverty. It was the first time most of us in that schoolyard had seen it up close. Our men were no different from American soldiers of other times. They possessed a basic generosity toward the very poor. Each left some food on his tray for the children to take to their mothers, who waited quietly and patiently at the rear of the yard. The children were remarkably good about waiting to eat until they returned to their mothers. Our food was strange to them. It was not their food and they did not know how to eat it. But they would eat anything. They took sugar from the bowls on the tables and poured it over everything—cereals, bacon, eggs, whatever. Later some were mildly sick.

As we waited for further instructions, we talked with other Marines in the schoolyard. Civilians milled around within earshot of our conversations, but everyone spoke freely about the 1st Marine Division's next move to the east coast of North Korea. Such openness contrasted sharply with the censorship and "hush-hush" attitude of World War II, when the slogan "A slip of the lip will sink a ship" was taken very seriously.

At noon on this second day, a sergeant major called out the names of five officers who were to leave immediately. We took our gear, and were driven to the dock at Inchon. On our way, we saw many Korean homes; they were small, one-room structures, with rice-straw roofs. In many cases the entire family—

parents, grandparents, and children, sometimes as many as 14 people or more—were standing in front of their hut. We wondered how so many could live in such a small space. The oldest male present always wore a white kimono with a small black horsehair hat; our driver explained that this dress indicated he was retired. Most of the Koreans had a pleasant, serene look, and gave us a friendly wave as we passed.

We arrived at the docks and waited. Since the tide was out, there was nothing else to do. The tides, with their 27-foot variance, are among the most impressive in the world. This factor was the main argument against MacArthur's plan to invade at Inchon harbor. I could see firsthand that the interval separating the tides would have left those invading quite literally high and dry with support impossible should the North Koreans counter the invasion.

Nightfall saw the tidal waters return. Thereupon we were taken aboard a Higgins boat, a small personnel carrier, out into the harbor.

The first person we met after boarding was Colonel Lewis K. "Chesty" Puller, regimental commander of the 1st Regiment, 1st Marines. There was no doubt who was in charge—Chesty Puller, the Marine Corps' most decorated man ever, with 53 personal medals. His nickname came more from his carriage than from the size of his chest. He was not a large man. Puller had a classic bulldog face, and held himself totally erect. At one time he had a large chest for a man of 5'10", but by then it had fallen, although he had yet to acquire a stomach. There he was, in his undershirt, smoking a pipe.

He was a rare man, Puller. If you took all the noncoms in the Marines and polled them as to what they thought an officer should be, they would have been unanimous in selecting Puller. Their admiration for him was fantastic; it showed and Puller knew it. In his presence, his men adhered to all military courtesies in addressing him, but out of sight they spoke of him as "Chesty," signifying he was one of them.

He was a brave man; many officers thought foolishly so. I was told he was reckless with human lives, that lives under him were no more than an extension of what he was trying to do with his own life. He went into places when other commanders simply would not go, and he insisted his men go with him. This was the Puller legend. I learned later he was aggressive and decisive, but not reckless.

Puller could talk with his men, the unique gift of great commanders. He could make them understand what he was trying to do. He left no doubt that, while he had no qualms about risking their lives, he had none about risking his own either. But it always had to be for a purpose, *a military purpose*, for he was 100 percent soldier.

He could analyze a tough situation and come up with the right answer. The tougher the situation, the better, for he had neither fear nor prejudice to clog his mental gears in battle. He was a basic man, a fundamentalist, who knew what the fundamentals of fighting actually were. He realized fully that without strong, well-trained NCOs, officers, and men under him, he could not be successful. Of course, he backed up his noncoms. They could count on it, knew it, lived with it. He understood them. He backed up his officers as well, but Puller did not identify as strongly with them as with his NCOs.

I never served with anyone so intent upon assuring that his men had the necessities with which to fight. These were limited to ammunition, food, clothing, and only one typewriter per battalion, the last-named to requisition more of these same supplies and to send out wounded and death notices. Cots fell into the frill category. You did not need to sleep on a cot to fight, so there were no cots. They took up space in the trucks. His trucks.

Puller was not a student like General Smith, but he had read history, all the history he could find about war. Unlike many generals, he did not let the atom bomb distort his sense of history. Puller knew what they forgot, that man himself is the changeless weapon of war, all the way from the time of spears to the age of guided missiles.

While I listened to Puller tell sea stories that night in the harbor, I remembered telling Ginny when I last saw her that if I were assigned to Puller, I would throw in the towel. But here I was, 50 days away from a law practice in Roanoke, proud to be a Marine, and prouder still to be in the Puller regiment, just like all the other Marines in his outfit.

I sipped a cup of coffee and listened to junior officers in the background rehash their experiences in the capture of Seoul, while Puller reviewed my personnel file. One, a property officer, griped because the others would receive medals, thus furthering their careers. Being a property officer would not help in later years for promotions, so he was saying. The sergeant major appeared, then announced in a loud voice:

"Captain William B. Hopkins, USMCR 010166. Colonel Puller to see you."

I got up, walked front, and stood at attention.

"At ease, Captain."

"Yes, sir."

"I see you come from Roanoke, Virginia?"

"Yes, sir."

"Where did you go to college?"

"Washington and Lee."

"A damn mink, huh?"

"Yes, sir, but I went to the University of Virginia Law School."

"That's no improvement!" When he said it, a broad smile, the well-known Puller smile, covered his bulldog face and put me at ease. I smiled with him.

I could see his one year at Virginia Military Institute had left its mark. The Washington and Lee campus adjoins that of VMI in Lexington, Virginia. On dance weekends, VMI students had to bring in their dates at midnight, sometimes as late as 1:00 A.M. Washington and Lee students, with no restrictions, oftentimes arranged late dates with those attending the VMI dances. A "mink" steals eggs from another's nest—ergo, the name given Washington and Lee students by the cadets.

Chesty continued, "You're assigned to the 1st Battalion, 1st Marines. Lieutenant Colonel Jack Hawkins is the commanding officer. The sergeant major tells me they've turned in for the night. Everyone's in the sack except the officer on the deck. He'll show you to your bunk. The Higgins boat should be here any minute now. Glad to have you aboard."

"Thank you, sir."

I picked up my gear and personnel file. By the time I reached the main deck, the boat was alongside to take me to the 1st Battalion's ship. It was an LST, long and barrel-shaped, designed to carry men, trucks, and other vehicles for unloading directly on the beach. Enjoying a shallow draft, the configuration of its design permits the doors in the front of the ship to open so that all can disembark by way of a ramp. An LST is probably best remembered for being unusually uncomfortable when sailing on restless seas. The officer of the deck showed me to my bunk. Everyone else seemed to be asleep.

"Do you have any idea where this crate is going?" I asked him.

"Sure, we're going to Wonsan, on the east coast. That's about 150 miles north of the 38th Parallel. We should be weighing anchor near noon tomorrow."

I could not sleep. As I lay awake, I reflected upon the events of the day and the past few months. Speculation about the intervention of China and the Soviet Union did not worry me. I believed both were afraid to engage the United States in an all-out atomic war. It was evident the North Korean Army was soundly beaten, and was coming apart at the seams. I expected the only action in the days ahead would be simple mop-up operations. There had been a number of new articles concerning Communist China's intention to intervene, but I too took these as bluff.

When I awoke at reveille, 2nd Lieutenant James Adair, the battalion adjutant met me. Adair was a friendly, knowledgeable officer, older than most lieutenants because he had come up through the ranks. He was tall and thin, and had a hollow face, with yellowish skin which reminded me of South Pacific days. There the Marines' skin turned the same color from taking Atabrine daily to prevent malaria. His eyes had a slant that often caused him to be taken for an Oriental.

He gave me a rundown of the meal schedule. All Navy officers, Lieutenant Colonel Hawkins, plus senior Marine officers on board, ate with the first shift, unless Hawkins desired to change the seating arrangements. At any rate, the colonel would see me at 1000 in the wardroom. That would give time to clear dishes and square things away for the day. Adair continued: "I'll introduce you to the officers at the second shift. When you come to breakfast, eat hearty. We're served only two meals a day."

At breakfast, I met the junior officers of "A" Company, Headquarters and Service, Weapons, TACP, two Korean interpreters, Captain Kim and 1st Lieutenant Suhr, and two news reporters, one a cameraman named Yoder, who was my frequent bridge partner in the evenings.

Lieutenant Colonel Jack Hawkins arrived for office hours on schedule. He was of medium height, very thin and youthful-looking for his 32 years. His dungaree jacket fit loosely, signifying considerable weight loss during the ordeal of Inchon-Seoul. Hawkins was a Naval Academy graduate from Texas. In a quiet voice, he said:

"You're assigned as company commander of Headquarters and Service [H&S] Company. 'A' Company and all your men are aboard this ship. 'B' company, 'C' Company, and most of Weapons Company are aboard other LSTs. I see by your personnel file that you're a senior captain. I'd rather not change the seating arrangements for meals. If you have any questions about your assignment, feel free to ask. Lieutenant Adair should be able to answer most questions."

"Thank you, Colonel. I guess I had better save my questions for later."

"Glad to have you aboard."

"Thank you, Colonel. Glad to be aboard."

My assignment pleased me. I expected to be promoted to major as soon as instructions from Washington reached the 1st Marine Division in Korea ordering me to take a physical examination. In the Marine Corps, a major serves a rifle battalion in the capacity of executive officer, operations officer, or Weapons Company commander. Serving as H&S company commander would give me the opportunity to learn all three jobs as each could be observed daily.

At noon we weighed anchor and set sail for Wonsan.

4

The Move to North Korea

We estimated we would be aboard ship seven days, since our ship had to go south from Inchon around the Korean peninsula, then north up to Wonsan. Before we left the harbor, Jim Adair introduced me to Master Sergeant Nicholas Fritz, the 1st sergeant of H&S Company, and to Master Sergeant Delmar Pruitt, the company gunnery sergeant. I spent an hour talking with each man. I knew that in the days ahead I would rely heavily on both in managing the company.

Fritz was a soft-spoken man whose face wore a smile most of the time. He had an average build and dark skin. He had enlisted in the Regular Marine Corps in Pennsylvania prior to World War II, was married, and had two sons. The 1st sergeant handles all administrative duties for the company commander. Fritz did not have to refer to his records to tell me the exact number of men aboard, the vacancies in each section, and the name and location of all sick or wounded. In our first conference, I could see he was on top of his job.

Pruitt, the company gunnery sergeant, executed the orders of the company commander. He was 5′10″, had an oval-shaped face with a mustache, and always appeared neat and well-groomed. Pruitt was about 20 pounds overweight. Most of his excess weight was around the middle, suggesting he had consumed more than his fair share of beer at Staff NCO clubs in the States before coming to Korea. From letters written and received, he appeared happily married, with no children.

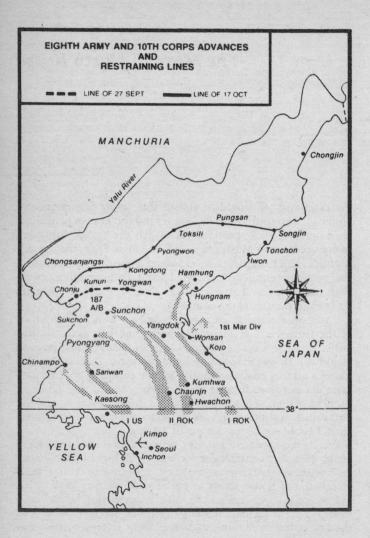

EIGHTH ARMY AND 10TH CORPS ADVANCES
AND
RESTRAINING LINES

▬ ▬ ▬ LINE OF 27 SEPT   ▬▬▬ LINE OF 17 OCT

MANCHURIA

Chongjin

Yalu River

Pungsan

Toksili   Songjin

Pyongwon   Tonchon

Chongsanjangsi   Koingdong   Hamhung   Iwon

Kunun   Yongwan

Chonju

Hungnam

187
A/B   Sunchon

Sukchon

Yangdok   1st Mar Div

Pyongyang   Wonsan

Chinampo   Kojo

SEA OF
JAPAN

Sariwan

Kumhwa

Chaunjn

Kaesong   Hwachon

38°

I US   II ROK   I ROK

Kimpo

YELLOW
SEA

Seoul
Inchon

Pruitt had also enlisted in the Regular Marine Corps in New York State prior to World War II. Unlike many Marine veterans, he wore no tattoo, not even the pierced and bleeding heart with the inscription, "Death Before Dishonor." Pruitt had a strong, resonant voice, yet he seldom yelled at his men. He was an articulate speaker, and only occasionally used profanity. Initially Pruitt impressed me as a transplanted businessman. He looked no part of the John Wayne—type Marine master sergeant, but I learned he was equally effective at getting his job done. Both Fritz and Pruitt were in their early 30s.

I searched for a place to exercise, but found no unused space aboard. Most of my time was spent in the officers' wardroom reading books and magazines, writing letters to Ginny, or conversing with the officers. I learned early that "Gook," meaning any North Korean soldier, and UTA, "up to the ass," meaning abundance, were the most frequently used expressions in conversation. In the evening, I usually joined a bridge foursome or read. I had determined not to forget the law on this tour of duty, as I had during World War II. I had packed three books: Wigmore on evidence, a Horn book on torts, and a Horn book on contracts.

After the first evening meal, I talked at length with the two Korean interpreters, Captain Kim and 1st Lieutenant Suhr. Kim stated that he was a lawyer in Seoul. He had been practicing only a short time, and was very much interested in reading my law books. He noticed that I had taken one out of my pack. I loaned him the Horn book on torts. Kim spoke broken English and did not seem to comprehend completely when we talked.

Suhr was the antithesis of Kim. He had graduated from the University of Shanghai, spoke beautiful English, and knew a great deal about international affairs, especially the United States. Although he was well informed about countries he had never visited, he most enjoyed discussing Korea.

After the evening meal, we talked for a long while. I took advantage of Suhr's willingness to air his views on Korea, which gave a perspective not found in textbooks or military information bulletins. Suhr referred to his native land as Choson, "Morning Calm," revealing a native preference for eastern beauty and order. We reviewed the peninsula's location and size—south of Manchuria and the USSR, extending 525 miles in length and up to 200 miles wide in parts. This shape, plus the ruggedness of the eastern coast, affects the tides, which are only two to three feet in the east and anywhere from 20 to 30 feet on the western shore. In the west, the estuaries and tidal flats make navigation difficult, as had been the case with the Inchon landing.

"Your newspaper reporters talk about the industrial north and agricultural south," Suhr said. "The truth is there are very few manufacturing plants in Korea, either north or south. Agriculture and fishing are the predominant industries of both areas."

Suhr strongly supported Syngman Rhee and the ROK government. He admired Rhee's devotion to the achievement of a united, independent Korea—an unflagging and lengthy devotion, which affected Suhr far more than anything else we previously covered.

On the second day at sea, I was reading in the wardroom when mealtime began—that is, the serving of the first shift of officers. I made it a point to be present thereafter, because I enjoyed listening to the ship's captain, a lieutenant commander. Like Charles Dickens's Mr. Fezziwig, "He lit up the room with his presence." A paunchy, jovial Irishman, he told another of his sea stories each day while the officers ate and laughed. In a loud voice he gave detailed accounts of each experience. Listening to such sea stories is a fringe benefit of service with the regular Navy, and I took full advantage.

One day he told about a large group of more than a hundred French prostitutes he had to take from the island of Corsica to the southern part of France. He began, "It was near the end of World War II. All my men remember this as the best of all our war duty assignments. The head madam came aboard with a boy toting piles and piles of luggage, and wanted to know where the captain's cabin was. Having been shown my quarters, she looked at me and in heavily French-accented English said, 'These are my quarters! Unload my gear, boy. This is my room until we reach France!'" At this point, everyone was laughing. Before he finished, his face grew serious, and shaking his head he said, "You know, I had one hell of a time getting her out of my cabin when we reached France!"

During the entire voyage the atmosphere was relaxing and convivial. Occasionally we speculated on the intent of the Chinese. We doubted they would send troops to Korea—there was no evidence indicative of their plans at this time. They were afraid of our atomic bombs, we thought. Each time the subject was broached, we concluded that Russia and China didn't want to start World War III over Korea.

The battalion's operations officer was Major David William Bridges from Florida. Of medium height and build, he was the efficient, studious type. He appeared more interested in the big picture and events around the world than did the other Marine officers aboard. Colonel Hawkins leaned heavily upon Bridges when making decisions. Bill Bridges had a map upon the forward bulkhead of the wardroom which showed the movements of American and ROK troops, and each time he received news on the radio he updated it. Marked by red-top pins with a streamer designating the military unit involved, the movement was always forward and steady. On October 14 the ROKs proceeded along the east coast north of Wonsan. They crossed the 38th Parallel on October 1, and captured Wonsan on October 10.

I asked Major Bridges for his version of my duties as the company commander of H&S, as I was not fully acquainted with the job description. He replied that my principal duty was selecting, establishing, and defending the command post. The command post, or CP, is the nerve center of the battalion. H&S is a hodge-podge of many diverse groups: the intelligence section, the administrative unit, the operations section, motor transportation and supply, a guard platoon, the medical unit and the communications platoon. When he stated that the TACP unit was also assigned to H&S, I was taken aback.

"What on earth is TACP?" I asked.

"TACP stands for Tactical Air Control Party," Bridges replied. "You will find this the most effective development made by the Marine Corps since World War II. I suggest you talk to Captain Barrow about this—he's used it most successfully. Bob surely will get a major medal for his performance at Yongdung-po and Seoul. Captain Robbie Robinson is the officer in charge of our battalion TACP, a unit consisting of two air officers and 12 enlisted men."

Captain Robbie Robinson was an aviator. He was a youthful-looking officer, about 5'11", and came from California. Because he went on many missions with "A" Company, and was a great admirer of Barrow, he preferred to reside with it. He joined the battalion at Inchon and until then was unacquainted with the ways of ground Marines in battle. At Yongdung-po, he asked Barrow to tell him what was happening. After Bob explained that "A" Company was in front of the division and surrounded by North Korean soldiers, he replied, "I'm sorry I asked you. Now I'm scared!" If he really was scared, other officers of "A" Company said he never showed it.

Robbie explained the air support operations. Every Marine infantry battalion carried with it a Tactical Air Control Party. When the ground commander needed air support, the TACP officer communicated by radio with the Tactical Air Direction Center. The ground officer designated the target, the nature and description, the time desired, the call signs and frequencies, the specific number of planes requested, and the identification of the front lines and vehicle markings. When the attacking aircraft reported on station, the unit commander received instructions from the aviator in the air to mark the front lines. Cloth panels were laid on the ground for this purpose. Before any strike, the ground officer and aviator verified all instructions. Normally, a white phosphorus shell designated the position to be attacked.

At mealtime, the second shift of officers rehashed experiences at Inchon, Yongdung-po, and the capture of Seoul. They frequently discussed Bob Barrow, partly because he didn't eat with this shift, but more importantly because he exhibited great leadership in handling his company. Bob Barrow was raised a few miles north of Baton Rouge, Louisiana, attended school at LSU and Tulane, and enlisted in the Marine Corps in 1942. A muscular 6'4", he served briefly as an assistant drill instructor at San Diego before going to officers' school. After being commissioned a second lieutenant in 1943, he spent most of his World War II combat duty fighting with the Nationalists in China against the Japanese. He was unmarried.

Barrow visited the wardroom only at mealtime. He had a soft-spoken southern accent, but said little. Like the others, he enjoyed listening to the ship's captain expound. His sharp features, narrow chin, and piercing eyes etched a picture of a highly intelligent man. While aboard ship, I gleaned my impression of him, with the exception of his physical appearance and confident bearing, from his officers. They talked admiringly of the firm, friendly way he handled his company.

"He knows how to make the right decision under fire," one said, "and once he's got his mind made up, he's not going to let the higher-ups pressure him into making a wrong move. Captain Barrow knew that railway station at Seoul had gooks inside. The big brass wanted to announce Seoul had been secured. They kept pushing the Skipper to take us on in there, but he wouldn't order us forward until an air strike had been called. Damn, we were lucky!" he exclaimed. "That station had gooks UTA. Half our company would've been wiped out if we'd advanced before that air strike!"

From listening to them talk, I could see that Barrow's performance at Yongdung-po and Seoul clearly pushed his stature above the hedgerow of other competent Marine officers of his rank.

On the third day at sea, we received news of an important top-level conference between General MacArthur and President Truman at Wake Island. After the meeting, we received very little information, although Truman announced that it was "a most satisfactory conference," while in Washington the Republicans labeled it "a political ploy to get votes for Democratic Congressional candidates in November."

The Top Secret transcript of the meeting reported that MacArthur anticipated an end to all "formal resistance . . . throughout North and South Korea by Thanksgiving." A short time later, he made the same announcement to the press: "It is my hope to be able to withdraw the 8th Army to Japan by Christmas." This uniformly optimistic attitude encouraged plans for rehabilitation.

During the meeting President Truman asked, "What are the chances for Chinese or Soviet interference?"

"Very little," MacArthur replied. "Had they interfered in the first or second months it would have been decisive. We are no longer fearful of their intervention. We no longer stand hat in hand. The Chinese have 300,000 men in Manchuria. Of these, probably not more than 100,000 to 125,000 are distributed along the Yalu River. Only 50,000 to 60,000 could be gotten across the Yalu River. They have no Air Force. Now that we have bases for our Air Force in Korea, if the Chinese tried to get down to Pyongyong there would be the greatest slaughter.

"With the Russians, it is a little different. They have an Air Force in Siberia, and a fairly good one, with excellent pilots equipped with some jets and B-25 and B-29 planes. They can put 1,000 planes in the air with some 200 to 300 more from the 5th and 7th Soviet Fleets. They are probably no match for our Air Force. The Russians have no ground troops available for North Korea. . . . Russian Air is deployed in a semi-circle through Mukden and Harbin but the coordination between the Russian Air and the Chinese Ground would be so flimsy that I believe Russian air would bomb the Chinese as often as they would bomb us. *Ground support is a very difficult thing to do. Our Marines do it perfectly. They have been trained for it. Our own Air and Ground Forces are not as good as the Marines, but they are effective. Between untrained Air and Ground forces an air umbrella is impossible without a lot of joint training. I believe it just wouldn't work with Chinese Communist ground and Russian air. We are the best."* (Italics added.)

MacArthur put his finger on the key to successful tactical air support of ground forces: "It is impossible without a lot of joint training." Contrary to MacArthur's view this joint training had not been emphasized between the U.S. Army and the U.S. Air Force for the five-year period prior to the Korean War. Before the meeting ended, MacArthur thanked all for the support he had received. "No commander has ever had more co-operation from all branches of government than I," he affirmed.

Everyone aboard ship shared MacArthur's optimism. MacArthur was a frequent subject of conversation in our wardroom, and all applauded him. Everyone seemed to know that he ordered the Inchon landing over the objections of other branches of the Armed Services. Never before had I been among Marine officers who sung his praises with such fervor, and for the first time I found myself joining the chorus.

Each day at mealtime more was said about "A" Company. An examination of its background helped one to understand its success. In August 1950, "A" Company, approximately 120 officers and men with an authorized strength of 228, was stationed at Camp Lejeune, North Carolina, as "A" Company, 1st Battalion, 2nd Marine Division. All the officers and staff NCOs had World War II combat experience. When ordered to the West Coast it became "A" Company, 1st Battalion, 1st Marines. After the company arrived at Camp Pendleton, an addition of 45 Regulars from various posts throughout the country and 55 Reserves from Oklahoma City, Tucson, and Los Angeles, brought the company to full strength. It was the first company to plant the American flag in the capital of South Korea.

The company executive officer, Lieutenant Dick Wilson, was a Reserve from Los Angeles. A bachelor with many girl friends, he was known throughout the company for his huge appetite for food and the large quantity of letters, both written and received. A quiet, steady officer, he never appeared ruffled by anyone or any situation.

Lieutenant William A. McClelland, leader of the 1st Platoon, came from Philadelphia. Tall, fearless and dependable, he was a mustang—an officer who rose from the ranks—who had served as a combat sergeant during World War II. McClelland was highly respected by his men. He never made a display of temper, and was very discerning about the needs of his troops.

Lieutenant Donald R. Jones from Illinois was another mustang who during World War II served as a sergeant in a machine gun platoon. He led the 2nd Platoon. Beginning as a private with the Marine Raiders during the early part of the war, he had his full share of combat duty in the Pacific before being wounded at Okinawa. Jones was very energetic and alert. He had the reputation of being everywhere at once in a fire fight, constantly exposing himself to enemy fire, but somehow never getting hit—a real fighter among fighting Marines. In discussions at mealtime, he stressed that a leader must lead. "When you have a fire team or squad leader who refuses to move forward in the face of enemy fire," he insisted, "the platoon leader must get with him and shove him forward."

Lieutenant John J. Swords, the platoon leader of the 3rd Platoon, was from upstate New York. He was an ensign in the U.S. Navy during World War II. He was belligerently sentimental about his troops, and had a good sense of humor.

Staff Sergeant Ernest J. Umbaugh was the platoon sergeant for the 1st Platoon. A rugged, tough NCO from Iowa, he was known as a very devoted family man. Staff Sergeant William Roach, the platoon sergeant for the 3rd Platoon, was a salty Marine who was called to active duty with his PFC son from the Los Angeles Reserve Unit. His son, while serving with the 9th Marines, was severely wounded during the Seoul operation, and had to be evacuated to Japan. Aboard ship, Roach couldn't get news about him. Lieutenant Swords said, "Roach doesn't give a damn about his own welfare, but he sure does worry about that son of his."

The company gunnery sergeant, Technical Sergeant King D. Thatenhurst, came from Birmingham, Alabama. He was 6'5" and weighed 240 pounds—not an ounce of fat on his body. During World War II, he had earned five Purple Hearts. Two Purple Hearts exempted one from service in Korea. Thatenhurst had to fight to stay with the company when it left the West Coast. "A" Company officers described him as a practical, hard-working, extremely loyal individual, who served as Barrow's right arm.

Sergeant Bennedette served the company as supply sergeant. He hailed from New York. He was one of the Marines who had been captured by the Japanese on Wake Island during World War II, and stayed in prison camps for the remainder of the war.

Corporal Frank Lescoe, a wireman from Maine, was short, dark, and always smiling. He was one of an unsung group. It is hard work to put the wire in, and dangerous to maintain, particularly when trouble-shooting. Inspecting a wire between the lines often causes shooting from both friend and foe.

Corporal Joe Leeds, a fire team leader in the 2nd Platoon, had been raised in an orphanage in New Jersey. Quiet and fearless, he fought as if he had the biggest stake of all.

Corporal Billy Webb, a squad leader in the 3rd Platoon, was a Reserve from Oklahoma—handsome, smart, and utterly fearless.

Sergeant Harry Spies from New Jersey was the section leader in the Machine Gun Platoon. "A" Company officers claimed that at Yongdung-po and Seoul he constantly displayed his bravery, a dynamic, explosive, inspiring type of courage. Spies was full of ingenious schemes for killing the enemy. He was always the first to reach his destination, remaining there to rebuke others for being late.

His top machine gunner, PFC Guy Tucker, from West Virginia, kept all around him entertained with his chatter and homespun humor. He spoke with a thick mountain accent. A skilled gunner, he was very cool and effective in combat. PFC Robert Carter from Augusta, Georgia, acted as a fire team leader in the 1st Platoon. An all-state football player, he was rugged and full of fight.

Next to "A" Company, Chesty Puller was the subject of most conversations. "He ordered us to advance down the main street of Seoul," an officer explained, "and when Colonel Hawkins advised that our intelligence reports said there were snipers in the buildings, Chesty bellowed, 'Hell, Hawkins! Snipers got no business holding up a column!'"

"What did you do?" I asked.

"Silly question!" he said grinning. "We advanced as ordered."

"Well, what about the snipers?"

"They came down out of the buildings and gave up," he laughed.

The occasion prompted another to joke, "You know Chesty doesn't need an R3 [Plans and Operations officer] for his attack orders."

"How's that?"

"All he needs is a map, a writing stick, and a straight edge."

With no space aboard for exercise, the men gathered daily beside a truck or truck bed, any available place that could be found. There they cleaned their rifles, machine guns, and other weapons, not because they needed to, but because it gave them a means of fighting boredom.

On October 19, the ship's radio announced that Pyongyang, the North Korean capital, had fallen to the 1st Cavalry Division without serious opposition. Bill Bridges appropriately stuck a pin on our map in the wardroom. On the east coast, the red-top pins showed the ROKs pushing northward beyond Hamhung. At mealtime all agreed the worst was over. Most felt that the North Korean operation was an all-expense-paid adventure, with little personal risk involved—like China duty after World War II.

Captain John Coffey, the Battalion 4 (Service and Supply), issued me a nylon sleeping bag. John had a boyish face, and had married a girl from Portsmouth, Virginia, a friend of my sister's. Friendly and competent, he did a fine job of anticipating our needs.

Our sleeping bags were unique. During World War II, the Navy became particularly concerned about the effect of Arctic or near Arctic waters upon the sailors when torpedoed. Regardless of clothing, the sailors could not survive the cold shock. It was observed that the seal could swim in the coldest waters without freezing. Upon examination it was found the seal has two layers of skin that hold the heat on the inside like a thermos. Food eaten converts to heat energy. The nylon sleeping bag consisted of two layers which held heat inside on the same principle. It, too, acted as a thermos. Once the bag was punctured, however, most of its protection against the cold was lost. An elastic band made the bag fit tightly around the face. The hood covered the face, yet permitted one to breathe freely.

On our fifth night at sea, I talked at length with Kim and Suhr after dinner. Suhr did most of the talking, while Kim listened. Suhr proudly proclaimed the Rhee government had initiated compulsory education that year for all children in South Korea. Although there were many public schools in the south, the Presbyterian and Catholic missionary schools gave the best education. Most of our interpreters had come from these church schools. Suhr boasted that the first metal printing type was invented by the Koreans in the late 1300s, and that a phonetic alphabet was devised in 1438. This alphabet simplified their written language. "Korea would be a great nation now, had China and Japan left us alone," he concluded.

After Kim and Suhr retired, I wrote a letter to Ginny. Jim Adair remained in the wardroom. While sipping a cup of coffee he began: "You know, it's hard to understand why a man like Captain Kim will not take prisoners."

"What do you mean by that?" I replied, somewhat stunned.

"When a North Korean prisoner was entrusted to his care in Seoul, Kim would take him up the street and kill him by shooting him in the back of the head."

"I find that hard to believe!" I replied skeptically. I went to bed thinking that Adair was putting me on. Nevertheless, I lay awake for hours just thinking about it.

The next morning after breakfast, I asked the battalion chaplain, Lieutenant Commander Jones, if Adair's statement was true. When he answered in the affirmative, I asked if Suhr had done the same thing.

"No, he's different," he replied.

Later in the day I told Adair that I could no longer sit near Kim at the dinner table. As far as I was concerned he was a murderer. Thereafter I confined my questions about Korea to Suhr.

Sometime during the night before we were due to arrive in Wonsan, I woke up. Our ship had slowed and I felt it making a turn. The next morning, we were told that Wonsan harbor was heavily mined. We would have to circle until the harbor was cleared by mine sweepers. We circled for five days. Our delay was labeled "Operation Yo-Yo" by those aboard.

Near the end of our voyage the food supply ran low. Everyone cheered when news came over the loudspeaker the night of October 25 that we would be landing at Wonsan the next morning. After eleven days at sea we looked forward anxiously to getting on land again, especially onto North Korean soil.

While we were making our journey Douglas MacArthur unilaterally changed UN policy for the conduct of the war in Korea. On October 17 he proclaimed a new restraining line, running north of Chongju to Songjin on the east coast, well above the Korean "waist" between Sinanju and Hungnam, the best defensive line north of the Parallel. A week later, on October 24, he did away altogether with the restraining line for non-Korean UN forces. When the Joint Chiefs informed MacArthur that this was not in consonance with their directive of September 29, he replied by citing Secretary of War Marshall's personal message of September 29, telling him to feel unhampered in his operations. His action, he said, was justified by military necessity; his ROK forces were weak and badly led. The Joint Chiefs failed to overrule MacArthur, a grievous error. By permitting him to disregard their policy directive without prior justification, they surrendered to him authority they should have retained.

5

Trouble at Kojo

Chesty Puller was waiting for us when we finally disembarked on October 26. Prior to our arrival, Wonsan had been occupied by ROK troops. These men had pushed north. Puller ordered the 1st Battalion to move immediately by train to the town of Kojo on the east coast, forty miles to the south where rice, ammunition, and other supplies for the ROK troops were stored.

There were supposedly some North Korean troops in the area. Puller's comment to Colonel Hawkins regarding that possibility amused me. "Hell, Jack, there's not a damned thing down there to worry about," he said, "but if the Commies do hit you, you can beat the hell outa' them!"

Soon after we got aboard the train, I met Captain Wes Noren, the commander of "B" Company. Noren had enlisted in the Marine Corps in 1939 and had come up through the ranks. He was from Milaca, Minnesota, of obvious Scandinavian ancestry. He was blond and muscular, weighed 165 pounds, and was of medium height. He held himself erect; his character was written on his face and bearing.

I could readily see why Fritz and Pruitt greatly admired their former company commander. They were always saying about him, "He's good people!" Wes looked and acted as a Marine officer should. He introduced me to all his junior officers. We chatted a bit before I walked through the train to meet Captain Bob Wray, the commander of "C" Company. Wray was an ex—

Marine Corps aviator from Oregon. Though he had not served with ground troops for very long, he had an appetite for learning. He had obviously gained the respect of his men, and was in the process of becoming a good field officer.

We arrived at Kojo in midafternoon. It was a small fishing village flanked by white beaches and sparkling blue water in the bay. Kojo appeared untouched by modern civilization; it was unspoiled and undamaged by the war. One lone, narrow road from north to south ran through the middle of the village. No road led to the west, only foot trails. The railroad bed coming from the south closely paralleled the dirt road except that it turned left about 500 yards before reaching the village. A few hills and rice paddies surrounded the village for the first few miles from the sea. Five miles inland the hills developed into mountains.

The ROK officers who met the train assured Colonel Hawkins of a tame assignment. They admitted, however, that small bands of escaping North Korean People's Army (NKPA) soldiers sometimes raided the village for rice. They added that they had scoured the hills without finding any trace of organized resistance. After we left the train, Colonel Hawkins pointed to a large hill about 1,500 yards northwest of the village. There he ordered me to establish the battalion command post. After only a few hundred feet my jeep slowed to avoid some chickens pecking rice kernels from the high grass in the middle of the road. Before leaving the road, the jeep stopped abruptly to miss running over a shoat that was dozing in the autumn sun.

H&S deployed on the hillside to avoid concentrating the men into a prime mortar target. I located the battalion aid station near the road and railroad, on a flat piece of ground 200 yards east of the command post. Since an outside kitchen would not be established, the cooks dug in near the aid station. In battle the cooks would become litter bearers. The battalion switchboard was placed in a small ravine, away from Hawkins's foxhole. A phone line connected the foxhole to the switchboard. The supply unit occupied an area near the road and railroad, approximately 100 yards north of the aid station. The men of the guard platoon formed a half-circle on the west side of the command post, so that H&S would not have to rely upon the rifle companies for defense. By nightfall, everyone's foxhole was deep enough for protection in case of a fire fight. My men were expert craftsmen; each knew his job and did it without any reminders.

When I joined the Marine Corps in 1940, the entire Marine Corps then consisted of only 52,000 officers and men. I was tremendously impressed at the time with the professionalism of the individual enlisted Marine regular. Rapid expansion during World War II had watered down the Marine Corps ranks, but here, ten years later, I saw we had come full cycle. Again the regulars of the 1st were true professionals. The officers were especially competent. A large number of the officers of the battalion had come up through the ranks. They had earned their bars through leadership and acts of valor in battle. For a combat officer, personal courage is essential. A diploma from West Point, Annapolis, or some other college doesn't assure this quality.

This was my first night of sleeping on the ground since World War II. It was a crisp October night, football weather in the States. A thin layer of ice covered the water in the rice paddies nearby. The ground was hard. I was still soft. Lying there in my sleeping bag, I felt I was literally freezing to death. Try as hard as I might, I could not sleep that night.

"A" Company, "B" Company, and "C" Company, with parts of Weapons Company attached to each, occupied areas at varying distances from the command post. They were anywhere from 1,000 to 5,000 yards away. Each company deployed in separate company or platoon defense formations. Our intelligence information did not call for the tight battalion perimeter defense we used later. The perimeter defense is similar to that seen in western movies, where the wagons form a circle before a fight with the Indians. Here mortars, artillery, and command post do not occupy a place on line; instead, they stay well inside the circle.

The next morning, all companies began reconnoitering the area, interviewing North Korean civilians through interpreters, and digging better foxholes. Major Bates, the Weapons CO, positioned the heavy weapons to cover the best potential targets. Our men watched in amusement as the ROK soldiers crowded into gondola cars. Many had their women, children, and chickens with them on their ride back to Wonsan.

Major Bridges sent me on a patrol to reconnoiter for a new command post. The vicinity he had in mind supposedly contained a church near a schoolhouse approximately a mile to a mile and a half from our present position. Jim Adair and two rifle squads accompanied me. It looked quite plain on the map, but after searching for half the day, my patrol could find neither church nor schoolhouse. We later learned our maps were inaccurate. They were acquired from the Japanese and were pre–World War II vintage.

When we approached camp upon our return, we saw everyone looking at the top of the hill. A large group of Koreans had gathered around the community cemetery. At the foot of the hill, another group of Koreans with picks and shovels had assembled.

Chaplain Jones was walking in circles, despairingly wringing his hands. He exclaimed, "A horrible thing is about to occur! A South Korean youth group in charge of political activity has searched Kojo and weeded out the Communist North Koreans—about 65 to 70. Those at the top of the hill are now being forced to dig their own graves. After the graves have been dug, they're to be executed!" Pointing, he continued, "Those at the foot of the hill with picks and shovels are neighbors who will bury the Communists after the execution."

Many young Marines around the CP appeared excited at the prospect of watching a mass execution. This attitude shocked me. I couldn't imagine civilized people shooting prisoners, political or otherwise, only a day or two after their capture. Without waiting for orders, Jim Adair ran to the top of the hill. He told the South Korean youth group they could not shoot the prisoners. I ordered a squad to go with him and give him backing. A noncommissioned officer was dispatched to the foot of the hill to instruct the neighbors to stay put.

After considerable argument, the political prisoners came back down the hill. Most were weeping. One was a boy of 12. They were taken to the rail station, placed on the train, and went to Wonsan for further interrogation.

"Why the 12-year-old boy?" I asked. "Why was he to be executed?"

"When the North Korean Army came through the village he was seen passing a hand grenade to one of the soldiers," was the reply.

A few hours later, near dusk, Lieutenant Paul Vnenchak, our communications officer, came running to the CP, completely out of breath. He had been out with his wire crews, he told Colonel Hawkins, driving along beside a rice paddy two miles away at approximately 35 miles per hour, when they had been fired upon. One bullet struck his jeep driver in the middle of the forehead. The jeep went out of control, then overturned. Vnenchak was thrown safe. He crawled back to administer first aid but found his driver was dead. Paul then crept along the ditch on one side of the road, keeping himself out of sight of North Korean soldiers on the opposite side. After crawling for some distance, he made a run for it, not stopping until he reached the command post.

While Paul related this incident, word came that one of his wire crews in the vicinity of Wes Noren's "B" Company about two miles south of Kojo had been fired on. Wes had placed his three rifle platoons on three small hills jutting up from the rice fields. Each hill afforded good observation from any approach. Because of the water level, however, foxholes could not be dug in the rice paddies themselves. A few minutes later, we were told that no member of the wire crew was killed or wounded. These first few shots should have warned us of worse things to come, but no one seemed too perturbed at nightfall.

Night brought darkness—a different kind of darkness, the kind I had not experienced since World War II. No lights, no fires anywhere—only the stars to break the pattern. There had been a few fires in the distance the night before, but not now. I crawled into my sleeping bag shortly after dusk. Exhausted from lack of sleep I dozed off immediately. I woke to the sound of nearby gunfire from almost every direction.

At 2200 heavy firing began in Wes Noren's Baker Company area, followed by rifle shots near "A" and "C" Company positions. Sixty millimeter mortar shells, periodically lighting up the sky, showed North Korean soldiers coming forward to the attack. In many cases enemy infiltrated within grenade-throwing distance before being detected.

Near daybreak, a lieutenant from "B" Company arrived at the CP and reported that his platoon had been overrun. Some of his men had been bayoneted in their sleeping bags. Enemy soldiers had passed through the sentries without observation, even though the machine guns managed to level in on target afterward killing large numbers. The lieutenant said, "I think that most, if not all, of my men have been killed." The buddy system had failed in the lieutenant's platoon because the buddy on duty was not awake. Fighting continued until daybreak.

Colonel Hawkins sent a radio message asking for reinforcements. Helicopters were requested for air evacuation and an LST for water evacuation of the wounded. Due to transmission difficulty, the message did not reach the 1st Marine Headquarters until 0700. When morning came, most of the North Koreans evaporated into the hills. They left scores of their dead behind, together with large numbers of wounded and others that we took prisoners. Our battalion suffered heavy casualties. All the companies except H&S were hit hard. Our first report showed that we suffered nine killed, 39 wounded, and 34 missing in action. This was especially disturbing since our strength was already down to less than 720 officers and men due to casualties suffered at Yongdung-po and Seoul.

Wes Noren's Baker Company was the hardest hit. Bob Barrow sent a platoon to help evacuate the wounded. They were carried in ponchos through rice paddies, knee-deep in mud and water. Midmorning, when most of the wounded had been recovered, about 200 North Korean troops who had stayed behind in Kojo suddenly ran across the rice paddies heading west. Marines of "A" and "B" Companies combined with the gunners of Fox Battery to kill almost half without return fire. The survivors escaped to the hills.

Colonel Hawkins sent another radio message at 1000. "Received determined attack from south, north, and west from sunset to sunrise by large enemy force, estimated at 1,000 to 1,200. . . . Civilian reports indicate possibility 3,000 enemy this immediate area. . . . If this position is to be held, a regiment is required. . . . Harbor in our hands and ROK LST has been here. Shall we hold or withdraw to north? ROK supply dump removed. Request immediate instructions. Send all available helicopters for wounded."

After interrogating the first few of our 83 prisoners, we found the North Koreans planned to make another major attack after sundown. The prisoners informed us the North Korean 5th Division command post was located a few miles south near the town of Tonchon, although some units of the NKPA's division were further south. The total strength of the division was estimated at 7,000 to 8,000 men. Colonel Cho Il Kwon, the former director of the Communist Party in Wonsan, commanded those attacking us. His unit was trained in China and fought against the Japanese in World War II.

In Wonsan, after conferring with Division and Corps Headquarters, Colonel Puller ordered the 2nd Battalion to Kojo. It was due to arrive after midnight, or early the next morning. All through the day helicopters worked away efficiently, evacuating the wounded, a major step forward since World War II. Most young Marines don't think of the likelihood of dying in battle; death always comes to the other fellow. Being wounded, however, is something expected by many, if not by most. Care for a wounded Marine—the best care—is essential. When a Marine is wounded in the front line, his platoon and company commanders will risk more deaths and wounded in order to save the one. This all-out attempt to rescue the wounded is one of the foundation stones upon which U.S. Marine esprit de corps is built.

In keeping with tradition, men in each company concentrated on retrieving dead, wounded, and missing. By day's end, the morning figures were revised to 23 dead, 47 wounded, and four missing. Hawkins seemed very upset by this turn of events. We spent the additional time in preparation for the second attack, expected by nightfall. The battalion CP was relocated onto another hill diagonally across from our previous station. This time all the rifle companies formed a tight perimeter around the command post.

Before we moved our positions, the head of the South Korean

youth group called on Hawkins. The Korean expressed his displeasure with the action Adair and I had taken the day before in preventing the mass execution. "It was wrong to stop us. Now I will have to return to South Korea," he complained bitterly. "There is no other choice. I have lost face."

Colonel Hawkins listened, but said nothing to Adair or me.

As we packed our gear for the move, a large group of people—women, children, and older men—somewhere between 800 and 1,000 in number, came walking up the road toward us. When they reached a position about 300 yards away, Colonel Hawkins ordered them to turn back. We shouted, but not comprehending, they proceeded on. Hawkins ordered us to fire if necessary to force them to take another route. I told him I thought they were civilians.

"Yes," he agreed, "but they may be shielding North Korean soldiers."

When shouting failed, I ordered gunners to put tracer bullets in two of our machine guns and fire over the heads of the gathering. One gun fired low, wounding a few civilians. Although our corpsmen rendered assistance to the injured, I have always felt a pang of conscience about this unnecessary injury. After the tracers were fired, the civilians turned back and moved to a small peninsula outside Kojo. There they stayed for the next few days. I never learned why they were going north. My guess is that they came from Tonchon to escape the North Korean soldiers.

Our new command post occupied ground on a steep hill commanding a good view of the surrounding area in daylight. We established a tight perimeter defense by late afternoon. The loss of men the previous night and the apparent size of the enemy force created a tense situation throughout the battalion. Everyone expected a major assault soon after dark. Although we had received word from Wonsan that the 2nd Battalion was coming to our assistance, we knew it could not arrive before midnight, perhaps not until the next day. Tension grew as the sun lowered toward China.

An hour before sunset, Chesty Puller and his bodyguard,

Bodey, arrived via helicopter. Chesty asked the mortarmen whether they had enough ammunition.

"Yes," they replied.

"That's fine. You'll get the chance to use those things tonight." Puller grinned.

He walked around the line, chatting, smiling and asking questions of riflemen and machine gunners. Again he queried about enough ammunition.

When they answered, "Yes," he cautioned, "Now don't waste it! Wait until you're getting Commies with it. Let 'em get in close. Don't waste ammo. Get your share! Remember, you don't hurt 'em if you don't hit 'em!"

Within the hour, Puller replaced fear with determination. Before his arrival the men genuinely felt on the defensive. Now the 1st of the 1st hoped the North Koreans would come again so they could "mow 'em down."

While the colonel was inspecting the defenses, Bodey came to the command post to dig Puller's foxhole and prepare his evening meal. Bodey had killed a large bird, a gull of some sort, on the beach. He dressed and prepared it, then proceeded to cook it for Puller's meal. Since he had no utensils, he used his helmet. He made a fire, then poured water into the helmet. It didn't take long for the green paint inside the helmet to peel off in the water as it boiled.

Fritz, Pruitt, and others around the command post were digging foxholes. Whenever they took a break, they passed by Bodey to inspect his progress. As the bird cooked, the water grew darker from the peeled-off paint. Nevertheless, Bodey continued, totally oblivious of the effect the green paint was having on the end product. The men began to speculate.

"He's trying to make points with the colonel," someone commented.

"I wonder if Chesty will eat it when he sees it?"

"If Chesty eats that, he'll eat anything!"

"Chesty's stomach is just like Chesty; it can hold anything," another replied.

"I bet he eats it."

"I bet he doesn't," one countered.

"I'll take that bet. My tonight's C rations against yours."

"You're on."

Puller climbed the hill and arrived at the command post. The men stopped digging to watch his reaction. Bodey took the bird out of the helmet. The outside skin was almost as green as the water. "I can't eat that thing!" Puller exclaimed.

"Pay off! I told you so!" somebody declared.

"Okay, you win."

The men returned to digging. "If Bodey had boiled water in the helmet before cooking the bird, then poured the water on the ground, then cooked the bird in fresh water . . ."—such was said by many to be the school solution. Others adhered to their belief that you just can't cook a gull in a helmet, period.

Puller opened a can of cold beef stew, and sat on the ground beside his foxhole, near mine. He began eating. Looking to the side, he spoke. "Hey, Roanoke, how's it going with you?"

"I've no complaints."

We struck up a lengthy conversation about life at the mouth of the Rappahannock River where it enters Chesapeake Bay. Chesty's home at Saluda, Virginia, was located on the south side of the river. Ginny and I often visited her aunt and uncle, Adelaide and Charles Tennant, on the north side at Wind Mill Point.

I then told him I had served with his brother, Sam Puller, twice—once in Basic School at the Philadelphia Navy Yard at the beginning of World War II, and again in the Pacific with the 3rd Marine Division.

"He was killed in Guam, you know," Puller said.

"Yes, sir."

"Did you like him?"

"Yes, sir."

"I miss him; I miss him." He frowned, his voice trailing.

I changed the subject. "You know, Colonel, there is one thing I can't understand. It doesn't make sense that the 1st Marine Division was sent to Wonsan in the first place. To be more explicit, after capturing Seoul, we were near the 38th Parallel on the west coast. It seems we should have been sent north up the west coast, with an Army division and ROK troops coming up the east coast. We wouldn't have tied up all those Navy vessels transporting people and equipment. That shipping could have been used for hauling ammunition, clothing, food, and other necessary supplies."

"It makes sense to me," he replied. "How many divisions does the Army have here?"

"Five or six, I think."

"Who's in charge?"

"The Army—no, General MacArthur."

"The Marines captured Seoul, didn't they? That's the capital of South Korea, isn't it?"

"Yes, sir."

"Well, if you were running this show and you were Army, would you let that one Marine division capture both capitals? Pyongyang is only a hundred miles north of the 38th Parallel."

"I see your point, I guess."

Darkness came again. All talking ceased. We kept close vigil through the night. No attack came. The North Koreans had apparently received enough punishment the previous night.

Shortly after midnight the 2nd Battalion arrived. The next day I talked to Robbie Robinson. "Why weren't your planes used to hit the North Koreans when they made a run for it from Kojo?"

"Our communication system was faulty," he replied. "That's unusual. We don't bring planes in close unless we know exactly what we're doing. We can't take a chance on dive-bombing our own troops. We did bomb Tonchon. If the gooks were where the prisoners said, we did a good day's work."

Sergeant Orville Jones, who accompanied Puller on most occasions in Korea, came to Kojo with the 2nd Battalion. Jones and Bodey found Irish potatoes in a cellar in Kojo. They roasted a few for Puller's dinner the second evening. Bodey prepared a roast pig to go with the potatoes. The men around the CP warned Bodey that our information bulletins said Korean pork was unfit for human consumption.

"Whaddya mean, it's no good?" Bodey protested. "Five minutes ago he was running down the road, a good healthy pig!"

The pig was eaten by Puller and others with no ill effects.

The next two days and nights in Kojo passed without incident. After continuous probing by patrols going miles in all directions, it became apparent the enemy had abandoned the area. We cleaned up, then went aboard an LST and returned to Wonsan. With all our searching, we never found our four missing men.

While aboard ship, Suhr said to me, "Captain, I make it a point not to ask personal questions, but I couldn't help overhearing that you live in Virginia."

"That's right," I answered.

"I have a sister going to school there. Her name is Hannah."

"Oh, you do," I said.

"You may not recognize the place because it is a small town—Salem, Virginia. She goes to Roanoke College."

"My gosh, Suhr, this is a small world! I know all about that school. I went there myself one year. My law firm represents Roanoke College. Mr. James C. Martin, the senior partner, graduated in the Class of 1898."

Suhr's eyes lit up. "That's my father's class! Give me that man's name again."

"James C. Martin. As soon as we get to Wonsan, I intend to write Mr. Martin about your father," I assured him. "Give me some details about your family—Mr. Martin will be extremely interested and would certainly like to know about your father."

We talked about Suhr's father and family for the rest of the trip. It was not until we approached Wonsan that I realized I did not see Captain Kim at Kojo. He apparently left us at Wonsan, never to return.

6

Enter the Chinese

After less than a week in Kojo we arrived in Wonsan again shortly after noon on November 1. When our ship was unloaded, we boarded trucks and drove through the middle of the city. Koreans of all ages, many with American flags, lined both sides of the streets waving and cheering as we passed. I turned to Suhr and told him I was delighted with the tremendous reception.

"Captain, do not be deceived by what you see on their faces," he answered, looking somewhat disgusted. In all my later contacts with North Korean civilians, I was never able to justify this cynical view of Suhr's.

Wonsan was a drab city with a population of 90,000, but to an American observer it appeared to be scarcely one-fifth that size. Too many people crammed into sparse home space accounted for this misconception. It had been bombed, though there were few military targets. The spots with the largest shell holes were in civilian areas. The oil storage tanks near the harbor were prime targets, and most of these had been destroyed by our planes. There were few other military targets worth destroying, certainly no industry of use in war. Regrettably, Tokyo headquarters continued to assign missions to the B-29s.

We took up defense positions on the western side of Wonsan. The CP was established on a small hill, the top of which formed a plateau, with good observation in all directions. As at

Kojo, H&S formed its own perimeter around the CP. The rifle companies, in contrast with Kojo, established separate defense perimeters in close proximity to us. Patrols accompanied by interpreters were immediately dispatched in all directions. Foot patrols covered the nearby area, while motor patrols traveled five to ten miles away.

Shortly after we arrived, my morale got a tremendous boost. At mail call I received a number of letters—a month's accumulation, mostly from Ginny. She had arrived at Rocky Mount, had written every day, and was anxious to hear from me. I passed around the enclosed baby pictures, the first ones that I had seen. Ginny also enclosed clippings from the *Roanoke Times* and *World-News*, of items I would not likely see in Korea. I knew she must have received my letters by this time, for I had written her every day since my departure except while in Kojo.

When the patrols returned near the end of the day, each had the same story to tell. They talked extensively with civilians who reported they had not seen a North Korean soldier for days. Suhr convinced us the civilians were giving the straight scoop. Patrols were again sent out the morning of the second day, and returned in the afternoon with the same message.

Midmorning the second day we received word of General Smith's wisest military decision in North Korea—CURFEW! Marines were ordered off the streets and away from the North Korean places of business by nightfall. We were further informed that military police would patrol the streets of Wonsan at night. Any Marine caught after dark without a proper explanation would be court-martialed.

Important as these moves proved later, they caused little comment throughout our battalion. Most agreed there was nothing to see or do in Wonsan, anyhow.

General Smith recognized the importance of good relations with civilians. In addition to curfew, he ordered each Marine battalion to have one officer designated as the political officer for contact with the local governments. Colonel Hawkins assigned Jim Adair to this position for our battalion. Each time we moved into a new location, it was Adair's duty to contact the local officials and inform them of our presence, along with our rules and regulations, so as to eliminate possible friction between the Marines and North Koreans.

Since the enemy was not around, there was little activity other than patrolling. To fight boredom, the men read everything from comic books to *Readers' Digest*. The overseas editions of *Time*, *Newsweek*, and *Life* were especially popular. Swapping sea stories, a favorite pastime of Marines in any war, and following the progress of the war outside our zone were top subjects for discussion. Everyone seemed to have an appetite for news of other Marine units in the field.

Near sundown many officers gathered regularly at the CP to talk until it was time to bed down for the night. At the first gathering, Lieutenant Vnenchak reported he had heard a radio broadcast which said that some Chinese volunteers were assisting the North Koreans on the western front. We speculated about what this meant. Most thought it would have no significant bearing on the war's outcome.

On the second night at Wonsan, we griped about the water's taste. Each battalion had an engineer platoon assigned to it. One of its functions was the operation of a water purification unit, although the water could not be used until tested by the battalion medical officer. The battalion surgeon added drops of iodine to keep the germ count within acceptable standards. To offset this heavy iodine taste, many drank only tea and coffee. When we gathered at the CP the second night, the officers used the occasion to chide the doctor.

"Doc, do you *have* to empty all your iodine bottles into that lister bag?"

"Oh, I've got a few left."

"I'll bet that iodine you've got left isn't as strong as what you've got out there in that water bag."

"My iodine is a little stronger," he replied defensively.

"Seriously, Doc, how do you expect us to drink this stuff?" someone spoke up.

"You can do without if you want. This is a populous area. The Koreans use human excretion for fertilizer. The germ count in this water is heavy, regardless of how many times you put it through that purification unit. I can lower the iodine drops, but there are a damn sight more germs than typhoid running around in this water! You've taken a shot for typhoid, but you haven't taken a vaccine to cover the rest of the germs."

"But, Doc, the water at Kojo tasted all right."

"That's because the germ count was low there. You supply me with a nice mountain stream away from people, and I'll take away the iodine."

On November 4 Puller assigned Bob Barrow to guard a truck convoy of 34 vehicles. The vicinity of Wonsan was relatively secure. The main enemy activity centered on the road west to Majon-ni. Thirty miles of twisting, treacherous road led westward from Wonsan to this crossroads of a transportation network that ran south to Seoul, west to Pyongyang, and east to Wonsan. Our 3rd Battalion, occupying a beleaguered perimeter there, needed supplies. For a week the road had been closed by the enemy. The road rose from a few feet above sea level at Wonsan to a height of 3,500 feet a few miles east of Majon-ni. At least 25 miles of road was controlled by the enemy, because of the narrow, precipitous route bordered by high ground on both sides. Marines labeled this area "Ambush Alley."

For added safety, the truck convoy needed to negotiate the entire distance during daylight hours. One platoon of engineers, one 81-millimeter mortar section, and a section of 75-millimeter recoilless rifles reinforced Barrow's "A" Company. He reasoned that because so many roadblocks required engineering equipment, it would be advisable to put the engineer platoon in the lead, followed by a rifle platoon.

The convoy departed Wonsan at 1530. They encountered four undefended crater roadblocks which were speedily filled by the engineers. At the fifth roadblock, however, they were ambushed by Red Koreans occupying the steep heights paralleling the narrow, winding road. With dusk approaching, Bob decided on a return to Wonsan. The trucks turned around safely on the narrow road.

As the enemy fire increased, Bob ordered lights out. In the growing darkness, a truck loaded with 20 Marines missed a hairpin turn, plunging over the edge. The accident occurred at one of the few places where the vehicle could land on a wooded shoulder instead of hurtling through space to the rocky floor several hundred feet below. Lights were turned on and the convoy got back without further incident. Bob's losses amounted to 24 men injured, 16 by the accident, and five vehicles destroyed.

"That was my fault," Puller said to Barrow upon his return. "I started you off too late in the afternoon."

At 0830 the following morning Barrow started out again. He put into effect a new tactical plan, based on the premise that the guerrillas would be waiting as usual for the sound of approaching trucks. This time he prepared a surprise. His infantry platoons took turns leading the column on foot, keeping a thousand yards or more in advance of the vehicles.

When Lieutenant Don Jones's platoon rounded a bend near the scene of the previous ambush, his men completely surprised a large group of North Koreans who had gathered to eat. The ambushers were ambushed! In short order, Jones's men killed 51 and captured three of the 70 or so Communist soldiers. The Koreans failed to return fire. The convoy had no further trouble, arriving at Majon-ni in early afternoon.

After spending the night at Majon-ni, Bob returned the next morning with 619 prisoners who had accumulated at the Majon-ni stockade. The captives were packed into open trucks covered with tarpaulins. Bob took this precaution in order not to advertise the nature of his cargo while passing through "Ambush Alley", the prisoners outnumbered their keepers by three to one.

Simultaneously with the return of "A" Company, Colonel Puller ordered "E" Company 2nd Battalion to proceed to Munchon-ni which straddled the highest pass along "Ambush Alley." North Koreans ambushed "E" Company four miles short of its objective. "A" Company arrived just as the shooting ceased; however, "E" Company suffered eight killed and 38 wounded. Helicopters evacuated the critical casualties, while Barrow brought back the lightly wounded and the prisoners to Wonsan without further interference.

On November 7 a large number of Marine replacements arrived to bring all companies in the battalion up to full strength. The guard platoon of H&S was increased to 40 enlisted, plus one officer. First Lieutenant Brice (Gus) Geisert, a bachelor from California, about my size, joined us as executive officer. Gus was a quiet, unassuming man who performed his duties with a minimum of fanfare. He wrote and received letters from only one girl back home, which led me to believe he intended to marry her upon his return. Corporal William Miracle, from New Jersey, a tall, resourceful individual, was added as my jeep driver. Miracle was quite fittingly gifted in the art of scrounging food.

Our nightly meetings now centered on the Chinese entrance into the Korean War. We had learned that the 1st Cavalry Division had suffered heavy losses in an engagement with the Chinese at Unsan on the western front on November 1. Earlier, on October 26, an ROK Division had been hit hard by the Chinese in the same area and driven back.

Who were these soldiers? How were they led? How could they inflict heavy casualties on a unit such as the 1st Cavalry Division? Some historical background is needed to give proper perspective.

In 1911 Dr. Sun Yat-sen had led the revolution which established the Republic of China the following year. Sun Yat-sen's political entity, the Kuomintang Party, attracted to it two men of similar backgrounds but widely different personalities, Chiang Kai-shek and Mao Tse-tung. After Sun's death in 1925, Chiang Kai-shek made himself commander-in-chief of the National Revolutionary Army, and in 1927 had turned on the Shanghai Workers' organization, killing some 300 Communist and labor leaders. Six days later he organized his own national government in Nanking.

On August 1 of that year, at Nancheng, the Communist Party's central committee organized an insurrection of officers against the Kuomintang, giving birth to the People's Liberation Army. That winter Mao Tse-tung was elected commander of the Red Army, which then consisted of a few thousand half-starved, miserably equipped men.

"Without a people's army, the people have nothing," Mao insisted. "Political power grows out of the barrel of a gun!"

Lin Piao, a Whampoa Military Academy graduate, gave the Communists their first major victory over Chiang Kai-shek's Nationalist troops. In line with the military doctrine developed in Sun-tzu's *The Art of War*, written about 400 B.C., he lured five enemy regiments into pursuing his Red Force into the mountains in Yungshin country. By erecting a roadblock at a narrow pass held by one-third of his force, then sending a small force to the enemy's rear to prevent escape, the major portion of Lin Piao's command swooped down from both sides of the entrapped Nationalists, cutting them to pieces.

The tactics employed at this victory of Lungyuankou on June 23, 1928, became Lin Piao's preferred strategy. A quarter-century later he used the same against the ROKs and the 1st Cavalry Division on the western front in North Korea. The Communist troops formed a "V," termed "Hochi Shiki," into which they allowed enemy forces to move. The sides of the "V" then closed around the enemy while another force moved below the mouth of the "V" to engage any forces attempting to relieve the entrapped unit being systematically annihilated.

When Chiang launched his Fifth Bandit Suppression campaign in 1933, the Chinese Reds planned their celebrated Long March, which became one of their most cherished traditions. Breaking out of Chiang's encirclement in October 1934, they took a circuitous 6,000-mile route to avoid Nationalist armies. Of 90,000 who started, only 6,000 were left a year later when the Communists reached Yenan in Shensi Province. There Mao alternately fought against and negotiated with the government.

After the Japanese marched into Peking on August 8, 1936, Chiang Kai-shek and Chou En-lai concluded a united front agreement, whereby Mao's Red Army became the 8th Route Army of the National Revolutionary Army. Soon after V-J Day, with the Japanese no longer a menace, the grapple for mastery between Chiang Kai-shek and Mao Tse-tung began anew. As a result of the arms and other assistance supplied by the United States, Chiang held a tremendous material and numeric advantage. But his failure to train and discipline his army, as U.S. Lieutenant General Joseph W. (Vinegar Joe) Stilwell had urged during the war, proved his undoing. In contrast, Mao's soldiers had been properly indoctrinated for the inevitable war ahead.

Early in 1948, the "year of decision," the People's Liberation Army captured Yenan in northern China along with thousands of government troops. The most crushing Communist victory of all came with the surrender of Tsinan, capital of Shantung, and its garrison of 85,000 to 100,000 Nationalists. By the early spring of 1949, the military collapse of the Nationalists had gone so far that the enemy controlled the major centers of population and the railroads from Manchuria south to the Yangtze Valley. Chiang Kai-shek abandoned the mainland for Formosa. Mao then consolidated his position.

When warned of the might of the United States, Mao declared, "The atom bomb is a paper tiger. We have the spiritual atom bomb. Weapons decide nothing. Man decides everything."

After the United States failed to heed the Chinese Communist warnings that American troops not cross the 38th Parallel, Mao sent his armies into North Korea. Lin Piao commanded those on the western front, Sung Shih-lun those in the north central part of North Korea which would engage the 1st Marine Division.

A stocky man, 5'8", with ramrod posture, Sung Shih-lun had much sharper features than most Chinese. At 45 years of age, he was a veteran of 23 years of combat. He had been handling troops since his graduation from Whampoa Military Academy at the age of 22, was regarded as one of Mao Tse-tung's finest generals, and was a veteran of the Long March. At the beginning of the Korean War, his army was positioned on the coast to invade Formosa. In August 1950, however, his troops were ordered to their home base in Shantung Province adjoining Manchuria, prior to their entrance into North Korea.

Stars and Stripes reported the presence of the Chinese Communists in battle on our side of the Taebaek Mountain range. The 7th Marine Regiment moved northwest from Hamhung to relieve the 26th ROK Regiment, which had been engaged in heavy fighting with this new enemy near Sudong.

Before moving out, Colonel Homer Litzenberg, the 7th Regiment's commanding officer, told unit commanders that this was the first time that Marines would be engaged in battle with the Chinese Communists. Although outnumbered by the enemy, the Marines must win. His men established positions at dusk on November 2, less than a mile south of the town. That night, bursting flares and bugle calls signaled a double envelopment attack by the Chinese. Lieutenant Colonel Ray Davis's 1st Battalion was the lead unit. Dawn the next day revealed a confused and alarming situation in the valley south of Sudong. Chinese and Marines shared the low ground between the 1st and 2nd Battalion command posts. Four enemy tanks were among Davis's men. PFC Red Duncan of Roanoke said later: "The first thing I saw near daybreak was the turret gun of a Chinese tank pointing straight at me from only a few yards away. I tell you, I got to one side in a hurry!" Several 3.6 rocket launchers eliminated the tanks in short order.

Litzenberg relied on the superiority of his supporting arms to tip the scales and regain the initiative. For the next few days, the 7th Regiment pressed forward to Chinhung-ni, exchanging fire with the retreating Chinese 124th Division. By the morning of November 7, all contact was broken. Later we learned the heavy losses sustained by the Chinese had rendered this division militarily ineffective. Roanoke Marines had participated in the first American victory over the Chinese Communists.

It was in this engagement that Marines established the tactical principle that would be used successfully to fight the enemy in the weeks ahead. To nullify Chinese night tactics, regardless of how large the penetration or infiltration, the defending Marine unit had only to maintain position until daybreak. With observation restored, superior American fire power and air cover would invariably melt the Chinese mass to impotency.

The 7th Regiment's experience had revealed a second enemy even more devastating than the Chinese Communists, however—the cold. Daily morning reports listed Marines suffering from frostbite, in some cases very severely. Frostbite is an injury to the skin or underlying tissue where actual freezing occurs; mild frostbite produces only swelling and reddening of the skin, but severe cases affect deep tissues, including bone, which may culminate in loss of the frozen part. Experiments conducted during World War II showed that frostbite could be treated by very rapid thawing of the still-frozen part in warm water. To combat the morale-breaking effects of the cold, General Smith—in addition to ordering the best available clothing from the States—had "cold-weather teams" lecture on survival in sub-zero temperatures.

Destroying their enemy's morale held top priority with the Chinese Communists. Mao Tse-tung had defeated the Chinese Nationalists, who had far more men and material, because Chiang Kai-shek's soldiers lacked the will to resist. Now, on the western front in Korea, they made what seemed to us an unusual move. American prisoners captured at Unsan were treated to hot food, cigarettes, and propaganda, then released to come back into our lines, on the theory that they would proceed to undermine the resolve of their fellow soldiers. The returning Americans, however, were immediately sent to Tokyo, to be interviewed by General Willoughby's intelligence section. This action denied them the opportunity to discuss their experiences with fellow soldiers at the time.

On November 8 we received orders to move. We were to defend the airfield below Wonsan which had been constructed by the Japanese. South of the airfield, the land was level for miles. On the north side of the strip and immediately adjacent to it was a hill that ranged from 50 to approximately 200 feet, reaching its greatest height at the western end of the runway where it made a sharp, almost 90° turn northward. A narrow-gauge railroad track bordered the south side of the wide concrete runway. A line of well-camouflaged hangers and storage huts ran parallel to the hill on the north. Tufts of crabgrass shoved through the concrete at various places, indicating the runways had been used only sparingly since World War II.

We dug foxholes halfway up the hillside, beginning at a point approximately 200 yards from the end of the runway. The entrenchments rounded the hill's elbow for approximately another 200 yards to give us good visibility over the plains that stretched a few miles west and many miles south. H&S occupied that portion of the defense line at the hill's elbow.

Daily the weather grew colder, and I grew tougher. I no longer minded sleeping on the ground, without the comforts of shipboard or civilian life. The cold, however, caused me to be uncomfortable many times while awake.

Midmorning on November 10, Chesty Puller brought Lieutenant Colonel Donald Schmuck to our battalion, and introduced him as our new commanding officer. Colonel Hawkins seemed pleased he was being sent back to the States. Colonel Schmuck was a bachelor, a short, stocky man, raised and schooled in Wyoming. During World War II he served with distinction and retained his regular commission after the war. A military man from the word go, he was energetic and determined. It did not take Schmuck long to know his company commanders and the key personnel in his battalion.

Two days after Schmuck assumed command, Suhr was asked by Division Intelligence to interview Chinese prisoners captured at Sudong, who were being held in the Division Compound at Wonsan. Suhr spoke fluent Chinese, although he protested that he didn't know all the dialects. He returned late in the afternoon, visibly shaken.

"My gosh, Suhr, are you sick?" I asked.

"No," he replied. "but I must go to Seoul immediately."

"I'm sorry. Has there been a death in your family? You look really worried."

"Worse. The Chinese are in North Korea in force. They're here to stay. My father is getting old. He needs me. I must get him out of Seoul and take him south."

"Suhr, I don't get it."

"You will!" he responded, with obvious agitation. "All through history, we Koreans have been like pawns on a chessboard. Some greater power has always made the moves. History is repeating itself. We can no longer call the shots. The fight is now between the Americans and the Chinese—maybe the Russians, too. They're here, Captain! They're here in force, and they're here to stay!"

"Look, Suhr," I argued. "We don't get that kind of information about them from Tokyo headquarters. Those Chinese are volunteers."

"No, they're not!"

"They're just trying to save face."

"No, Captain, you are wrong!" he said emphatically.

"Suhr, how many prisoners did you interview?"

"Two. But there were many more."

"What rank were they?"

"One was what you would call a noncommissioned officer, one a private."

"Suhr, in Tokyo they have the big picture. We send information daily to MacArthur's headquarters. They have the big picture there that we can't see here. Those two prisoners are too dumb to know the Chinese Communists' intentions."

I will always remember Suhr's reply. "Yes, Captain, they're too dumb to lie, too! Besides, I talked to the other interpreters. All prisoners are saying the same thing. I'm leaving. My father needs me!"

He talked to Colonel Schmuck and other officers of the battalion before leaving.

"Goodbye, and good luck, Suhr," we said as he departed.

"He was one good interpreter," all agreed.

"Yes, but what an ego. Thinking he knows more than the intelligence section in Tokyo."

No one in our battalion seemed to share Suhr's deep concern about Chinese intervention, despite Prime Minister Chou En-lai's public warning of China's involvement. Now the captured enemy had verified Chou's words. We continued to believe what we chose to believe, the more so because the reports we got came from our commander-in-chief, General of the Armies Douglas MacArthur.

7

We Battle the Cold

"The thermometer reads 15° right now," Pruitt announced at breakfast on November 13.

"We can't fight this cold without better clothing," Fritz added. "And, things are going to get a damn sight worse. Each day the morning report shows more Marine frostbite casualties up north."

Everyone now complained about the cold. It was obvious that our clothing, though normally considered heavy, was inadequate for a North Korean winter. It was apparent the situation would worsen in the days ahead. As the weather grew colder, fur-lined parkas were requisitioned by John Coffey. When they arrived, there were not enough available for all the companies. Colonel Schmuck made the decision to issue parkas to one company at a time. The rifle companies were first, followed by weapons, then H&S. I did not like this decision, because one man will freeze as fast as the other. Whatever the company designation, the temperature and exposure to the elements were the same for all. Hindsight tells me that Schmuck was correct, for someone had to be left out when there were not enough to go around. If half the men in the same company had parkas while the others did without, there would have been even greater morale problems. But the men of my company complained bitterly about the cold. Day in, day out, almost every minute of the day, we were uncomfortable.

On November 14, the 1st Battalion was ordered to come out of defensive positions and go into bivouac near the airfield for further transportation to Chigyong, approximately 50 miles north of Wonsan. We were relieved by a battalion of the 3rd Army Division. South Korean soldiers were used to fill the division's depleted ranks. All the officers and the senior NCOs were Americans; the majority of the lower ranks were South Korean.

Before the Army took over our defensive positions, a kitchen was established on an apron at the end of the airfield. I talked to some of their company officers. One captain was very unhappy when I asked about interpreters.

"You must have many, with so many Koreans in your ranks."

"No, we don't."

"Well, how do you communicate?"

"We don't," he replied abruptly. "The high brass that thought this thing up never read about the tower of Babel. All those South Koreans know how to say is 'more chop-chop.' Eat! They're the goddamndest eaters you ever saw!" The men were eating while we talked.

"If I weren't standing here, some of those men would come through that chow line three or four times," the captain said. "And, damn near half of them are named Kim. You have to point if you want one to do something."

I was thankful that I didn't have to serve under such a handicap.

A few hours after sundown, the Army men who took over our positions began to fire sporadically into the dark. By midnight, all weapons, including the machine guns, were engaged in shooting. Firing did not terminate until daybreak. When dawn arrived, no enemy bodies were found. This was because none were around.

Later in the morning, stretcher bearers carried out the body of Second Lieutenant John C. Trent of Memphis. Trent had been the captain of Army's 1948 undefeated football team. A graying, weeping master sergeant with a thick southern accent accompanied the body. "I been in this man's Army mor'n half my life, and this is the most fucked-up unit I ever seen. We burnt out three machine-gun barrels last night, and nobody ain't seen nothing!" He paused. "Right here is the finest young officer I ever seen. He's been trying to straighten out this shitty mess—and look what happened! Trouble is, we'll never know whether he got kilt accidental or on purpose. Cain't nobody say there ain't some gooks among them ROKs."

"Why don't you send them back to South Korea then?" I asked.

"The big man over in Tokyo conjured up this one—ain't nobody going to buck what *he* says," the sergeant replied.

Early in the war, MacArthur ordered General Walker to sweep up South Korean replacements to fill the ranks of the depleted Army divisions. He later described this expedient in his reminiscences as the "so-called buddy system which proved so successful." That statement seems to prove, however, that the gulf separating MacArthur from the fighting man in Korea was far wider than the combined breadth of the Sea of Japan and Honshu Island. The United States Army official history speaks more accurately: "They were civilians, stunned, confused and exhausted. Only a few could speak English. Mainly garbed in the shirt, shorts, sandals and cloth shoes they had on when caught, these pitiful refugees were dealt out, a hundred at a batch, to each infantry company and artillery battery in the division. Such fundamental problems as the use of Western-style latrines had to be explained in sign language and then demonstrated by the numbers by American instructors."

Near noon on November 15, we were told that at daybreak the next morning we would ride north to Chigyong in open flatbed cars aboard the train now waiting alongside the airfield. The extreme cold caused Marines from the other companies to taunt those of H&S about not having fur-lined parkas. Each time one of my men complained, a man from Weapons or a rifle company cried out, "Semper Fidelis!" or sometimes the abbreviated version, "Semper Fi!" "Semper Fidelis," the U.S. Marine Corps' motto, means "Always Faithful." But when one Marine complains about his lack that another possesses, he is usually answered by the cynical version of the motto, meaning, "Fuck you, man, I've got mine!" Many times during the afternoon, the riflemen had yelled, "Semper Fidelis, ole buddy boy!"

An hour before sundown, Fritz and Pruitt came running.

"Captain, Captain, have you noticed that train?"

"Sure, it looks like any other Korean train."

They persisted. "But have you noticed one thing very unusual about it?"

"No."

"Captain, there's a guard on one of the cars!"

"What's so unusual about that?"

"Well, have you ever seen a guard out here guarding ammunition, this lousy chow, barbed wire, or anything else!"

"I can't say that I have."

Pruitt elaborated. "That guard on that one car tells me something . . . it really tells me something, Captain! Otherwise, they wouldn't have a guard. Look at him. He's walking around just that one car, the boxcar . . . not one of those damn flatbeds we're to ride!"

"What are you suggesting, Pruitt?"

"Cap'n, the guard around that boxcar is a red flag. I don't understand why you officers don't recognize a red flag when you see one. It was the same way in World War II, when we had our rest camp at Guadalcanal, of all places. A major was sent down to Melbourne to bring back whiskey for the officers. Now this major was smart, see . . . so after he bought the whiskey, he packaged it in tubes made for 81-millimeter mortar shells. He saw the tubes were carefully placed aboard ship and he watched his cargo all the way back to Guadalcanal. The major wasn't concerned about anything but those mortar tubes. And every day he inspected them. You know what happened?"

"Go ahead, I'm listening."

"When the ship arrived at Guadalcanal, the major supervised the unloading of those mortar tubes. Now Captain, that was the brightest red flag you ever saw! Why in hell would a major be so concerned? The tubes were unloaded aboard a Higgins boat, then brought ashore. When the mortar tubes got there, the crane operator caught on. A sergeant who had been aboard ship had given him the high sign. That crane operator carried one of those tubes up as high as he could get it, then . . . oops! He 'accidentally' let it fall. Marines standing around hauled asbestos in every direction, thinking the mortar shells might explode. But, no! The tube broke open, and there it was, Cap'n—officers' whiskey! The officers had plenty, but we got our share! Captain, the guard around that boxcar is a red flag!"

"Pruitt, do you think there's whiskey aboard that car?"

"I'm not saying, but it's something good. Why else would it have a red flag on it?"

"Pruitt, let me say this to you and Fritz both. I know what you've got in mind and I say no! Remember, all Marines have been trained in marksmanship. I'd hate to have a first sergeant or gunnery sergeant shot by a Marine marksman. Leave that car alone, whatever you do."

"Look Captain, there are two things wrong with this war," Pruitt complained. "It's too damn cold, and there's no officers' whiskey to confiscate. Captain, aren't you freezing to death?"

"Yes, Pruitt, I'm hurting; I'm really hurting, but we'll make it somehow."

"Everybody else in the Company's freezing, too. I'd just as soon have a Marine shoot me through the ass as freeze to death out here!"

I gave the admonition again as the two walked away. At dusk, however, Fritz came back in real excitement.

"Captain, we've found out what's aboard that car!"

"What, Fritz?"

"Fur-lined parkas—fur-lined parkas, UTA! There's enough to outfit the entire company!"

"Look, Fritz, for God's sake, leave that car alone!" I insisted. "Regardless of how cold you are, I don't want a dead first ser geant! You take parkas off that boxcar, and that guard will shoot you without blinking an eyelash."

"Captain, this cold would freeze a brass monkey's balls off!"

"Well, I don't want to see you or Pruitt going after those fur-lined parkas, Fritz. That's a sure way of becoming a noncombat casualty."

Night came. The temperature dropped. It was the coldest day of the year thus far. The recorded temperature reached 10° Fahrenheit. We had sweaters, gloves and regular combat gear— but no parkas. We had our sleeping bags. These would keep us from freezing, though many times we could feel the cold even inside the bag. I crawled into my sleeping bag and tried to sleep. An hour or two later, I heard Fritz calling. He was trying to find where I was sleeping. After locating me, he began.

"The men are cold outside their sleeping bags. They're going to have a hell of a time on the ride to Chigyong in the morning. They'll freeze for sure on those flatbeds."

I gave Fritz no encouragement as he walked away. Try as I might, I couldn't sleep after that. Near midnight, a voice called, "Captain Hopkins! Captain Hopkins!"

I was lying in my sleeping bag, shaking from the cold and thinking about the tough ride the next day. Fritz came nearby.

"Captain! That poor guard on the train doesn't have a parka. He's having one hell of a time to keep from freezing. Pruitt has helped him, though. He's made a fire at the other end of the train to keep him warm. He's brewed up a pot of coffee and is down there talking to him. You know that poor guy would freeze to death if he stayed next to that boxcar. It's just too cold without a parka!"

"How far down is the guard, Fritz?"

"Oh, I'd say 20 to 30 cars away. I already have a group of men out there. If you'll permit us to go to the back side of that boxcar, there's no light—no way he can see us! We'll get enough parkas to outfit the whole company. Pruitt'll whistle if there's any problem."

In a shivering voice, I consented. "Okay, Fritz, you win. Go ahead."

Immediately Fritz whistled. The detail, already assembled, went to the back side of the car. Each box contained eight parkas. Enough boxes were thrown off for all of H&S, including the TACP unit—almost 200 parkas. As the boxes arrived, each man stood in line to receive his issue. It seemed the entire company knew what was coming off before I did, for everyone was dressed and ready. Fritz, with company roster and flashlight in hand, did a thorough job of making sure the truck drivers, cooks, supply persons, everyone, was outfitted that night. The boxes were then thrown in a pile and burned.

Fritz ordered, "Now everybody pull the tags off your parka tonight. Do it tonight!" he repeated. "Do you hear. Tonight! I don't want to see one damn tag tomorrow morning. Some nosey bastard might ask where you got that new parka if it still has a tag on it."

Persons, some distance away from our bivouac, called, "Why the fire?"

"We're just trying to keep warm. Nothing to worry about."

Before returning, Pruitt put extra logs on the fire for the guard at the end of the train. Fritz gave him his parka when he arrived. Sleep came easily the rest of the night. We awoke early in the morning, boarded the train with all our equipment, and rode north to Chigyong. En route, I realized that without parkas we would have had some frostbite cases for sure, because the temperature had dropped to 8°, with the wind-chill factor making it worse. We may have prevented frostbite by getting into our sleeping bags as we rode, but space was not available on the flatbeds for each person to do this.

When we arrived at Chigyong, we unloaded our equipment, trucks, gear, and tents. Then we proceeded to another bivouac on high ground outside town. There we would wait until we received orders to head north. We were told we would move into the mountains a few days hence.

Corporal Miracle went on a scrounging mission soon after our arrival. Our money was worthless; we could only barter. Cigarettes were the best medium for trading. Miracle used them to procure eggs, potatoes, onions, vegetables, and ham— our first good food in Korea. Our mess sergeant did the best he could with powdered potatoes and eggs, and other G.I. chow, but try as he might, the food was still tasteless. Supplementing the Marine Corps menu with fresh produce made mealtime enjoyable again. After we erected our pyramidal tents, for the first time since we had been in Korea, Miracle traded cigarettes for an urn with enough charcoal briquettes to keep warm inside.

Both Fritz and Pruitt proved to be good cooks, although Fritz deferred to Pruitt, since he seemed to enjoy preparing food most. For breakfast our second morning at Chigyong, Pruitt served ham and eggs, with french-fried potatoes and onions. Although there were only five in our tent, enough french fries were cooked to feed a squad. Near noon, Jim Adair came by.

"Captain," he said shaking his head, "I can still smell the stench!"

"Stench! These potatoes and onions smell good, Jim!" I exclaimed. "And you followed your nose right on in here! Have some french fries—Pruitt cooked them up this morning—more than we could eat."

"That's not what I'm talking about," Adair replied. "Man's inhumanity to man never ceases to amaze me!"

"You're not making sense, Jim! What gives?"

"I met with the town officials of Chigyong this morning, and they showed me to their jail. The black hole of Calcutta has got nothing on that place! Political prisoners are packed in so tight that it's damn near impossible for anyone to sit down. They're all in one room."

"Go on . . ." I nodded.

"Hot! That room must be 105° Fahrenheit if it's one degree! And there are no toilet facilities in that room. The men have relieved themselves all over the place. I've never smelled such a stench! It's still in my nose—I promise you!"

"You mean right now?"

"Believe me, I can still smell that damn jail! I told the town officials that was no way to treat prisoners. They answered by saying, 'You should see what they did.' They took the pro–Syngman Rhee Koreans, put them in a cave, diverted a small stream into the cave, and drowned them! That's what they did!" Adair shook his head. "They tried to take me out and show me, saying some of the bodies were still there. Their families had yet to claim them. I said no. I'd seen enough for one day."

"I don't guess there's anything you can do about it, is there, Jim?"

"Nope! We've been told to cooperate with the local governments, not run 'em. But, damn! I hate to see any living creature treated that way. I don't care who they are!"

I changed subjects. "I get the impression that 75 percent of the Koreans around here don't have any interest in this war. They just want to be left alone so they can live somehow."

"You're right, Cap'n," Adair replied. "Except that I'd raise your figures to 90 to 95 percent! Surviving through the winter here is a chore in itself. But have you noticed   most of these people look contented anyhow."

"They do, don't they!" I agreed. "That reminds me of a saying by an old neighbor when I was a boy. 'Son, if you ain't never ate ice cream, you don't miss it none!'"

"I guess that's it," Jim laughed. "That explains it," he said as he helped himself to more french fries.

"Put a little more salt and ketchup on that batch," Pruitt said as he handed him the salt.

Pruitt and I inspected the company area as soon as Jim departed. A holiday spirit prevailed among our men. It had been announced earlier that we would remain in bivouac for our entire stay in Chigyong.

"I guess there aren't many Chinese or gooks left to fight," one said as we passed by.

"Our main enemy now is the cold," I agreed.

We learned that 7th Regiment Marines reaching the mountain plateau at Koto-ri on November 10 met with a minus 8° temperature, worsened by a 20- to 30-knot wind. Over 200 men in various degrees of collapse turned into the aid station for treatment. The medical officer reported the men were dazed and stunned. A number of cases had a very low respiratory rate. Stimulants were required in addition to warming in order to restore normal functioning. Afterwards, in more severe weather, the shock reaction did not reappear.

Nearly eight centuries earlier, the harsh mountain winters further west prompted Genghis Khan to say, "No one fights in the land of the Mongols in wintertime!" The latitude of the north-central Korean mountains does not suggest the severity of the cold. The explanation comes from the fact that in wintertime Siberia harbors the largest cold air mass in the world. Prevailing winds push this cold mass eastward across the mountains of North Korea. Temperatures of 30 to 40 degrees below zero are experienced frequently. We were advised that those occupying high ground near the Yalu could expect an average daily temperature of 41° colder than George Washington's army had experienced at Valley Forge. Fortunately, when we were fully dressed, our winter clothing gave us protection unavailable to Washington's troops.

The best protection against cold is several layers of clothing. We were issued three sets of "long johns," or wool underwear. OD trousers and a flannel shirt were worn over the underwear. A high-necked sweater, buttoned to the chin, and a second pair of trousers formed a third layer. The second set of trousers required suspenders and were tucked into our boots to keep out the cold air. Another layer was added by a warm and roomy field jacket with a detachable hood. Our heads were covered by a cap which keeps the head warm without restricting the helmet. A jacket hood went over the helmet and buttoned around the chin so that most of the face was protected. Mittens with a trigger-finger opening were supplemented by regular gloves. Our clothing was completed by a fur-lined overcoat or parka.

This outfit, with changes, plus the nylon sleeping bag, cost the Marine Corps $153.46 per person in 1950. Still, the feet were vulnerable to frostbite. The felt insoles in the boots or "shoe pacs," as they were called, invariably became wet from perspiration. When a Marine stood still, the sweat froze into a film of ice between his foot and the inner sole. If he did not remove this felt insole, he fell victim to frostbite. The greatest danger came when a Marine got overheated on a forced march, stopped to rest, and did not have an extra set of felt insoles.

We walked extensively while in Chigyong, but there were no forced marches. Throughout our stay, we felt free to travel the roads both north and south without taking a patrol along. Intelligence reports from Tokyo headquarters indicated that the Chinese had disappeared along with the North Korean soldiers. Still, one always kept his personal weapon at his side.

On November 2, General Willoughby reported to Washington about the Chinese intervention. His estimate of Chinese strength along the Manchurian border proved to be amazingly accurate. He concluded with a warning: "Although indications so far point to piecemeal commitment for ostensibly limited purposes only, it is important not to lose sight of the maximum potential that is immediately available to the Chinese Communists. Should the high-level decisions for full intervention be made by the Chinese Communists, they could promptly commit 29 of their 44 divisions presently deployed along the Yalu, and support a major attack with up to 150 aircraft."

These disclosures, together with the news of the 1st Cavalry Regiment's defeat at Unsan, caused the Joint Chiefs to call on General MacArthur for his views. They requested his earliest interim evaluation of the situation in Korea, and its implications in light of what appeared to be overt intervention by the Chinese.

MacArthur replied, "It is impossible at this time to authoritatively appraise the actualities of Chinese Communist intervention in North Korea." He then posed four courses the Chinese might follow, one course being all-out intervention.

On November 5, General MacArthur directed two weeks of maximum air efforts. The Far East Air Force in Japan was ordered to eliminate the Korean end of all international bridges on the Manchurian border. Beginning at the border progressing southward to the battle line, excepting only Rashin and electric power plants, his B-29s were ordered "to destroy every means of communication and every installation, factory, city and village." For the first time, MacArthur authorized the use of incendiaries.

The next day he notified Army authorities that he intended to have his B-29s take out the international bridges across the Yalu near its mouth between Sinuiju and Antung. Acting on President Truman's instructions, the Joint Chiefs ordered MacArthur to call off any bombing within five miles of the Yalu.

MacArthur protested: "Men and material in large forces are passing across all bridges over the Yalu from Manchuria. This movement not only jeopardizes, but threatens the ultimate destruction of the forces under my command. The only way to stop this reinforcement of the enemy is the destruction of these bridges and the subjection of all installations in the north area supporting the enemy advance to the maximum of our air destruction." He warned, "Every hour that this is postponed will be paid for dearly in American and other United Nations' blood."

Truman authorized MacArthur to go ahead on November 8,

but to bomb on the North Korean side only. The aerial attacks against the bridges continued through November, but the results were disappointing. By the end of the month, the air effort had succeeded in cutting four of the bridges and in damaging most of the others. By then, the Yalu was frozen solid in most places and the Chinese had built pontoon bridges across the river at critical points. The ice would not thaw again until spring.

Taking advantage of the removal of the five-mile restriction, the Far East Air Force proceeded under MacArthur's direction to destroy the small cities, towns, and villages between the Yalu and the 8th Army battle line, plus a few towns in northeast Korea. There was no military justification for this war against the civilians. By November 28, the Air Force estimated that destruction of the centers of population was as follows: Manpojin, 95 percent; Kanggye, 75 percent; Hoenyong, 90 percent; Namsi, 80 percent; Chosan, 85 percent; Sakchun, 75 percent; Huichon, 75 percent; Koindong, 90 percent; and Sinuiju, 60 percent. Most of the surviving men, women, and children who were left homeless by this burning and destruction moved south to the western side of the Taebaek Mountain Range. Those in the northeastern tip of Korea came southward along the east coast. Few if any came through the Chosin Reservoir area where we were located.

What would have happened if the bridges had been destroyed has been debated more times than the long count in the second Dempsey-Tunney fight. Those who take MacArthur's side would fare better if he had not issued his communiqué of November 9 to the Joint Chiefs saying that he could keep the number of Chinese reinforcements crossing the Yalu low enough with his air power. This, he felt, would enable him to destroy those Chinese already in Korea. MacArthur was determined to launch his attack on November 15 and to keep moving until he reached the border. For 16 days after his November 9 communiqué, he was unbending in his optimistic outlook. The Joint Chiefs warned him, "This new situation indicates that your objective, the destruction of the North Korean armed forces, may have to be reassessed." MacArthur retorted in strong terms that any course of action short of complete destruction of the enemy would be tantamount to abject surrender and a breaking of the faith with the peoples of Asia.

General Willoughby reiterated the claim that only Chinese volunteers had entered Korea. Probably no more than a battalion of volunteers from each division identified thus far was actually in the country, he said. The defeat of the 1st Cavalry Regiment was explained by saying that it had failed to put out adequate security. According to Willoughby, the 1st Cavalry was overrun by a small, violent surprise attack and scattered during the hours of darkness.

On November 7, Marine General Smith advised Major General Edward Almond, commander of the 10th Corps, that due to winter, the UN forces should hold enough terrain to provide for the security of Wonsan, Hamhung, and Hungnam. Smith believed that we should not attempt to hold positions on the plateau north of Chinhung-ni. Almond agreed partially, but added Hagaru at the foot of the Chosin Reservoir. By November 11, however, Almond had changed his mind, seemingly in agreement with MacArthur.

At the time, General Smith commented that MacArthur's and Almond's attitude appeared to be one of "extreme optimism or extreme pessimism; there did not appear to be any middle ground." Ignorant of Smith's concerns, we at Chigyong reveled in Tokyo's optimism.

8

Into the Mountains— Smith's Dilemma

When we think of modern war, we think of men armed with guns, tanks, airplanes, and other weapons, locked in battle with a similarly armed opposing force. We talk most about the strategies that commanders use to outwit or outmaneuver their adversaries. More often than not, however, wars are won or lost over the question of supply. If the general in the field does not have ammunition, food, and clothing for his troops at the right place and at the right time, he cannot employ his forces as he would like. Logistics dominate strategy. The more protracted the war, the more dominating logistics become.

The mission now assigned to the 1st Marine Division posed tremendous supply problems. Only one road wound through the mountainous terrain to the division's final objective. From the 38th Parallel to the Yalu River the mountains of Korea are similar to those of West Virginia. They are characterized by endless rows of steep hills and narrow valleys, ideal terrain for Chinese Communist "Hochi Shiki" tactics. In contrast with West Virginia, however, the mountains in central North Korea are very bleak-looking because most of the heavy growth has been removed. Although the Koreans blamed the Japanese for the absence of trees, the harsh winters were the main culprit, and the lack of good topsoil worsened the problem.

This area is sparsely populated; the homes of the natives are primitive. At first glance, the countryside may impress the visitor as that of a third-world nation, but the ubiquitous presence of electric power generating facilities, much of the power originating at the Chosin Reservoir, partially dispels this notion. This reservoir, among the largest in the world when it was built, is a tribute to the ingenuity and frugality of the Japanese.

The maps of Korea circulated in the English-speaking world at this time were of Japanese origin. They showed the waters of the Chosin River, flowing north to the Yalu, being dammed to form the Chosin Reservoir. Our Korean interpreters spoke of both river and reservoir as "Changjin," but we adopted the name shown on the maps.

Unlike most such projects, the Chosin turbines generate electricity in the direction opposite to the river's flow. The reservoir itself, being approximately 3,000 feet above sea level, provides the water that is pumped upward, then south, through large steel tubes called penstocks, towards Hamhung and Hungnam. This water is lowered by gravity to different levels where turbines are activated along the route. The same water is used over and over again for the generation of electricity until it nears sea level.

The area between the Chosin Reservoir and the Yalu is trackless waste. The Yalu itself runs through a gorge-like channel, rimmed by high mountains on both sides until it reaches the lower west coast area. This barren countryside presented the Chinese troops with severe logistical problems that we did not recognize at the time. The People's Liberation Army had been trained to live off the land; food was obtained from friendly farmers in exchange for work. Until the Korean War, this army had never been outside China, yet initially it did not make the necessary adjustments in its supply corps to meet this changed situation. "An army moves on its stomach," but there was very little food north of the Chosin Reservoir to the border.

Although the whereabouts of massive Chinese troops could not be located, the evidence of their presence continued to mount. On November 8, a Marine patrol captured a Chinese prisoner of the 126th Division near the Chosin Reservoir. He stated that "Red China would commit a total of 24 divisions against United Nations' forces in Korea." Marine airmen making nightly strikes from the first through the ninth of November at Sinuiju reported a steady stream of trucks from Antung,

Manchuria. They described southbound traffic as "very heavy," "tremendous," and one convoy was reported to be "gigantic." This information was all relayed to MacArthur's headquarters in Tokyo.

On November 14, two civilian draftsmen, formerly employed by the traffic department of the Pyongyang Railway Depot reported to 10th Corps intelligence a continuous flow of Chinese soldiers through Manpojin, beginning on October 12. One of them estimated that 80,000 Chinese had passed through the border town. Chinese officers told the two men that 200,000 to 400,000 Chinese soldiers were scheduled to enter Korea. Military plans, however, continued to be made as though these reports did not exist.

What does a military commander do when ordered to do something that he knows is wrong? Does he owe his first allegiance to his superior, or to his troops? This was Oliver Smith's dilemma. He knew that if every general refused to carry out orders whenever he doubted their wisdom, many of the decisive battles in history would have reached a different conclusion. Yet Smith strongly believed that the scattering of his forces, now demanded by Generals Almond and MacArthur, would ultimately lead to the destruction of his 1st Marine Division. He commented at the time, "I have little confidence in the tactical judgment of the 10th Corps, or in the realism of their planning." And, in reference to the conduct of the war in Korea, he said, "There is a continual splitting up of units and assignments of missions to small units which puts them out on a limb. This method of operating appears to be general in Korea. I am convinced that many of their setbacks here have been caused by this disregard for the integrity of units and time and space factor."

In sharp contrast with MacArthur and Willoughby, General Smith was deeply concerned about what he considered "unrealistic planning and the tendency to ignore enemy capabilities when a rapid advance was wanted." On November 15, he wrote a letter to General Clifton B. Cates, Commandant of the Marine Corps. It said in part:

"So far our MSR [main supply route] north of Hamhung has

not been molested, but there is evidence that this situation will not continue. . . . Someone in high authority will have to make up his mind as to what is our goal. My mission is still to advance to the border. The 8th Army, 80 miles to the southwest, will not attack until the 20th. Manifestly, we should not push on without regard to the 8th Army. We would simply get further out on a limb. If the 8th Army push does not go, then the decision will have to be made as to what to do next. I believe a winter campaign in the mountains of North Korea is too much to ask of the American soldier or Marine, and I doubt the feasibility of supplying troops in this area during the winter or providing for the evacuation of sick and wounded."

In conclusion, Smith reiterated his doubts about his wide-open left flank and the prospect of stringing out a Marine division along a narrow, twisting mountain road for 120 miles from Hungnam to the border. A part of this road ran from the port city of Hungnam to the hamlet of Yudam-ni, on the western side of the Chosin Reservoir. Smith was particularly concerned about that portion of the road from Chinhung-ni through Funchilin Pass to Koto-ri. As he described it:

"The road between Chinhung-ni and Funchilin Pass is similar to that part of the Tioga Pass in California, east of the pass. It was cut out of the side of the mountain and had numerous hairpin turns. For the most part, it was one way with a turnout at intervals. Numerous places along the road the ice had formed from springs that had overflowed the road and had frozen."

The distances and miles to the hamlets, towns, and cities along the road are as follows: Hungnam to Hamhung, eight miles; Hamhung to Oro-ri, eight miles; Oro-ri to Majon-dong, fourteen miles; Majon-dong to Sudong, seven miles; Sudong to Chinhung-ni, six miles; Chinhung-ni to Koto-ri, ten miles; Koto-ri to Hagaru, eleven miles; and Hagaru to Yudam-ni, fourteen miles. A railroad paralleled the road as far as Chinhung-ni. Beyond Chinhung-ni the railroad was destroyed beyond repair.

Smith made determined preparations for the Chinese intervention. Where the road was too narrow, he directed Lieutenant Colonel John H. Partridge, commanding officer of the Marine 1st Engineer Battalion, to strengthen and widen it for use of tanks and heavy vehicles. He selected Hagaru, at the base of the Chosin Reservoir, for the building of an airstrip. This town would serve as Smith's advance CP, and supply base. In the meantime, supplies could go by rail to the railhead at Chinhung-ni. From there they were trucked north over the road. Colonel Partridge began constructing the airstrip on November 20. He placed his men on an around-the-clock, seven days a week work schedule.

Smith deliberately stalled the 1st Marine Division's advance in order to prepare for its supply. As a result, we stayed at Chigyong four days longer than originally anticipated. This time was used to clean our gear and clothes. For the first time in North Korea we took body baths inside our tents, without freezing in the process. Fritz and Pruitt obtained empty stainless steel five-gallon sugar and lard containers from the galley. We cleaned our clothes by boiling them in soap and water, then rinsing them with cold water in our helmets. Clotheslines were strung inside the tents; when hung outside the wet clothes froze immediately.

The third morning in Chigyong I decided to visit Hamhung and Hungnam. Since our clotheslines were filled to capacity, I had little else to do. Miracle and I drove first to Hamhung. It was more modern than Wonsan. In the middle of the city there were two paved streets scarred with large potholes made by our trucks and tanks. We saw no vehicle larger than a bicycle driven by a civilian. Overhanging electric wires lined each side of the street. There were many two-story buildings of brick, stucco, or concrete. The 10th Corps occupied two of these. Otherwise the city appeared as drab as Wonsan. Soldiers and Marines walked along the sidewalks and side streets. After driving through the streets for a while, we went to Hungnam, the port city.

We saw the port, but not much city. There were American ships in the harbor, and a few destroyers were anchored in the distance. The ocean front was lined with many one-room homes capped by straw roofs and a few stucco and concrete buildings. First Marine Headquarters was located in a two-story stucco building that had once been an engineering college. There was not much else to be seen.

I took the occasion to check with regimental headquarters for orders concerning my promotion to major. I was told that no orders had been received from the Commandant of the Marine Corps. While there, I also hastily examined the personnel records of my men. I was not surprised to find that Pruitt had a high GCT score, one which would have qualified him for entrance to a good eastern college had he so desired.

As we drove back to Hamhung, two Korean prostitutes waved to us from the side of the road. They were the only two I saw in Korea. Miracle stopped the jeep. The two young Korean girls were heavily painted. Neither could say more than a few choice words in English. By coupling these with suggestive gestures, they dramatically made their pitch. Even though we got no closer than ten feet, a strong smell of perfume permeated the air. As we drove away, a truck stopped behind us.

When we returned through Hamhung near the middle of the day, the business district was filled with people. We stopped and chatted with soldiers and Marines along the streets. Everyone seemed to be looking for something to do or to buy; they could find neither. The city was swollen with refugees. Many carried their belongings in packs, A-frames, or man-drawn carts. Where they found places to sleep at night remains a mystery to me.

While walking along the streets, I met two officers who had come over with me on the *U.S.S. General Walker*. When I told them that I'd been assigned to the 1st Battalion, 1st Marines, one immediately spoke up.

"Oh . . . you were with that unit that got men bayoneted in their sleeping bags at Kojo!"

"Yes, and I'm with one hell of a good unit, too, the best I've ever served with," I told them. "But that incident has been advertised by division headquarters more than anything else we've done!"

"Don't take it to heart," he replied. "Can you think of a better example as a warning to others?"

"No, I guess not," I said as I returned to my jeep.

We returned back at Chigyong shortly after noon. Fritz and

Pruitt had cooked a good meal of fried ham and eggs, and french-fried potatoes and onions topped with catsup. As we ate, we talked about our trip.

We no longer gathered around the fire at the CP to exchange jokes and stories at nightfall, as had been done in Wonsan. Instead, most of the Marines stayed in their tents, although there was visiting from tent to tent to swap ideas and stories. Some officers and the ranking NCOs of H&S frequently visited our tent. Conversations centered on life in the Marine Corps, mostly personal experiences.

A sergeant from Camden, New Jersey, who enlisted in the Marines in 1941, told his story: "Shortly after I volunteered for the Marines, I was sent to boot camp at Parris Island, South Carolina. Within one hour after I crossed that bridge from Beaufort to Parris Island, I knew I'd made the biggest mistake of my lifetime. After boot camp, when I came home to Camden on leave, I didn't admit to my buddies what a helluva mistake I'd made. A year later when I came back home again, I found myself too much a part of the damn Marine Corps to condemn it. Here I am in this godforsaken cold country. The hell of it is, I wouldn't be satisfied being anyplace else!"

On one occasion, while watching Pruitt cook french fries, I asked, "Pruitt, I've often wondered why you stayed in the Marine Corps after World War II."

"I figured it was the best thing to do . . ."

"Didn't you think about getting a job on the outside?"

"I thought about it, but not seriously. I like Marine Corps life—I've got a good wife; we don't have to worry about our needs; I enjoy my friends. What else is there, Captain?"

"Not much," I nodded. "But did you ever consider officers' school?"

"No, not seriously," he answered.

"I'm surprised."

"Oh, about five years ago, my company commander at Camp Lejeune asked if I'd like to go. I said I'd think about it. I didn't have to think long to know I didn't want to go."

"Why not?"

"I couldn't see where I'd better myself."

"Oh."

"Being a Marine master sergeant gives me everything I want . . . self-esteem, respect from others, good companions. If I'd become an officer I'd have been separated from my friends."

"Yes, but you'd have made new friends."

"Sure, but they wouldn't have been one bit more interesting than the ones I've got."

"I see, so you volunteered for this," I said.

"Oh, no, I didn't! I volunteered to ship over after World War II. When I decided to stay in, I couldn't see five years ahead. Captain, I've never met anybody that could see five years ahead. I surely didn't volunteer for this; it's against my principles to volunteer."

"Yeah, I know the Marine Corps' principles for success—get a receipt for it, shoot the shit, and never volunteer!"

"Yep, that's it exactly!" Pruitt replied as he placed the potatoes on a paper towel.

Near the end of our stay at Chigyong, Miracle and I again visited Hamhung. This time, the road was crowded with thousands of people walking to the city. It took at least twice as long to drive the short distance as it had previously.

When we arrived at Hamhung, we learned that Syngman Rhee and his wife were visiting the city. He was to make a speech that day. I was astonished to find North Koreans would walk to Hamhung to see the president of South Korea. It had been my experience that people don't come to see or hear a man they don't like. Five years of Communist rule had certainly failed to indoctrinate the majority of North Koreans.

This was not surprising. Americans stood tall in Korean eyes because of their liberation from Japan. Korea had not been occupied or exploited by Occidentals as had many other Asiatic countries. Her tradition of private ownership of land and property, and a social structure built strongly around the family, made other systems of government appear more appealing than communism to the average Korean.

The friendly civilian attitude was apparently not recognized at Tokyo headquarters, for during the lull in combat action the bombing and burning of towns and villages continued with intensity. This was a terrible mistake on our part. Strafing or bombing that kills civilians backfires. Its negative worth can be measured in direct proportion to the number killed. While the civilian population may be unable to retaliate with guns, it will surely do so in other ways. This retaliation may be in the form of land mines and booby traps placed along your path when you least expect them. Or it may be in the form of misinformation concerning the whereabouts of the enemy. You don't win a war by multiplying your opposition.

Our bombing and burning of the small cities, towns, and villages along the Yalu, with its slaughter and displacement of men, women, and children, did not and could not aid our cause militarily. No ground commander in Korea requested it. Our enemy was both an idea and an army. Indiscriminate killing strengthens the will of the enemy to resist, and makes communism appear to the unfortunate survivors as their only salvation. In addition, this type of warfare flagrantly violates the accords reached at the Geneva Convention which obligate belligerents to protect civilians. But people and nations with power often establish their own rules in dealing with another.

Those in MacArthur's headquarters did not seem to understand the nature of our foe in the field and shape their plans accordingly. Even though three-quarters of the world's population belonged to the underdeveloped and developing countries, more of the military capacity of the United States was built to fight against advanced societies. A strategic air force is essential to conquer an industrial nation, but it had little if any value in North Korea or China during 1950. A chemical factory making fertilizer may be a prime strategic target when located in a hostile Germany. Ammonia and its derivatives can be used to make explosives. The same fertilizer factory in Hamhung had little military significance. North Korea had a few steel-working plants, but no steel-making facility. Although one plant made explosives for the Japanese in World War II, the North Koreans lacked the know-how to readily convert the fertilizer plant to war use.

To justify the bombing of communities with few or no military targets, some rationalized that the Asiatic placed little value on human life. This depended on whose life. Koreans placed a high value upon their own lives, although many placed a low value on the life of another, especially the enemy's.

In 1950, the average Korean realistically held lower expectations of life than an American. A mother with many children expected to lose half or more of them before they reached maturity. The masses could not afford immunization shots for cholera, typhus, tetanus, smallpox, or typhoid fever. Parents might see a healthy child run in and out of the house one day, then watch him die a few days later from one of these diseases, simply because medicine was unavailable. Despite these low expectations of life, Koreans hated those who killed or abused them just as much as citizens of the western world do when abused. People react as people the world over.

While we bivouacked at Chigyong, MacArthur completed plans for the occupation of all of Korea by UN forces. Across the Korean peninsula on the western front the 8th Army had difficulty lining up forces for its attack north. MacArthur's use of all available ships to transport 10th Corps personnel to the east coast, instead of carrying supplies, caused General Walker's 8th Army to experience a serious supply shortage. The shortage began in late October, and remained acute through the middle of November. Walker was forced to postpone his attack northward and he notified General MacArthur the 8th Army needed 4,000 tons of supplies per day in order to sustain an offensive. It was not until November 20 that the combined efforts of our supply agencies began to pay off so that this required figure could be achieved. On November 22 Walker notified MacArthur that the logistics in the forward area of the 8th Army had been solved and that he had rescheduled his attack for November 25.

On November 20 MacArthur issued an order to the troops which again indicated that he expected simply an occupation, rather than a fight, in the move to the Yalu. It said: "Elements of minimum size only will be advanced to the immediate vicinity of the geographical boundary of Korea. No troops or vehicles will go beyond the boundary between Korea and Manchuria, or between Korea and the USSR, nor will fire be exchanged with, or air strikes be requested on, forces north of the northern boundary of Korea. Rigid control of troop movements in the vicinity of the northern boundary will be exercised. Damage, destruction or disruption of service to power plants will be avoided. No personnel, military or civilian, will be permitted to enter or leave Korea via the Manchurian or USSR border. Commanders will insure that the sanctity of the international border is meticulously preserved."

The deployment of the 10th Corps and the 8th Army created a situation where if the Chinese should attack in force, the possibility of total disaster was inherent. Because of the intervening mountains neither the 10th Corps nor the 8th Army could come to the aid of the other. Had MacArthur read Mao Tse-tung's *On the Protracted War*, the ordeal that awaited the 8th Army and the 1st Marine Division might have been avoided.

Before 1949 China had been one thing—afterwards, she was something else. Those in authority in Washington and Tokyo recognized this. Not understood, however, was the Communist Chinese soldier who had brought about this change. He was indeed unlike the mercenary who served under the Chinese warlords familiar to the west, or the well-equipped but ill-led soldier of Chiang Kai-shek, for whom our military leaders had little respect. He was a fighter now, and his officers knew what they were doing.

Early on the morning of November 22, Wes Noren moved his "B" Company north to the railhead at Chinhung-ni to relieve the 3rd Battalion, 5th Marines, guarding the division supply dump. The next day, Thanksgiving Day, the rest of our battalion joined "B" Company. Before we left, Pruitt and I inspected the premises to insure that all slit trenches had been covered, dirt from the foxholes replaced, and the area left in shipshape condition. Whether in bivouac or in the line, it was standard procedure for Gus Geisert or myself to inspect our company area for cleanliness each day. Either Fritz or Pruitt always preceded us. Seldom did we find anything to complain about. Only on the first day of our arrival at a new area did we experience even minor problems. Sometime during this day, Pruitt usually approached.

"Captain, those cooks are using mealtime again as an excuse for not digging foxholes. And those damn fly boys want to know why they have to dig holes when there's no enemy around!"

"What did you tell them, Pruitt?"

"I told them it's orders. And we don't want any Bolsheviks around here! But I'd expect you'd better give both groups an extra shove."

Fritz and Pruitt took great pains to load my jeep with the empty sugar and lard cans, a pick and shovel that had been confiscated from somewhere, a large box of fresh potatoes, onions, and other odds and ends that might add to our comfort. Among these last were the recent overseas editions of *Time*, *Newsweek*, and *Life*. The November 13 and 20 editions of *Life* had many pictures of captured Communist Chinese soldiers. A solemn-faced Pruitt studied the pictures for hours as he rode north, sitting on the back seat of my jeep.

The ride to Chinhung-ni proved interesting. The flat terrain continued until we reached Majon-dong, where hills began forming into mountains. They had developed on both sides of the road by the time we reached Sudong. Except for the lack of trees, the six-mile drive from Sudong to Chinhung-ni reminded me of a visit to a West Virginia coal mine. The route through the narrow valley, with a railroad bed on one side of a small stream and a dirt road on the other, looked the same. In West Virginia, the rail line usually stops at the coal tipple. Here it stopped at Chinhung-ni.

When we arrived at Chinhung-ni in late afternoon, the men of the 5th Marines were standing beside the road, ready to leave for Yudam-ni. They had been served Thanksgiving dinner. Due to the lateness of the hour, the battalion commander decided not to travel north until the next day.

When darkness came, many warming fires alongside the road signaled our presence. Had Chinese been suspected in the area, there would have been no fires. I picked out a spot near a fire tended by the battalion executive officer. I enjoyed listening to him reminisce about the Marine brigade during the early fighting in South Korea.

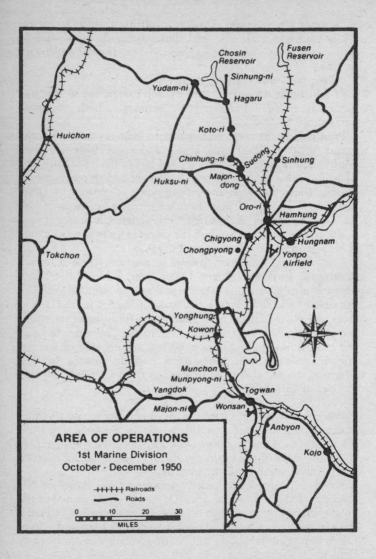

AREA OF OPERATIONS

1st Marine Division
October - December 1950

+++++ Railroads
— Roads

0   10   20   30
MILES

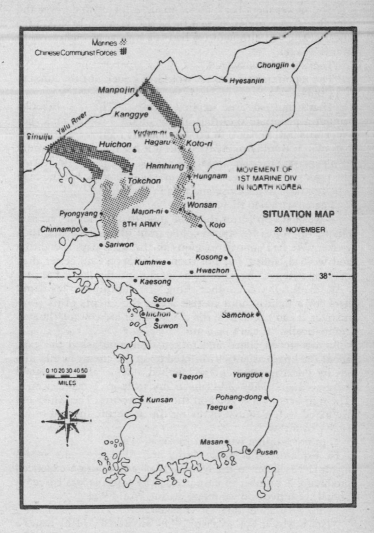

Marines ·:·:·
Chinese Communist Forces ▦

Chongjin ●
● Hyesanjin

Manpojin ●

Kanggye ●
Sinuiju ● Yalu River
Yudam-ni ● Koto-ri
Huichon ● Hagaru ●
Hamhung ●
Tokchon ● ● Hungnam

MOVEMENT OF
1ST MARINE DIV
IN NORTH KOREA

Wonsan ●

Pyongyang ● Majon-ni ●
8TH ARMY ● Kojo

SITUATION MAP

20 NOVEMBER

Chinnampo ●
● Sariwon

Kumhwa ● Kosong ●
● Hwachon

Kaesong ●   38°

Seoul ●
Inchon ● Samchok ●
Suwon ●

0 10 20 30 40 50
MILES

Taejon ●   Yongdok ●

Kunsan ●   Pohang-dong ●
Taegu ●

Masan ●
● Pusan

"The newspapers back home made a lot of to-do over the fact that Army troops arrived in Korea with 2.6 bazookas instead of the 3.5, although we had the 3.5 at the end of World War II," I said.

"That's so," he answered.

"The reporters said the 2.6 wouldn't knock out the Russian T-34 tank."

"That's not so!" he replied firmly. "The 2.6 bazooka wouldn't penetrate the front armor of the Russian tank, but you could still knock it out if you had the right team firing the bazooka. It would disable the tank if it hit the tracks. It would also penetrate the side armor. Of course, the 3.5 would destroy the tank if you got a good hit from any direction, but the men who fire have to get close and this is dangerous."

"I agree with you there."

"A weapon's no better than the man that's firing it," he said raising his voice. He sipped coffee from his canteen cup, then spoke. "We had enough weapons in the early days of fighting and we had bodies, but not men. A weapon's no better than the man firing it," he repeated as he put another log on the fire.

"And I'll tell you another thing," he continued. "It's damn hard for a fighting unit to rise above the talents of its commander. It can't be done if the commander is a coward," he said emphatically. "It can't be done!"

As we sipped coffee and talked, someone asked the exec about the huge casualties inflicted upon the enemy by all units in the Pusan perimeter. He laughed, "Most of the captured were civilians. They didn't have any weapons when captured. The numbers looked good on the daily reports. The killed and wounded were counted by using the scientific method of casualty counting."

"I'm not familiar with that method," I said.

He explained that many Army and Air Force units used a formula based on so many rounds of ammunition expended producing X number of casualties. The formula was based on casualties killed and wounded during World War II.

"Well what about targets?" I asked.

"That's why it was so absurd!" he answered. "Many times a unit would fire away when there were no enemy in sight! The report the next day, though, showed lots of enemy casualties, although ammunition had been expended needlessly."

The press consistently reported the estimated casualties given by the unit commander, with no questions asked. It was my observation that UN reports of enemy killed and wounded remained unreliable throughout the war.

We sipped coffee until almost midnight before bedding down.

9

Sung Shih-lun's Trap

When we awoke at daybreak the morning of November 24, the Marines of the 3rd Battalion 5th had already moved north. As the men began to stir, a PFC nearby spoke out.

"Hey, Jim, where's it at?"

"This is Chinhung-ni."

"Hell, Jim, I didn't ask you the name! Where is it at?"

Both men were standing on the road and were looking in all directions. There were no homes in sight. A disabled Chinese tank of Russian make stood between the creek and the road. The tank looked in good condition; there was only one small hole in its left side. The inside was ripped to shreds, an obvious casualty of a 3.5 bazooka shell. Across the creek was the railroad.

"There it is, right over there!" Jim said, pointing to the railroad station about 30 feet long, 20 feet wide, and seven feet high. Beside the station were three large pyramids of supplies, each 20 to 30 feet in height, covered by canvas tarpaulins. The supplies bulged from beneath the covers, three or four feet from the pyramid's base. Approximately 70 yards south on the same side of the railroad track were 50-gallon drums, nearly 200 in number, equally divided between gasoline and heating oil. This was the largest collection of military supplies north and west of Hamhung.

Rolling ground stretched west of the railroad for about a half-mile in diameter. Roughly 1,000 yards south of us, on the western side of the stream, were four or five mud homes with rice-straw roofs which could not be seen from the road.

"So this is Chinhung-ni, Jim?"

"Yep, this is it!" He paused, then raised his voice. "Another goddamned swinging place!"

Literally and figuratively Chinhung-ni was a wide place in the valley.

Before breakfast, Colonel Schmuck gathered together his company commanders and staff for a reconnaissance of the area. As we walked someone suggested that we use the same foxholes the 5th Marines had occupied.

"No," Schmuck replied. "This area can be defended best by placing all men and weapons on one side of the road and railroad." (The 3rd Battalion had dug in on both sides.) "We don't need that division supply dump inside our perimeter to defend it. We need to control all approaches to those supplies."

After we completed our survey, Schmuck decided that our best protection would be to place all men and weapons on the western side of the railroad. Targets in the valley, running north-south, could then be adequately covered by our heavy weapons. When complete our defense perimeter took the shape of a bowl with our heavy weapons concentrated near the center and bottom of the bowl—a 360° target range. Rifle company personnel were placed on the line on a 50 percent alert basis. One man was to stay awake in each two-man foxhole, with inspecting teams making the rounds to insure this was being done.

Before noon, we began to dig foxholes and pitched warming tents 50 to 100 feet behind the perimeter so that men could guard their respective positions on the buddy system. Small oil-burning stoves had been issued immediately prior to leaving Chigyong. One stove, plus a fuel-oil can, was allotted to each tent. Warming tents were essential now, as the temperature was dropping to zero or below each night.

The battalion CP tent was erected on the reverse slope of a hill inside the perimeter near the railroad. The intelligence section established a checkpoint on the road to interview civilians. Squads of the guard platoon alternated daily with members of the intelligence section. Interpreters were also rotated. Schmuck made a roster of his staff officers and myself to stand watch in the command tent four hours each day—two hours during daylight and two hours at night.

H&S Company formed part of the perimeter nearest the supply dump. The battalion kitchen was established close to the center of the perimeter. Hot meals were served twice daily to all troops. In early afternoon, Pruitt and Miracle came into our tent with all the canned goods they could carry.

"I've heard Marines say that within days after arriving at Parris Island they thought they'd died and gone to hell," I said. "You two look like you've just died and gone to heaven."

"Goddamn, Cap'n! That supply dump has food, clothes, and ammunition UTA!"

Pruitt explained the supplies were stacked in three piles at the railhead. Food was in one pile, ammunition in another, and clothing in the third. Clothing consisted of socks, shoe pacs, sweaters, shirts, trousers, boots—every kind of necessary winter clothing.

"But, Cap'n, there are no parkas!" Pruitt said.

"Well, Pruitt, I have you and Fritz to thank for mine," I laughed.

"And let me tell you one thing," Pruitt continued. "There are advantages to serving with the Army. Most of that food over there was bought by an Army quartermaster. Look here! Look at these cans of boneless chicken! And there's plenty more where they came from. Can you imagine a Marine quartermaster buying boneless chicken? Hell, he'd rest in purgatory for eternity rather than do a thing like that! The men might enjoy the taste."

"I take it you don't think Marine quartermasters buy good food."

"You're exactly right, Cap'n. They've been trained to be tighter than a bull's ass. They buy by the pound instead of by taste! I'll bet every one of those stainless steel containers of lard was bought by some Marine quartermaster."

"I agree with you, but we couldn't wash our clothes without those lard cans."

"Cap'n, let me show you this." At that, Pruitt pulled out a small bottle. "Look."

"Steak sauce!" Fritz exclaimed.

"What good is steak sauce, Pruitt?" I asked. "We haven't seen a steak since we've been here. Even you and Miracle haven't scrounged up a steak!"

"I know, Cap'n, but there are lots of things this steak sauce will add taste to." Shaking his head, he continued, "There's no pogey-bait. Anyhow, we couldn't find it. Another thing—there's no officers' whiskey!"

"You didn't really expect to find officers' whiskey, did you?"

"No, I guess not. I've said it before, and I'll say it again—it's a piss-poor war where there's no officers' whiskey to confiscate."

The food was spread on the deck. In addition to boneless chicken and steak sauce, there were crackers, tomato ketchup, cans of tuna fish, pickles, fruit cocktail, pineapple chunks, and grapefruit juice. Pruitt frequently received packages of assorted cheeses from his wife; he graciously shared them with others in the tent. However, his taste in cheeses was different from most in that he insisted, "It's got to smell bad or bite back at you to taste right!" I was among the few who agreed with him. A variety of cheeses were available most of the time.

In midafternoon, Fritz announced that the kitchen had been established and the cooks were thawing turkeys for "the best Thanksgiving dinner ever." The next day was Saturday, November 25.

Foxhole digging proceeded slowly. The ground was frozen hard for about five inches. Only after removing this five-inch crust did digging become easy. By nightfall everyone's foxhole was deep enough for protection against a mortar attack, but still too shallow to give much elbow room. With the exception of Bob Barrow, however, no one in the battalion considered the Chinese a formidable enemy. Although I never heard him comment about Tokyo intelligence reports, Barrow clearly felt the Chinese Communist threat was more dangerous than we had been led to believe. He respected the Chinese.

Many 1st Marine Division Regulars had served in China before, during, or after World War II. Barrow served there, in a team of four Americans working with up to 1,500 Chinese Nationalist guerrillas. They operated against Japanese communication lines in the corridor from Hankow to Canton. While on China duty, Barrow lived off the land and was out of touch with headquarters for the last eight months of the war. "The war was over nine days before we got word of it," he recalled. "I had never heard of such places as Iwo Jima and Okinawa till well after the war. I was astonished to learn about the atomic bomb!"

Barrow frequently talked about the beautiful mountains and the rugged and very underdeveloped country just south of Chungking Lake in Hunan Province where he spent most of his duty. Walking 25 or 30 miles a day for five days, staying five or six days in friendly Chinese farmhouses, Barrow came to know and admire the amiable, hardworking hinterland Chinese. He warned: "They are intelligent and highly adaptable."

Unknown to MacArthur or the Joint Chiefs, on October 14, 1950, the Chinese began sending infantry divisions into North Korea. Between October 14 and November 1, some 180,000 troops from the Chinese 4th Field Army crossed the Yalu into Korea. More than two-thirds of this force had been near the Korean border in Manchuria since July 1950.

In overall charge of this army was Marshall Peng Teh-huai who made his headquarters at Mukden, Manchuria. Under Peng was Lin Piao, who at age 21 gave Mao his first major victory over the Nationalists in 1928. Lin Piao commanded those who initially crossed the border and were aligned in front of the 8th Army.

In late October and early November elements of the Chinese 4th Field Army battled with the ROKs, the 1st Cavalry Division, and the 7th Marine Regiment. The Communists labeled these moves as their first-phase offensive. In each engagement our troops took prisoners—96 by the 7th Marines. Many of these prisoners appeared in the November 15 and 22 issues of *Life* magazine.

The withdrawal of Red Chinese forces seemed to mystify

intelligence sources in Tokyo. In retrospect, the uncensored press gave more useful and indeed more accurate information than did MacArthur's daily intelligence summaries to his commanders in the field. On November 9 the newspapers carried accounts that had been reported by Marine aviators of the numerous enemy vehicles crossing the border from Antung, Manchuria, into Korea: "Pilots say Red troops continue to pour across the border even in the face of the Reds' unexplained pull-back."

Although Chinese news releases and MacArthur's headquarters referred to Chinese troops in North Korea as Chinese volunteers, *Newsweek* stated: "Of 150 Chinese prisoners captured, not one said he was a volunteer." The record of prisoner interviews filed daily in Far East Command Headquarters at Tokyo confirmed the *Newsweek* report.

The veteran war correspondent Don Whitehead, with the 8th Army troops on the western front, reported on November 13, "The cold winter is beginning, and our troops are not prepared for it. In January, the temperatures average six degrees below zero." On November 15, Marines arrived at Hagaru in 15° below zero cold and found it undefended. Two Chinese soldiers surrendered. They confirmed civilian reports that the Chinese were deployed in large numbers a few miles northwest of Hagaru. The constant trickle of refugees arriving daily in Hamhung told of Chinese displacing them from their homes.

Beginning on November 7, Smith's intelligence section established contact with hamlet, village, and town chiefs. All reported enemy sightings. These civilian reports proved to be our most reliable source about the Chinese. In person or by phone, they told of the presence of numerous Chinese in the Chosin Reservoir area. The enemy numbers were sufficient to cause Smith deep concern, though not undue alarm. Records in Tokyo indicated that the Chinese outnumbered the Marines in our zone, but not to the extent revealed later. Yet on November 17 MacArthur insisted to Ambassador Muccio there could be no more than 30,000 Chinese troops in Korea!

After Sudong, Marines failed to learn the whereabouts of the Chinese Communists' 9th Field Army, which was there setting its trap. This force of 12 divisions was commanded by General Sung Shih-lun, whose specific mission was "to annihilate the 1st Marine Division," then to move south and take Hamhung.

Sung Shih-lun had studied the writings and tactics of Mao Tse-tung, especially Mao's often-quoted sixteen-word tactical credo adopted from Sun-tzu: "Enemy advancing, we retreat; enemy entrenched, we harass; enemy exhausted, we attack; enemy retreating, we pursue." Over-simplified as this may seem, Mao wrote in his book *On the Protracted War*, "We have always advocated the policy of luring the enemy to penetrate deep precisely because this is the most effective military policy for a weak army in a strategic defense against a strong army."

Luring the Marines deep was the keynote of Sung's strategy. He skillfully went about his mission. After the Marines arrived at Yudam-ni, Hagaru, and Koto-ri, Sung planned to surround each unit, then blow up the bridge behind them at Funchilin Pass, making escape impossible. This bridge, three and one-half miles south of Koto-ri, was the key point on the only road leading back to Hamhung. It spanned a formidable chasm, estimated at more than 1,000 feet in depth. Marines would be able to take arms and equipment neither to nor from the Chosin Reservoir without rebuilding the bridge. Sung did not intend to give them the chance to do that.

An analysis of Sung Shih-lun's troops shows them contrasted sharply to those of the 1st Marine Division. The Chinese division was composed of about 10,000 men on paper; in actuality it contained 7,500 to 8,500 personnel. Three divisions made an army. Each division was composed of three regiments plus an artillery battalion, an engineer company of about 100 men, a 150-man transport company, a 100-man guard company, and a 60-man communications company. Because of the mountainous terrain, Sung could not bring his artillery battalion, essential to every division, into the Chosin Reservoir vicinity.

Sung's men depended on a wide assortment of weapons, most of them American, captured from the Chinese Nationalists. His command combined peasant soldiers recruited by the Communists and former Chinese Nationalists. Perhaps the most distinctive feature about his soldiers was the lack of any official provision for an honorable discharge. Once the Chinese peasant became a cog in the military machine, he remained there until he was killed or captured, became a deserter, or was incapacitated for active service. Recruiting officers, however, had little difficulty in filling their ranks with those inured to hardships from birth.

A Marine officer who had served in China recognized one of the prisoners captured at Sudong as a former Chinese Nationalist. "What are you doing fighting for the Communists?" he asked. "I remember you as being on the Nationalist side when I was in Tientsin."

"They feed me," was his simple, honest reply.

Once his command was assembled at Antung, near the Yalu River, Sung informed his soldiers through speeches and pamphlets that the Americans planned to invade China and that they were being sent to fight alongside their North Korean brothers to save the homeland from the Imperialists. After this indoctrination, Chinese girls passed out apples, cigarettes, and small gift packages to the soldiers.

When Sung's men crossed the Yalu, each soldier was given a four-day food supply of rice, millet, or soybeans to carry in his pack, and only 80 rounds of ammunition. Afterwards, food had to be procured locally from the North Koreans. Although each soldier was warned not to take food or molest the civilians in any way, the lack of an adequate supply system left him no choice but to steal from the North Koreans. This accounted for the constant flow of refugee families to Hamhung-Hungnam. When his supply of ammunition had been expended, the Chinese soldier had to do without.

Each Chinese wore a two-piece reversible mustard yellow and white uniform of quilted cotton and a heavy cotton cap with fur-lined ear claps. Issued to the troops just before crossing the Yalu, the quilted cotton blouse and trousers were worn over the standard summer uniform and any other layers of clothing the soldiers may have acquired. The first Chinese Communists we saw had canvas shoes with crepe rubber soles.

Later arrivals wore a half-leather shoe, or even a full-leather boot. Most Chinese carried a shawl-like blanket in addition to the small pack containing food and personal belongings.

Bob Barrow's statement about the adaptability of the Chinese proved correct. Sung's men quickly observed that planes in our particular area did not bomb North Korean homes. The Chinese concentrated in such areas. Later we learned that they hid in Korean homes during the day, sometimes as many as 40 to 60 in one small hut.

From the start, Sung's troops had other serious handicaps. At best, the infantry received little help from supporting arms. A primitive communications system also accounted for critical shortcomings. The radio net extended only down to the regimental level, and telephones only to battalions or occasionally companies. Below the battalion, communications depended on runners or such signaling devices as bugles, whistles, flares, and flashlights. The consequence was a tactical rigidity that proved fatal many times in the Chosin Reservoir campaign. Commanding officers had little or no option below the battalion level. Once committed to the attack, a battalion usually kept on as long as its ammunition lasted, even if events indicated it was beating out its brains against the strongest part of the 1st Marine Division's defense line.

Sung's troops epitomized the Chinese Communist strategic aims summed up years before by Mao Tse-tung. The North Korean mountainous terrain was especially adapted for Mao's operational principles, although it severely penalized his troops logistically. "Make wiping out the enemy's effective strength our main objective . . . in every battle, concentrate on absolutely superior force, encircle the enemy completely . . . do not let any escape from the net . . . strive to draw the enemy into mobile warfare."

Mobile warfare restricts the use of the terrain for cover, inhibits effective firepower, and prohibits artillery when advancing units move beyond the range of their fixed emplacements. Luring the 8th Army and 10th Corps units into mobile warfare was not necessary. Tokyo Headquarters accommodated Mao's generals satisfactorily on that score.

MacArthur's plan called for the 8th Army on the west flank

of the Taebaek Mountain Range to proceed north with all deliberate speed. The 10th Corps was to move towards the Yalu on an ever-widening front in three columns, each separated from the other. No 10th Corps division could support the other in case of enemy attack. The plan for the already over-extended 1st Marine Division was an advance of 55 miles west of Yudam-ni to Munpyong-ni to remove Chinese pressure on the 8th Army, then north to the Yalu.

The viability of MacArthur's strategy hinged on the premise that the intelligence data fed to his headquarters by air and ground troops in Korea was clearly wrong. He had no alternative plan to contain the enemy, in the event that the unwanted information on Chinese strength proved correct.

Soon after we arrived in Chinhung-ni, Bob Barrow spoke to "A" Company concerning the Chinese. "The leadership of our new enemy is completely different from that which I knew in China, but there will be very little difference in the individual soldier. Unlike the Japanese, these soldiers are not fanatics; they will go about their business with resigned determination—but not of a sort that can't be broken. They will greatly outnumber us, but will not have the firepower that we enjoy. These peasant soldiers are accustomed to unusual hardships, both before and during service. They can walk great distances with ease, and hill climbing, the curse of the U.S. servicemen, is second nature to them. Their capacity to endure and exist on the most meager of diets will amaze you.

"Time will be our biggest enemy, for the Chinese is a highly adaptable type, and rather quick to learn. These people are unaccustomed to fighting Occidentals but they will learn new methods, adapt themselves to the new situation, and as time goes on, they will become a dangerous enemy. They are particularly fond of a fluid offense—they will not have many fixed objectives. If they can't destroy an enemy unit today, they will try some other time, or they will move on to another. And although they don't like the defense, once committed to it (and always with exceptionally good reason) they will make a damn good show. They can outwalk us and out-'fast' us, but they can't outfight us.

"Don't let this remark breed contempt, for a scabietic, bandy-legged, consumptive-ridden, poorly fed, inadequately clothed, illiterate, scared peasant is just about as capable of killing you as you are him. If their leaders can get enough 'trigger fingers' at the right place and at the right time, we will have our hands full."

As indeed we did. On Saturday morning, November 25, while Sung hastily assembled his "trigger fingers" to perfect his trap, we at Chinhung-ni eagerly prepared for Thanksgiving dinner. The day began well. We joked with the battalion surgeon about the water's taste. "Lose your iodine, Doc?"

"Nope! That water was tasting too much like Scotch whiskey. I was afraid some of you might become addicted!"

"This water tastes so good I'm afraid to drink it," another laughingly commented.

"I told you if you'd give me a mountain stream away from people I'd give you good water. And here it is!" he replied with a grin.

Fritz had not exaggerated in promising us a Thanksgiving feast. The menu included shrimp cocktail, stuffed olives, roast young tom turkey with dressing and cranberry sauce, candied sweet potatoes, fruit salad, fruit cake, mince pie, and coffee.

The men were served from two lines by a group of happy, smiling cooks and helpers. They realized that on this day alone and with this one meal they had regained much of their lost popularity with the troops. Some came through the lines a second and even a third time. One expressed his approval by saying, "You cooks done outdid yourselves today. Jamming all that good stuffing up them turkey asses makes it taste downright scrumptious!"

After dinner, I wrote Ginny a long letter telling her, among other things, how grateful I was that our country could serve such a meal to troops halfway around the world. I now received letters from her seven days after they had been mailed. This tremendous morale booster was a great improvement over the mail delivery in World War II. In the South Pacific theater it often took more than a month to receive a letter from the States. I wrote her further that all our men, including myself, were in excellent physical condition and good spirits. "The intelligence information from Tokyo is all good," I wrote. "Don't believe what you read in the newspapers about the Chinese. The reporters need something to write about. It makes good copy to have us fighting hordes of Chinese instead of the few which is actually the case!"

Near dusk, Jim Adair came by the tent, smiling from ear to ear.

"Cap'n, have you heard? We're going to be home by Christmas!"

"Don't hand us that bullshit!"

"It just came over the 'Stars and Stripes' radio station. MacArthur said that he's going to have the first troops home by Christmas. The communications platoon sergeant just told me. He heard it himself."

"Well, that doesn't mean the Marines will be going home by Christmas, but that's damn good news, Jim," I replied approvingly. "Pruitt, right now I'd like to join you in a drink of confiscated officers' whiskey!"

We laughed and joked until bedtime.

10

The Real World of North Korea

Fritz was the first in our tent to arise early on the Sunday morning of November 26. After he woke up he visited the battalion supply tent, pitched on a small ledge overlooking the division supplies. A thermometer hung on a pole outside the tent.

"The thermometer says it's eight degrees below zero," Fritz announced when he returned.

"No wonder I felt so cold in my sleeping bag last night!" I mumbled. "I was afraid I'd punctured a hole in it somewhere."

Slowly we unzipped our sleeping bags and began putting on winter clothes.

"That's the last of the potatoes," Pruitt spoke up. "They're no good once they've been frozen," he said as he picked them up one at a time. "I didn't think they'd freeze inside the tent. I shouldn't have left them so close to the canvas. From now on we'll store all food near the center of the tent."

When dressed, I joined a large gathering at the communication platoon's radio jeep to get the football scores over the "Stars and Stripes" radio station. Only a few games were broadcast, but after the scores the station aired a show of Glen Miller favorites. After listening to the news, I walked to the road.

The information gathered at the checkpoint on the road was, if true, alarming. North Korean civilians repeatedly told of seeing numerous Chinese about five miles southwest and west of our present location. The pedestrian traffic flowed from northwest to southeast, toward Hamhung. Seldom was anyone seen walking toward Koto-ri. The reason for moving was always the same; in order to survive, the Chinese took the Koreans' homes and food. On this day, we became concerned at last about Chinese in our vicinity.

On the night of the 26th, several Chinese groups made probing attacks in the western and southern sections of our lines. On the morning of November 27 Schmuck sent out a number of small patrols in an effort to locate the Chinese. In contrast to the 8th Army, constant patrolling was the trademark of the 1st Marine Division. To Schmuck it was a fetish. Fire teams and squads were sent on reconnaissance missions only. They were instructed not to fire upon meeting a superior force, but to return and give information on the whereabouts of the enemy. Units of platoon size and up constituted combat patrols. These normally took an artillery or mortar forward observer with them, to punish the enemy. Each day Schmuck accompanied a patrol. Most of his staff officers remained at the CP during his absence.

While we were sampling one of Pruitt's boneless chicken sandwiches, with a sprinkling of cheese, a dash of steak sauce, and a pickle on top, Fritz came into the tent. He reported that PFC Roach had escaped from the Navy hospital in Tokyo, bummed a ride on a plane to Yonpo Airfield and made his way to "A" Company.

"And you know, Cap'n, he's over there with his daddy right now!"

"Well, I'll bet his father's pleased to see him. He's been worried enough about that young man," I replied.

Early on the morning of the 28th, patrols were again sent out. Later in the morning, the paymaster flew in by helicopter. Fritz and Pruitt sent word throughout the battalion that he was aboard, and that anyone who wanted to be paid should come to the first-aid tent where the pay line would be established. I was amazed to see the long line of men, when cash had absolutely no use that I could think of at Chinhung-ni. That night in our tent while we were sitting on the deck, with the charcoal urn going full blast, I spoke up.

"Why in hell would anybody be getting money out here?"

"It's good for morale," Pruitt replied.

"Morale! You can't spend it!" I said.

"Captain, did you ever gamble with IOUs?" Pruitt asked.

"No."

"Well, it's no fun! There's gambling all over this battalion tonight. About three or four days from now, the same seven guys who always win will be sitting down playing cards for all that money you saw today. That damned Indian halfbreed in the Guard Platoon will be among those seven. He's a card rack if I ever saw one! Whether dice or cards, he stays on a hot roll."

"Captain, I know gambling's against regulations," Pruitt continued, "but in the service it's just as important not to know what's going on sometimes as it is to know what's going on! It's important not to know they're going to have the damnedest poker game over in Weaver's tent about four days from now."

"So, it's important not to know, huh?"

"I said sometimes, Captain. Sometimes it's important not to know. Take Captain Barrow for instance. He doesn't know young Roach is over there with his daddy."

"The hell he doesn't!" I answered. "Bob Barrow knows everything about 'A' Company! He knows the name of each man and what he's doing. Bob even knows the family background of some of his men."

"You're right, Cap'n. You're right. And that's the reason he doesn't know young Roach is there!" Pruitt said emphatically. "Captain Barrow knows you're not supposed to have father-son combinations in the same company and you're not supposed to harbor a Marine who's gone AWOL from the Tokyo hospital. But he also knows that Platoon Sergeant Roach is *one damn good* Marine and he's tickled pink at seeing his son again. So, Captain Barrow doesn't know young Roach is there!"

"Suppose the battalion sergeant major sends an inquiry about Roach."

"Oh, in that case, Captain Barrow will investigate. Then, in a few days he'll find him," Pruitt explained. "Oh, he'll find him anyhow, but he'll find him at the right time. Besides, the sergeant major isn't going to ask any questions because he's got a son of his own with the 5th Marines."

"Okay, Pruitt, I get you. Since it's important not to know, tell me who's the big winner after the game gets down to six or seven players."

"I'll let you know, Captain."

Shortly after dusk that evening, we repulsed another light attack on the perimeter, but again received no casualties.

Later that evening, when I stood duty watch in the CP tent, we learned that one returning patrol had definitely established Chinese in estimated battalion strength, waiting in a mountain valley to the southwest. The Communist troops were hiding in houses by day and probing by night, apparently in preparation for a determined attack. Our radio also reported the 8th Army was retreating. For myself and many others, November 28 and the morning of November 29 are the dates when we first began to think and live in the real world of North Korea. Until then, we believed Tokyo reports that spoke of Chinese volunteers and minimal opposition. In reality, the situation was quite different.

By November 24 the Chinese had moved 30 infantry divisions into North Korea. Seventeen were in the 8th Army sector and 12 were in the Chosin Reservoir area. The Chinese 124th Division, part of the 42nd Chinese Army facing the 8th Army, was so badly mauled by the 7th Marine Regiment that it was unable to engage in further activities during November and December. The Chinese and Korean Communist strength in Korea stood at between 270,000 and 340,000 men. Approximately 440,000 UN troops of vastly superior firepower faced them, although one-half of the UN forces were ROK troops; many were service troops.

A further breakdown in the fighting zones showed that approximately 150,000 Chinese combat troops opposed approximately 130,000 combat troops of the 8th Army consisting of the U.S. 2nd, 24th, 25th, and 1st Cavalry Divisions, the ROK 1st, 6th, 7th, and 8th Divisions, the British 27th Brigade, and the Turkish Brigade. In the Chosin Reservoir area, approximately 100,000 Chinese combat troops faced 24,000 men of the 1st Marine Division, including elements of the 7th U.S.

Army Division. The Chinese had an additional fourteen divisions of 140,000 men in reserve north of the Yalu River.

At this point, MacArthur was not impressed by the Chinese entry into the war. To initiate his final offensive, on November 24 MacArthur issued an optimistic communiqué. His message showed clearly that he thought the burning and destruction by his air force of the civilian center of population between the Yalu and the 8th Army front had aided our cause militarily.

"The United Nations massive compression envelopment in North Korea against the new Red Armies operating there is now approaching its decisive effort. The isolating component of the pincer, our air forces of all types, have for the past three weeks, in a sustained air attack of model coordination and effectiveness, successfully interdicted enemy lines of support from the north, so that further reinforcement therefrom has been sharply curtailed and essential supplies markedly limited. The eastern sector of the pincer, with noteworthy and effective naval support, has now reached commanding enveloping position, cutting in two the northern reaches of the enemy's geographical potential. This morning the western sector of the pincer moves forward in general assault in an effort to complete the compression and close the vise. If successful, this should for all practical purposes end the war, restore peace and unity to Korea, enable the prompt withdrawal of United Nations' military forces and permit the complete assumption by the Korean people and nation of full sovereignty and international equality. It is that for which we fight."

It is ironic that the greatest military victory of his career, the Inchon landing and capture of Seoul, resulted from MacArthur's insistence that ground troops, namely the 1st Marine Division, were essential for the interdiction of enemy supply lines. Yet this same MacArthur now concluded that his air force had effectively interdicted the supply lines of the Chinese! In jungle warfare and in mountainous terrain, air power alone cannot prohibit the movement of supplies to the front. Within earshot of several war correspondents, MacArthur told an 8th Army general, "If this operation is successful I hope we can get the boys home by Christmas." When we heard the news over "Stars and Stripes" radio, newsmen had already labeled this offensive the "Home for Christmas Drive."

On the western front, the 8th Army moved ahead in columns as scheduled. During the first 36 hours it encountered light resistance and registered ground gains of as much as 12 miles. This took the forward echelons beyond range of their fixed artillery emplacements. Sadly, unit commanders believed Tokyo intelligence summaries and failed to place combat patrols on the flanks of the moving column. UN troops thereby became prime fodder for Chinese "Hochi-Shiki" traps. In addition, they could not take full advantage of air cover, due to the lack of competent TACP teams.

Shortly after dark on November 25, strong Chinese forces struck suddenly and hard at General Walker's central and eastern units. The ROK II Corps at Walker's right scattered before the vicious onslaught. The IX Corps in the center held briefly, then gave ground. On Walker's left the II Corps, only under pressure at its east flank, withdrew in coordination with the IX Corps' rearward move. Walker's divisions failed to adhere to the principle that still might have turned the tide of battle in their favor—maintain position at night. With superior air power, daylight dramatically shifted the advantage to UN troops.

Walker notified Tokyo at noon on November 27 that the Chinese were attacking in strength, but it was too early to tell if the enemy meant to sustain its attack. The next day he reported that he no longer doubted the Chinese had opened a general offensive.

Sun-tzu observed: "If you know the enemy and know yourself, you need not fear the result of a hundred battles. If you know yourself, but not the enemy, for every victory gained you will also suffer a defeat. If you know neither the enemy nor yourself, you will succumb in every battle." MacArthur had fallen victim to the worst phase of Sun-tzu's pronouncement.

The Chinese indulged in an analysis of themselves vis-à-vis the enemy after each battle. Their evaluation of the 1st Cavalry Division, considered among the best of Walker's troops, is worth noting. On November 20, less than three weeks after the Chinese Reds' 39th Army had driven the 8th Cavalry Regiment from the Unsan area on the western front, the headquarters of the 66th Army, Chinese People's Volunteer Army, published a pamphlet entitled "Primary Conclusions of Battle Experiences at Unsan." It made several favorable comments: "The coordinated action of mortars and tanks is an important factor. . . . Their firing instruments are highly powerful. . . . Their artillery is very active. . . . Aircraft strafing and bombing of our transportation system is great. . . . Their infantry rate of fire is great, and the long range of fire still greater."

But then the pamphlet said the American soldiers, when cut off from the rear, ". . . abandon all their heavy weapons, leaving them all over the place and play opossum. . . . Their infantry men are weak, afraid to die, and haven't the courage to attack or defend. They depend on their planes, tanks and artillery. At the same time, they are afraid of our firepower. They will cringe when, if on the advance, they hear firing. They are afraid to advance further. . . . They specialize in day fighting. They are not familiar with night fighting or hand-to-hand combat. . . . If defeated, they have no orderly formation. Without the use of their mortars, they become completely lost . . . they become dazed and completely demoralized. . . . At Unsan they were surrounded for several days, yet they did nothing. They are afraid when the rear is cut off. When transportation comes to a standstill, the infantry loses the will to fight."

Although this Chinese Red view of our troops may be overly critical, MacArthur clearly overestimated American training and discipline. He apparently believed his 8th Army soldiers were efficient, battle-hardened troops, with their service in Korea making up for the lack of indoctrination and discipline before their arrival. Perhaps because MacArthur's naval and air forces gave us complete control of the sea and air in Korea, and he had witnessed the surrender of Japan without an infantry invasion, he grossly overestimated his air power's role in destroying infantry troops. The Chinese forces were simply the wrong kind of enemy for effective strategic bombing by air or tactical bombing that would prevent men and supplies from reaching the front. They were adept at camouflage. They lived off the land, and had few identifiable supply dumps—none that our intelligence sources could identify in North Korea.

Chesty Puller later described an incident that sheds some light on the faulty intelligence picture. On November 26, General Smith asked Puller to attend the next two mornings' briefings by General Almond at the 10th Corps Headquarters in Hamhung. Smith needed to be with the 5th and 7th Regiments at Yudam-ni. On the morning of the 27th, after General Almond gave his briefing, he said a plane was waiting for him. He hoped to return by early afternoon, but if he did not, he wanted the staff to care for some visitors from Tokyo: General Willoughby and his crew.

The next day, nothing was said about Willoughby's visit at the staff conference. After the meeting, Puller asked General Clark Ruffner, the 10th Corps chief of staff, what had happened. ·

"I don't think you want to know!" Ruffner replied.

"Then why in the hell did I ask you if I didn't want to know?" Puller snapped back.

Ruffner said, "Well, when Willoughby asked Almond about the Chinese, Almond replied that the 7th Marine Regiment had engaged in one hell of a fight with the Chinese Reds at Sudong, continuing on to Chinhung-ni."

"That's another goddamn Marine Corps' lie!" Willoughby replied.

"But the Marines took a large number of prisoners who are now in the prison compound at Wonsan," Almond said.

They flew to Wonsan. Willoughby saw the Chinese, then left without so much as a word before his return flight.

Every midnight, the Korean situation map was sent out from Tokyo with detailed positions of the enemy and friendly forces. The night before, the map showed UN, North Korean, and few Chinese forces. But on the night of November 28, it abruptly revealed one-half million Chinese troops scattered over the map, some of them as far as 100 miles south of the Yalu. Puller told his staff: "Now that's the fastest damned troop movement in the history of the world! You'll never see another such! And don't forget this lesson. Tokyo wouldn't admit that we had

Chinese fighting us even after the 8th Army was in flight, because some damned staff officer hundreds of miles away willed it to be so. You can't will anything in war!"

By November 28, all 8th Army units were in full retreat. Effective resistance on the western front had collapsed. MacArthur called an emergency council of war in Tokyo that evening. Generals Walker and Almond, hastily summoned from Korea, joined Hickey, Wright, Willoughby, and Whitney at MacArthur's American Embassy residence. In a meeting lasting from 9:30 P.M. until 1:30 A.M. MacArthur revised his strategy. He ordered Walker to make withdrawals as necessary to keep the Chinese from outflanking him. Almond was directed to maintain contact with the Chinese, but to concentrate the 10th Corps into the Hamhung-Hungnam area. The Chinese Reds were thus handed their greatest victory. Even though UN forces outnumbered the Chinese and possessed far greater firepower, they retreated before peasant foot soldiers who had little artillery and no air cover. In addition, these peasant soldiers were insufficiently supplied with the basics for fighting— food, clothing and ammunition. The shortages were partially remedied by the thousands of tons of military supplies abandoned by the 8th Army in its hasty retreat.

General Sung established his CP ten miles north of Yudam-ni. From there he directed the Chinese attack. With the rapid rearward movement of the 8th Army, and with the Chinese Communists in hot pursuit, fighting in Korea was narrowed down now to the vicious bloody battles between the 1st Marine Division and General Sung's 9th Chinese Army. This army group came by rail from Shantung Province, China, directly to the border in late October and early November, and started crossing at once. The 9th was comprised of three Chinese armies, the 20th, the 26th, and the 27th, each with three divisions. Each of these armies was reinforced by a division from the 30th Army, thus giving each army four divisions. The news media repeatedly spoke of "Chinese hordes" now engaged in Korea. The term was used so often that it became the subject of jest. Each time a patrol returned to camp, a Marine might ask, "How many Chinese hordes did you see today?"

General O. P. Smith's troubles were close at hand. When he awoke on the morning of November 28, his worst fear had been realized. With the 8th Army in full retreat, the gap separating his forward echelons from the elements of the 8th Army widened at a rapid pace. Chinese forces surrounded every battalion under Smith's command except one. Sung now readied his troops to spring the trap, and carry out his expressed mission of annihilating the 1st Marine Division.

General Smith established his advance CP at Hagaru. His 1st Marine Division was reinforced by three battalions from the U.S. 7th Infantry Division, a company of Royal British Marines, plus an assortment of Army engineers and service troops. Smith's insistence on securing his supply lines, as well as establishing bases for further operations in the frigid barren wastes of the Chosin Reservoir area, proved invaluable in the weeks ahead. He now readied his troops to engage the Chinese who were deployed around his units like a giant spider web.

An actual spider spins its web to trap flies or other insects incapable of resisting the spider's overpowering strength. Ultimately, it devours its prey. When a hornet is caught, the spider keeps its distance, lest it fall victim to the hornet's sting. But the strength of the hornet deteriorates proportionately to the time it remains confined, and unless it removes itself from the spider's trap, it, too, will be consumed.

The difference between untrained soldiers and trained, disciplined troops is equal to if not greater than the difference between the fly and the hornet. Sung's expressed mission was the annihilation of the 1st Marine Division. He knew his soldiers must soon test the stinging power of the Marines to prevent those in his net from escaping.

Before attacking, General Sung disseminated among his troops by pamphlet and lecture a composition, "The Bloody Path," by a captain of the Russian Navy. It said in part: "When in the summer of 1950 the American imperialistic marauders, the newly appeared pretenders to world domination, provoked the bloody holocaust in Korea, the Wall Street housedog, General MacArthur, demanded that the American so-called 'Marines' be immediately placed at his disposal. This professional murderer and inveterate war criminal intended to throw them into battle as quickly as possible for the purpose of inflicting as it seemed to him then, a final blow on the Korean people.

"In putting forward such a demand, MacArthur proceeded from the fact that U.S. 'Marine' units have been trained more than any other type of American forces for the waging of the unprecedented brutal and inhuman, predatory war against the freedom-loving Korean people.

"It was precisely to the U.S. Marines that the Ober-bandit MacArthur addressed the words:

"'A rich city lies ahead of you, it has much wine and tasty morsels. Take Seoul and all the girls will be yours, the property of the inhabitants belongs to the conquerers and you will be able to send parcels home.'

"The events in Korea have shown graphically that the Marine Corps stalwarts did not turn a deaf ear on the appeal of their rapacious axeman. They have abundantly covered Korean soil with the blood and tears of hundreds and thousands of Korean women, old people and children . . ."

General Sung's own battle message concluded by saying: "Soon we will meet the American Marines in battle. We will destroy them. When they are defeated, the enemy army will collapse and our country will be free from the threat of aggression. Kill these Marines as you would snakes in your homes!"

At the beginning of the series of battles between the Chinese and the 1st Marine Division, Sung had a heavy numerical advantage, as well as the availability of reinforcements. His greatest weakness was resupply. The Marines had the advantage of complete air cover and superior firepower. Smith's weakness was the scattering of his forces. His 5th and 7th Regiments were deployed at Yudam-ni for an attack west. The three battalions of the 7th Army Division occupied ground near and around Sinhung-ni on the east side of the Chosin Reservoir.

Puller's 1st Regiment guarded Hagaru at the base of the Chosin Reservoir, Koto-ri, 11 miles south of Hagaru on the main supply route, and Chinhung-ni, the railhead supply point ten miles south of Koto-ri.

The 43 miles of road from Chinhung-ni to Hungnam passed

through comparatively level terrain. But there were few straight or level stretches of road for the remaining 35 miles from Chinhung-ni to Yudam-ni, with the route from Chin hung-ni through Funchilin Pass to Koto-ri being the most difficult. Funchilin Pass represented an ascent of 2,500 feet from the railhead valley floor at Chinhung-ni for a straining jeep or truck. The road was a twisting one way shelf with a cliff on one side and a chasm on the other. Military historian S. L. A. Marshall proclaimed it the most dangerous defile in all of Korea.

The critical and highly vulnerable bridge in Funchilin Pass was three and one-half miles south of Koto-ri. At this point, water from the Chosin Reservoir was discharged from a tunnel into four large steel pipes that descended sharply down the mountain side to the turbines of the power plant. Where the pipes crossed the road, they were covered on the uphill side by a concrete gatehouse without a floor; on the downhill side was the one-way bridge over the pipes.

Between the cliff and the more than 1,000-foot drop, there was no possibility of a bypass. It was essential that the bridge be kept intact for the movement of vehicles, tanks, heavy weapons, and supplies to and from the reservoir area.

Smith did not have enough men available to guard this bridge and adequately defend the other vital areas assigned to Puller's regiment. Ridge's 3rd Battalion, reinforced, had the duty of guarding Hagaru, the advance supply base. Sutter's 2nd Battalion, reinforced, guarded Koto-ri, and Schmuck's 1st Battalion protected the division's supplies at the railhead at Chinhung-ni, in addition to patrolling the road to the north and south Puller's regiment was too thinly spread as it was.

Sung could read his map. The bridge at Funchilin Pass gave him his ace in the hole.

General Walter Bedell Smith, chief of the Central Intelligence Agency, could also read a map. He knew the terrain, and the size of the enemy forces, as well as our own, by virtue of reading the daily intelligence summaries. He commented pessimistically: "Only diplomacy can save MacArthur's right flank!"

I studied the latest snapshots of my wife and child. I mused, "Yes, Ginny has lost weight, a lot of weight because of worry. I won't criticize the news reports back home again soon. Ginny has cause to worry!"

11

Block-Parts

If you take a flat map
And move wooden blocks upon it strategically,
The thing looks well, the blocks behave as they should.
The science of war is moving live men like blocks.
And getting the blocks into place at a fixed moment.
But it takes time to mold your men into blocks
And flat maps turn into country where creeks and gullies
Hamper your wooden squares. They stick in the brush,
They are tired and rest, they straggle after the ripe blackberries,
And you cannot lift them up in your hand and move them.
    A string of blocks curling smoothly around the left
Of another string of blocks and crunching it up
It is all so clear in the maps, so clear in the minds
But the orders are slow, the men in the blocks are slow
To move, when they start they take too long on the way
The General loses his stars and the block-men die
In unstrategic defiance of martial law
Because still used to just being men, not block-parts.
                    —STEPHEN VINCENT BENÉT, *John Brown's Body*

The map, an essential planning tool, could not give MacArthur the ground view he needed for success in North Korea. Mountains, hills, and valleys all showed the same on his situation map. Villages, towns, and cities appeared as dots with funny-sounding Japanese names written underneath or beside each dot. The erasure of dots only inches away from the Chosin Reservoir by air force bombs and incendiaries was still too far distant from the battle zone to punish the enemy. After the bombing, pictures showing charred bodies of innocent victims became excellent material for the Communist propaganda mill.

    The multitude of hiding places in the hills, valleys, tunnels, and mine shafts in the vicinity could be appreciated only by those who were there. The warm, comfortable quarters in the American Embassy at Tokyo were simply too far removed from the reality of North Korea for MacArthur to identify with his

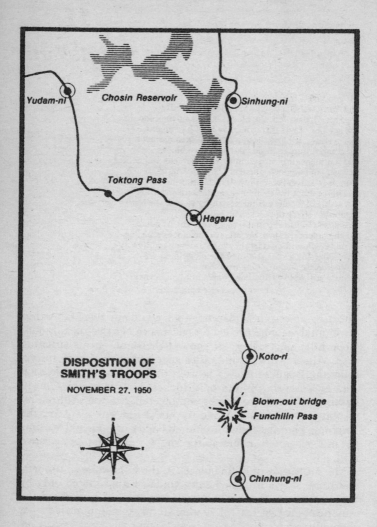

Yudam-ni

Chosin Reservoir

Sinhung-ni

Toktong Pass

Hagaru

**DISPOSITION OF
SMITH'S TROOPS**

NOVEMBER 27, 1950

Koto-ri

Blown-out bridge

Funchilin Pass

Chinhung-ni

men and the problems they faced. This distance alone created illusions. Furthermore, MacArthur commanded many who were not yet ready to function as "Block-Parts."

Not so with Generals Smith and Sung. Both shared one thing in common: men they could move like blocks on the map—men with a tradition of victory in battle. Sung's men had been at war with either Japanese or Chinese Nationalist soldiers for years. Smith's officers and NCOs cut their teeth fighting trained, resourceful, and fanatical Japanese soldiers in the islands and jungles of the Pacific. They had learned firsthand that effective firepower means "bullets hitting people." To their present situation this meant seeing Chinese before shooting at them. More important, Smith knew it took little blocks to make big blocks.

In 1940, the U.S. Army Infantry School at Fort Benning, Georgia, developed the fire team concept. A corporal was placed in charge of three men centered around a Browning Automatic Rifle (BAR) operator. This successful concept was adopted by both the Army and the Marine Corps. The Marines added an additional man as squad leader. Luckily the Marine Corps maintained this structure after World War II. Each infantry squad had three fire teams, each infantry platoon had three squads, and each company had three rifle platoons.

A Marine division differs from an Army division in other ways. It is unlike any army division in the western world. The Marine division carries its own tanks, air force, ground transportation, artillery, supply, and medical battalions, plus an engineering battalion with the ability to build bridges, roads, airfields, water purification plants, and so forth. The Marine division is self-sufficient. In fact, it is a small army.

On the morning of November 27, the 5th and 7th Marine Regiments moved west in the attack from Yudam-ni. They were met by heavy resistance from Chinese troops. The nights of November 27 and 28 saw the enemy counter-attack. The result was heavy casualties on both sides—disproportionately high for the Chinese.

By the night of November 28–29, when fighting broke off, the area around the Marines was strewn with Chinese dead. Inside the perimeter, the medical unit had its hands full. Seriously wounded Marines filled all available tents. The less fortunate were huddled side by side outdoors and covered with tarpaulins while lying on straw to prevent freezing. Primitive as this hospitalization appeared, "died of wounds" cases numbered no more than might have been expected under better conditions.

"Everything was frozen," said Lieutenant Commander Chester Lessender (MC) USN, the 5th Regiment surgeon, when interviewed by correspondent Keyes Beech. "Plasma froze and the bottles broke. We couldn't use plasma because it wouldn't go into solution, and the tubes would clog up with particles. We couldn't change dressings because we had to work with gloves on to keep our hands from freezing. We couldn't cut a man's clothes off to get at a wound because he would freeze to death. Actually, a man was often better off if we left him alone. Did you ever try to stuff a wounded man into a sleeping bag?"

The next day and night at Yudam-ni passed without major Chinese opposition, but continued sub-zero cold imposed a strain upon those on duty watch.

Keyes Beech wrote further, "Seldom has the human frame been so savagely punished and continued to function. Many men discovered reserves of strength they never knew they possessed. Some survived and fought on will power alone."

To understand the continuing fight between Smith's and Sung's troops, one must keep in mind the five locations of Smith's troop concentrations: Yudam-ni on the west side of the Chosin Reservoir, Sinhung-ni on the east side, Hagaru at the southern base of the reservoir, Koto-ri on the road south, and Chinhung-ni, the division supply dump, ten miles south of Koto-ri at the valley railhead. The division radio relay linked Yudam-ni, Sinhung-ni, Koto-ri, Chinhung-ni, and Hagaru. It provided us with a reliable communications system throughout the campaign.

When Smith received orders on November 29 to come back to the Hamhung-Hungnam area, his plan for withdrawal was simple. Troops at Yudam-ni and Sinhung-ni would move south to Hagaru. With the major portion of his command consolidated at Hagaru, Smith would proceed to Koto-ri with his entire division, less our battalion, intact. He would move to Chinhung-ni, and then to Hamhung-Hungnam.

There were two highly vulnerable locations along the Marines' route of withdrawal. One was Toktong Pass, where the main supply route wound its way up from the plain at the foot of the Chosin Reservoir, three miles north of Hagaru. The other trouble spot was Funchilin Pass, three and one-half miles south of Koto-ri. "F" Company of the 7th Marines occupied the high ground called Fox Hill at Toktong Pass. A company-size unit was not available to guard Funchilin Pass.

Smith commanded from his advance CP at Hagaru. His air force reported seeing the movement of large numbers of Chinese toward Hagaru. He knew they would attack soon. The problem was simply when, where, and with what strength.

In keeping with Smith's policy, the Marines won respect at the outset by allowing Korean residents all the privileges of self-government at Hagaru that could be reconciled with military security. The police department and town officials were allowed to continue functioning. In turn, they briefed the population about restricted areas and security regulations, particularly curfew. Korean civilians entering Hagaru through Marine roadblocks were searched before being taken to the police station where they were questioned by an Intelligence Section interrogation team. Second Lieutenant Richard E. Carey, the intelligence officer, was a newcomer to Colonel Ridge's battalion charged with the defense of Hagaru.

Carey instructed his agents to converse with incoming Koreans and learn everything possible about the enemy's situation. All refugees told the same story. Most came from areas north and west of Hagaru; the Chinese Communist troops had evicted them from their homes. Since the Korean civilians were untrained observers, their estimates of Communist numbers and equipment could not be taken too literally. Their statements agreed, however, that the enemy was in close proximity.

Carey decided to risk sending two agents on the dangerous mission of establishing direct contact. They planned a circuit of the perimeter. They would mingle whenever possible with the Chinese to determine the areas of heaviest concentration.

The results went beyond Carey's fondest expectations. Not only did the Korean agents return safely, but they brought back vital information: large numbers of well-equipped Chinese troops were stationed south of Hagaru. Since the Marine air force also reported unusual activity in this area, Carey assumed the enemy was concentrated there in division strength.

This answered the questions, "How many?" and "Where?" But when to expect the attack? Carey sent out his agents again to make direct contact. Upon reporting back, the agents said they talked freely with enemy troops, including several officers who boasted that they would occupy Hagaru on the night of November 28. The agents reported major enemy units were only five miles south of the perimeter.

Dusk was at approximately 1800. Complete darkness set in shortly thereafter. Adding an estimate of three and one-half hours for Chinese movements from the line of departure, the Intelligence Section calculated the enemy would attack in division strength as early as 2130 from the south and west.

Colonel Ridge accepted these Intelligence estimates for troop dispositions. As the main bastion of defense, the tie-in structure of "H" and "I" Companies extended to include the south and southwest sides of the perimeter, nearly one-third of the entire circumference. The new perimeter ran in a continuous line 2,300 yards in length, or more than a mile and one-quarter. Each platoon front averaged 380 yards. Supporting arms took up the slack for lack of numbers.

The Chinese attacked at the place anticipated, arriving an hour later than originally envisioned. Three red flares and three blasts on a police whistle signaled the beginning of the attack. As they came forward in waves, the Chinese were mowed down.

At about 0020, however, the enemy broke through one platoon area and penetrated as far as the company CP. Pandemonium ensued, with the sound of Chinese trumpets and whistles adding to the confusion. It became difficult to distinguish friend from foe. Observers reported tracer bullets were so thick they lighted up the darkness like Christmas trees. Some enemy troops made their way far enough inside to surround the battalion CP, the portable galley, and the provision tent. But once inside the battalion lines, the Chinese disintegrated into looting groups. They were either killed or captured.

During all the commotion, Marine engineers continued work on the airstrip under fixed lights. With or without Chinese, the engineers obeyed orders to work on a 24-hour, seven days a week schedule. A completed airstrip at Hagaru was an essential ingredient to Smith's plan.

Colonel Ridge had assigned a portion of the perimeter, East Hill, to an assortment of Army troops. The largest unit was Company "D," 10th Engineer Combat Battalion. It was composed of 77 American enlisted men and 90 ROKs. This unit arrived in Hagaru at noon, shortly before the enemy cut the mail supply route to the south. At 2130 Chinese overran the hill. More than half the UN soldiers became casualties. Here was another example of the difficulties imposed by the language barrier. American officers understood the ROKs had run out of ammunition. Later it was found that most of them had not fired a single shot, but continued to hold their firepower in reserve. Fortunately, the Chinese move on East Hill was a diversionary attack made only in company strength, with not enough numbers to carry through. Marines regained the hillside the next morning, but left the Chinese occupying the topographical crest of East Hill.

The story was tragic 12 miles north of Hagaru at Sinhung-ni. On the night of November 27–28, the Chinese hit the Army units hard. When the senior Army commander was killed, Lieutenant Colonel Don C. Faith took command of the three Army battalions. On the afternoon of the 28th, General Almond emerged from his helicopter. He immediately pinned a Silver Star on Colonel Faith and two other soldiers standing nearby. After Faith described his predicament, Almond spoke: "The enemy who is delaying you for the moment is nothing more than remnants of Chinese divisions fleeing north. We are still attacking and we're going all the way to the Yalu. Don't let a bunch of Chinese laundrymen stop you!"

After Almond departed, one of the soldiers who had just been decorated, wondered aloud, as he examined his medal, "What in the hell is this for?"

An officer standing nearby asked Faith, "What did the General say?"

"You heard him!" he blurted. "'Remnants fleeing north!'" Faith ripped the medal from his parka and threw it into the snow.

The Chinese Communists pressed their attack against Faith's battalions on the next two nights. Feeling he would be overwhelmed in his Sinhung-ni perimeter, on December 1 Faith attempted a breakthrough to Hagaru. In preparation Faith destroyed his howitzers and all but essential equipment. His convoy moved slowly, burdened with hundreds of wounded under the constant cover of Marine close air support. Losses of officers and NCOs along the way gradually deprived his units of leadership. At dusk, with the task force only four and one-half miles north of Hagaru, Faith fell mortally wounded. His units shattered into leaderless groups. The column ceased to exist as a military force. A tragic disintegration set in, as wounded and frostbitten men made their way across the reservoir ice in little bands.

Stragglers came into Hagaru all night. By the morning of December 2, 670 survivors had been taken into warming tents at Hagaru. Marine Lieutenant Colonel Olin Beall of the 1st Motor Transport Battalion led his truck drivers on a search for other survivors.

Marine truck drivers enjoyed the well-earned reputation of being the most accomplished thieves in the Corps, although they preferred the term "scrounger" to "thief." On this occasion, Beall's men scrounged up some light machine guns with numerous belts of ammunition which were put to good use. Machine-gun fire kept the Chinese pinned down while the truck drivers gathered the survivors, in many instances driving jeeps across reservoir ice frozen to a depth of 18 to 20 inches. The Marine Corps' demand that all service troops be trained for combat duty returned big dividends.

Of the 319 Army soldiers rescued by Beall's men, nearly all were wounded or frostbitten. Some were found wandering in

aimless circles on the reservoir ice in a state of shock. Rescue
work continued until the last of an estimated 1,050 survivors
of the original 2,550 Army troops were saved. Of this group,
385 able-bodied soldiers were organized into a provisional battalion and equipped with Marine gear. It is a tribute to these
survivors that they participated in the remainder of the fighting against the Chinese.

When news reached us at Chinhung-ni that wounded men
had been abandoned by Army troops, the reaction was bitter.
We did not know all of the circumstances when we first heard
about the ill-fated Faith battalions.

Our perimeter at Chinhung-ni stayed calm the night of November 28. On the morning of November 29, Wes Noren led a
reconnaissance patrol to search out the exact enemy positions.
They were reportedly to the west of us. At day's end, Noren's
patrol pinpointed the Chinese.

As a result, Schmuck ordered Bob Barrow's "A" Company to
attack west the next day to destroy the enemy in the valley.
After receiving orders, Barrow was worried that his men might
be running out of gas, since they had often been sent on single
company missions. Early in the morning, he called his men
together and mounted a 50-gallon oil drum to speak words of
encouragement. He realized his fears were unfounded. Eager-
ness showed on all faces. His men were ready to go.

Barrow's tactics followed Maurice de Saxe, who said in his
Reveries on the Art of War, "Those who wage war in mountains should never pass through the defiles without first making themselves masters of the heights." On each side of the
narrow valley to the west, there was a series of steep, rocky
ridges, difficult to negotiate. Barrow dispatched a reinforced
squad to each side. These men traveled near the ridge crest
paralleling the main body on the valley floor. In addition to
providing observation for artillery fire, these squads set the
pace for the main body's advance. Still more, they gave Barrow's men an absolute defense against a Chinese V-type
"Hochi-Shiki" trap.

The enemy were found occupying Korean homes. When the
first shots were fired, the Korean civilians separated them-

selves from the Chinese. Barrow methodically advanced his men by fire and movement until all resistance dissolved. Marine Corsair fighters wound up the pursuit, scattering the enemy into hiding.

The Chinese troops used a mixture of traditional and modern materiel. Some Chinese rode shaggy Mongolian ponies. The dead left behind were clothed in new padded cotton uniforms and armed with American weapons, presumably captured from the Nationalists. The Korean civilians came with our troops to camp. From there, they were sent to Hamhung.

Schmuck, Bates, and Bridges accompanied "A" Company. When they returned late that afternoon, they told of the day's events with great excitement. Their enthusiasm reminded me of returning duck hunters, each of whom had bagged his limit for the day. Of course, ducks don't shoot back. In this case, neither did the Chinese after artillery fire began raining upon them. Whether Chinese or American, you can't hurt your attacker when your back is turned toward your pursuer. The valley to the west remained quiet for many nights thereafter.

We received word this same day that the 1st Marine Division would consolidate in a perimeter defense around Hamhung-Hungnam. This news caused great disappointment throughout the battalion: it meant retreat. General Smith recognized the adverse psychological impact on his troops when he told a reporter, "Retreat, hell! We are just attacking in another direction!"

Late that evening, near midnight, Colonel Puller radioed Schmuck for a report on the events of the day. Schmuck briefed him on the elimination of the Chinese to our west. Puller then stated that Colonel Ridge was having one hell of a fight again at Hagaru.

"Ridge says he's not sure he can hold until morning," Puller continued. "He must think he's commanding WRs [Women Reserves]. He'll make it all right!"

Schmuck asked Puller how he was getting along.

"Fine! We have contact with the enemy on all sides."

Everyone in the command tent laughed at Puller's remark. We learned later that some Chinese got as far as Puller's mess hall tent before being killed. Puller's statement was repeated to me at least five times before 1000 the next morning. And each time, the men listening doubled up with laughter.

"Ain't that just like Chesty," one said. "Claiming he's in good shape while he's surrounded 'cause his men can shoot Chinks in every direction!"

At this time the morale of our battalion approached its highest peak. In part, this was because we had yet to experience significant casualties in battle against the Chinese. More important, however, we believed we were invincible. We had not received heavy pressure upon our lines, as other Marine battalions had.

Sutter's 2nd Battalion, 1st Marines, plus an assortment of Army engineers, service troops, a few British Royal Marines, and Marine engineers and artillery formed a well-entrenched defense perimeter at Puller's CP at Koto-ri that could not be successfully attacked without huge losses to the attacking forces. Since Puller's position was in no immediate danger, Smith ordered Puller to send some 900 men, 150 vehicles, and 30 tanks to the relief of Hagaru.

Puller christened the column "Task Force Drysdale," after its commander, Lieutenant Colonel Douglas Drysdale of the British Royal Marines, 41st Commando Battalion. The British Marines wore berets instead of helmets, the most distinguishing feature between us. Army troops plus George Company of our 3rd Battalion together with the Marine service troops, MPs, truck drivers, and signalmen composed the remainder of this force.

The Chinese occupied the heights on each side of the road about four miles north of Koto-ri. They permitted the head of the column to pass through before they descended from the hills. Only 300 of Drysdale's seasoned troops reached Hagaru. Of the remainder, 321 were killed, missing, or captured, and approximately 300 returned to Koto-ri. This fight, on the road that Marines called Hell Fire Valley, went to General Sung. The added 300 troops arriving at Hagaru, however, proved to be the difference on the night of November 30. In two attacks at Hagaru, Sung expended a full division without success, save holding the topographical crest of East Hill. Colonel Puller placed Drysdale's returnees in the defense perimeter.

Puller had his own way of getting his point across to unit commanders serving under him. When an Army captain asked him for the line of retreat in case he was overrun, Puller got on the radio with the 11th Marine Artillery. He gave the artillery commander the exact location of the captain's unit, the correct distance and azimuth, and then said, "If this unit starts to pull back from the line even one foot, I order you to open fire on them." Turning to the captain, Chesty grinned, "Does that answer your question?"

Another Army battalion from the 7th Division arrived at Koto-ri the night of December 1. The Chinese realized the futility of further attacks on Puller's stronghold.

Early in our move to the Chosin Reservoir, General Smith's intelligence unit became convinced, on the basis of civilian reports, that Chinese soldiers were moving through the countryside in columns of substantial size, harboring in native villages and mine shafts. Marine aviators discounted this view; daylight reconnaissance failed to show troop activity within the villages. Still, the civilian reports persisted. Finally, North Korean natives asked unit commanders to attack the nearby villages to destroy the Chinese invaders. Only after the Chinese cut our supply route and refugees streamed south did Smith order large-scale air bombardment of villages adjacent to the road.

At Funchilin Pass, the original concrete bridge blown up on the night of November 28 was repaired immediately by engineers from Koto-ri with a temporary wooden structure. It was blown up again, and replaced with an M2 steel treadway span. On the night of December 2, the Chinese blew up the bridge for the third time.

This time, however, Sung played his cards differently. He moved elements of the Chinese 60th Division into Funchilin Pass to prevent further replacement. Sung deployed one regiment along the mountain ridge on the northwest side of the pass. A second regiment was dug in on the south and adjacent to the bridge site. The third regiment he used for roadblocks and harassment purposes between Chinhung-ni and Majon-dong. Sung learned at Whampoa and thereafter the prime importance of holding critical points on strategic roads. Sun-tzu had drawn the appropriate analogy. "When a cat is at the rat hole, 10,000 rats dare not come out; when a tiger guards a ford, 10,000 deer cannot cross."

A gap of 24 feet had to be spanned for the Marines to come out with their vehicles, tanks, guns, and wounded. The Chinese Communists south of the bridge were not vulnerable to attack by Marines from Koto-ri. The attacking force could proceed to the gap, but no further without replacing the bridge. Chinese heavy weapons and machine guns were trained on this spot.

Smith recognized that Sung could be saving his main blocking effort for the ten-mile stretch from Koto-ri to Chinhung-ni. A mere platoon could do great mischief in such terrain. He designated the 1st of the 1st for the attack north to enable his engineers to rebuild the bridge. This meant we had to be relieved by an Army unit. The division's supplies at Chinhung-ni could not be left unguarded with so many hungry Chinese in the area. Smith made his request to General Almond. After conferring with Tokyo headquarters, Almond designated a column labeled "Task Force Dog," commanded by Brigadier General Armistead Mead, for our relief.

The afternoon of December 2, Schmuck led a reconnaissance patrol of three jeeps into the mouth of Funchilin Pass. Before leaving Chinhung-ni he sent a decoy platoon up the valley to divert attention from his movement on the road. He instructed this platoon to stay visible but not come within rifle range of the Chinese. Schmuck sighted large numbers of enemy on both sides of the road in Funchilin Pass. He called for artillery fire before returning to Chinhung-ni. Shells raking the hillside unquestionably eliminated many.

More important, his mission established Hill 1081, the "Big Hill," as the key terrain feature dominating the fields of fire at the bridge site. Chinese prisoners taken later by patrols confirmed Schmuck's analysis. As we had discovered previously, the Japanese maps were poor in detail. Schmuck's personal reconnaissance in all directions proved invaluable. His patrolling in the days ahead enabled him to fill in the voids on the maps. Distances on the maps were shown in meters; thus Hill 1081 measured 3,546 feet above sea level.

Our biggest problem was ascertaining the actual strength of the enemy to our north. On December 1, civilians at our road checkpoint estimated 10,000 Chinese were in the valley between us and Koto-ri. The returning patrol of December 2 reported the equivalent of at least two companies digging in on the Big Hill. A patrol coming back on December 4 reported numerous Chinese digging in across the narrow valley adjacent to the blown-out bridge. From this information we established the presence of large numbers of Chinese around the bridge site, but short of those claimed by civilians.

While we were searching for the enemy we did learn that they were taking the measure of us. A North Korean civilian reported to Division Intelligence he had been conscripted by a Chinese company of 175 men. He led them under cover of darkness to a spot on the mountainside overlooking our installation at Chinhung-ni. After carefully making an assessment of our positions during the day, the Chinese returned north again that night.

By November 30 the Marines at Yudam-ni felt the enemy had shot his bolt. At a terrible cost in killed and wounded, the Chinese had achieved nothing more than a few local gains. An attacking force is always placed at a distinct disadvantage in fighting an entrenched defensive force. Now it was time for the Marines to expose themselves to move south. The two Yudam-ni regimental commanders began joint planning for redeployment at Hagaru. General Smith recognized that the problems of the two commands could not be separated. He considered the assignment of command to the senior regimental commander, but rejected this course in favor of cooperation.

The Marines regrouped on the south side of the village of Yudam-ni astride the main supply route as a first step toward a breakout. Surprisingly, the enemy took little advantage of this readjustment when the men drew rations and ammunition. All equipment that could not be carried out was destroyed.

On December 1, a battalion was displaced overland on each side of the road between Yudam-ni and Hagaru to capture the high ground and prevent the main body from being ambushed by the Chinese. Each battalion was directed to join the main body again at Toktong Pass. Lieutenant Colonel Ray Davis, 1st Battalion, 7th, was assigned this mission on the south side of the road.

Davis's battalion clawed its way to the mountaintop in 16° below zero cold. For 36 hours the battalion beat back repeated attempts by the Chinese to destroy the main body. Finally, Davis's men began collapsing in the snow—oblivious to the cold, heedless of the Chinese bullets ricocheting off the rocks. Officers and NCOs had to shake and cuff the prostrate Marines into wakefulness. Davis's battalion reached Fox Hill at Toktong Pass at 1130 on December 3. Fox Hill had been successfully defended by only one company against overwhelming odds. The battalion on the north side of the road met only sporadic opposition. The move to Hagaru was made without incident.

Before entering the Hagaru perimeter, the survivors of Davis's battalion stopped short several hundred yards from it. His men closed ranks into a compact column. With shoulders thrown back, and shoe pacs beating a firm tread on the frozen road, Davis's Marines marched in at attention. In tribute to his outstanding leadership and the resilience of the men serving under him, Davis was awarded the Congressional Medal of Honor. Roanoke Marines suffered proportionately with the others in Davis's decimated ranks.

A combination of surprise, determination, trained and disciplined troops, and close air support caused the Chinese again to sustain heavy casualties. The last Marine unit entered the Hagaru perimeter at 1400 on December 4. More than 1,500 casualties, a third of them frostbite cases, were brought to Hagaru. Once inside the perimeter, a new air of confidence prevailed. Somehow the 1st Marine Division would succeed.

On December 2, the 2,900-foot airstrip at Hagaru was made available for planes. The runway took 12 days to build. Men on the firing line had found it difficult to reconcile bulldozers moving dirt under floodlights while a few hundred yards away a life and death struggle raged on the perimeter. The airstrip, however, proved its worth. From December 2 through December 6, 4,312 wounded and frostbitten cases were evacuated.

More than 500 Marines, mostly those previously wounded and returned from hospitals, rejoined the division at Hagaru. The same morning the airstrip opened, 12 replacements arrived at our CP. Among them was a tall, handsome, clean-cut sergeant, a Marine Reserve from Pennsylvania named Gordon. The sergeant major assigned him to "A" Company, where he became a squad leader in the 1st Platoon. Sergeant Gordon had recently received pictures from his wife of their new baby. He took great pleasure in showing the pictures to anyone and everyone who would take a look. He, as well as the other replacements, seemed pleased at joining our battalion.

Our sergeant major impressed me with his command presence, and with his efficient manner in handling the replacements. After watching him make the assignments, I returned to our tent.

"That sergeant major is one tough Marine!" I commented as I reached for a piece of cheese.

"He's not as tough as you think, Captain!" Fritz replied. "He worries about that son of his up north all the time. I'll bet he's sitting in his tent right now worrying if he makes it to Hagaru!"

Anxiety over the Marines "encirclement" was being strongly felt also in the United States. On December 4, the Communist radio in Peking broadcast that annihilation of the 1st Marine Division was a mere matter of time. Most stateside news analysts saw matters the same way.

On December 5, Major General William H. Tunner, USAF, the chief of the Combat Cargo Command, visited Hagaru. He offered his C-47s to General Smith for troop evacuation after the casualties were flown out, a gracious though impractical gesture. Smith explained that all able-bodied men would be needed for the breakout and that he could not abandon so much equipment to the Chinese. He failed to point out that to select Marines for the final plane embarkment would be difficult, indeed, because this unit would likely be killed or captured by the enemy.

Marines draw ammunition and rations before moving south from Yudam-ni. A string of Chinese dead encircle the defense perimeter.

On outpost at Koto-ri. Note improvised shelters for keeping warm.

Air drops at Koto-ri.

Prisoners being captured south of Koto-ri.

Marines inspecting Chinese dead.

Marine dead being loaded onto truck at Koto-ri.

Return of sniper patrol. Sgt. Albert L. Ireland leads Pfc. Linden L. Brown and Pfc. Robert B. Glover, Jr.

At northern side of the blown-out bridge blocking route to safety. Ridge across narrow valley, where Chinese Communists were dug in with machine guns to prevent replacement of bridge, is visible at lower left.

Chinese prisoners captured in valley near blown-out bridge.

Moving column nears blown-out bridge. At top right, note downed helicopter at point where road bends left to bridge.

U.S. Army's 92nd Armored Field Artillery Battalion, under Lt. Col. Leon Lavoie, providing excellent support to attacking infantry on morning of December 9, 1950.

Marines walking to safety after repair of blown-out bridge. Note deep cut and steepness of north face of Hill 1081 at right.

Pause for rest during march southward.

A dead Marine is strapped on hood of each jeep on march as the column stops for rest.

Supplies on beach at Hungnam awaiting shipment south.

Destruction of remaining supplies at Hungnam before departure.

With over two-thirds of his command concentrated at Hagaru, Smith planned next to move his blocks to Koto-ri. For
the first time, combat correspondents reported that the odds
had shifted in Smith's favor—that he would "break Sung's
hold"—but they predicted "final success will extract a heavy
price in blood."

12

On the Eve of Battle

Peace permits men to go their separate ways. War demands that thousands give their all to a common task. The Army, Navy, Air Force, and Marines all joined forces to extricate the 1st Marine Division and supporting troops from Sung's trap. The Air Force did yeoman service in making air drops of ammunition and needed supplies all along the route. In addition to supplying the troops and caring for the wounded, the Navy gave close air support from the carriers *Baedong Strait, Leyte, Valley Forge, Philippine Sea,* and *Princeton.* This proved invaluable each time the Marines took the offensive against the Chinese. The Army covered the escape route from Chinhung-ni to the south. Marine air and ground troops forged a bond of understanding that could never again be broken.

On the morning of December 6, I awoke early and, after getting a bite to eat, walked to the checkpoint on the road. A few Korean refugees were being questioned when I arrived.

"This road has 'one way' signs planted somewhere," the sergeant in charge said. "These Korean families keep going south. No one travels north except us Americans.

"Anything new?" I asked.

"No, sir. These people say there's a hell of a bunch of Chinese up there on the mountain, but that's nothing new."

"Do they say how many?"

"No, only lots and lots of them," he said, gesturing with his arms in a gathering motion.

I returned to the CP, then walked through the rifle company areas. As I passed through each area, men were sitting in front of their tents in small groups cleaning their rifles, machine guns, and mortars, chatting and joking as they worked.

As I came upon one group, a Marine was looking down his rifle barrel.

"Cap'n, I bet you've never seen a barrel any shinier than this one—I don't care how many rifles you've inspected! Take a look, sir."

As I held it up and peered through, I commented, "That's a clean-looking piece all right."

He smiled as I handed it back. "Cap'n, a bullet coming out of that barrel will tear the ass right out of a Chinese! And it won't be long now—will it, sir?"

"I don't know," I answered. "We haven't received orders yet."

As I continued walking, I could feel the rising tide of excitement among the men. I approached one group with a dismantled machine gun. Its parts were spread upon a poncho. The men were carefully washing each piece with gasoline. We had learned from experience that oil thickened in the cold and often caused the machine gun to fire sluggishly until it warmed up.

The sergeant in charge asked, "Cap'n, have you noticed something strange about this country?"

"Sure, there are lots of things different, but I wouldn't necessarily call them strange."

"Well, sir, how long have you been in the Marine Corps?"

"Ten years, including the Reserves."

"That's one year more than me. But have you ever been with a Marine unit where there are no dogs—our galley just attracts dogs."

"No, I don't believe that I have."

"Well, have you seen a dog since you've been in Korea?"

"No, I haven't," I answered. "I haven't even heard one bark."

"Nobody else has either."

"I guess these people are just too poor to feed anything other than their own children, anything that doesn't help them make a living."

I continued on until I came to the stream at the southern

part of the perimeter where there were a few mud houses with rice-straw roofs. Four women had broken the ice on a small pond. They were washing clothes and contentedly beating out the water with wood paddles on nearby rocks. "Each one seems to always use the same rock," a corporal said. "They come out here every day. They take their clothes inside to dry."

When I arrived back at the CP, communication men were testing radio equipment. Two had walkie-talkies strapped on their backs, and were standing about 100 yards apart.

"One, two, three, four, five—do you hear me? Over."

"One, two, three, four, five—do you hear me?" one repeated, as I moved toward my tent. When I walked inside, Pruitt was sitting on the deck writing a letter. A number of filled sheets of paper were scattered on the dirt floor beside him.

"Writing to your wife, Pruitt?" I asked.

"Yep!"

"My gosh, you've written five or six pages already! I've never seen you write that much before! All those to your wife?"

"Yep. I just heard that Cap'n Barrow found PFC Roach. Sent him back yesterday afternoon."

"Is that what you're writing about?"

"Nope, Cap'n. But that tells me something, that really tells me something. We're going to be up to the ass in Chinese before long."

"Bob Barrow hasn't received orders," I replied. "Colonel Schmuck doesn't know yet when we're going."

"Well, Cap'n Barrow's intuition is good enough for me. It won't be long now, Cap'n."

At midmorning, an advance party of officers of Task Force Dog arrived at our perimeter. They had been fired upon by the Chinese just before entering. A young guard in the back of one jeep was apparently hit and killed when the jeeps came within view of our camp. When I asked the battalion doctor where the guard had been hit, a corpsman piped up, "Captain, the bullet went in his mouth and out his ass!" The doctor explained the man died of heart failure; there were no marks on his body.

The Army officers seemed anxious to review the details of our defense perimeter. As we walked around, they examined the deep foxholes that had been dug upon our arrival and daily improved. Most were covered with dirt-filled bags on top of logs and were well camouflaged from the view of an approaching enemy. At varying distances in front, the men had strung double-apron and single-apron barbed wire fences, oftentimes connected by barbed wire concertinas. The Marines delighted in showing the trip flares and booby traps they had placed along the fence. We informed the officers we had received reports over our radio that barbed wire fences seemed to confound the Chinese soldiers. They invariably tried to crawl under the fence. One line lieutenant reported, "It's as if they have some superstitious dread of wire; it will stop them every time."

When we arrived back at the CP, I made the mistake of chatting about the effectiveness of Marine air power. Immediately, an Army officer spoke.

"Do you think that's fair? Is it fair for you to have your own air force when we don't have even one damned plane?"

I disengaged from the argument. I could see that neither of us would gain any knowledge from this line of conversation. After showing the officer who would occupy my positions around my company area, I decided to write to Ginny. In our tent, Pruitt had completed his letter and was preparing one of his specialties—an open-faced tuna fish sandwich. He mixed the tuna fish with mayonnaise and tomato ketchup to give it a meaty look and flavor and toasted the bread slice on one side. As always, a dill pickle was on top. We had found that bread would not freeze inside the tent when stored near the canvas. Instead, it stayed fresh for many days, much longer than normal.

"I hope we finish this food before leaving," I commented.

"I agree!" Pruitt replied, as he proceeded to make another sandwich.

Throughout the day, men continued to ready themselves by boiling their clothes, rinsing them with cold water in their helmets, and then hanging them up to dry on clotheslines inside their tents. Rifles, machine guns, mortars, and heavy weapons were cleaned, set aside, then cleaned again. Most took the opportunity to bathe while still inside a tent. In spare moments, we wrote letters home.

For the past few days, Barrow, Wray, and Noren had been frequent visitors at the CP. None wanted to be the last to get vital information about our next move.

Schmuck set the tone around headquarters, with his attitude of good humor and enthusiasm. A short man who appeared to strut, he was always decisive with his orders, and his mannerisms sometimes reminded me of Napoleon. This day while Schmuck was inside his tent, Bob Barrow made the officers outside laugh heartily by mimicking him. Each of Schmuck's gestures was exaggerated when executed by Barrow's 6'4" frame. Nonetheless Bob greatly admired Schmuck.

While waiting to see him, Bob told us about an incident the previous evening when he and Thatenhurst inspected sentries on the perimeter. Thatenhurst began rebuking Corporal Joe Leeds for not challenging. Leeds spoke up.

"Now, Gunny, don't go chewing our asses out. We knew who you were. There ain't two Chinese in the whole world as big as you two!"

"You can't quite separate yourself from your upbringing," Bob commented. "Leeds was raised in an orphanage in New Jersey, and he tries harder than anybody I ever saw. The least criticism bothers him though."

Conversation changed to the latest "Stars and Stripes" newscast. MacArthur's daily communiqués increased the estimated strength and capability of the Chinese. If one took them at face value, one could easily get the impression the Chinese were unbeatable. "Stars and Stripes" reported the enemy now had 800,000 men in the war. It had been an error in the first place to picture Red China as a paper tiger. It was equally wrong to picture it now as a full-grown beast. Mao's government had held full control of the Chinese mainland for only one year. However, the exaggerated strength reports didn't phase us at Chinhung-ni. No one appeared to be intimidated.

That afternoon we received word the enemy had cut the main supply route two miles to the south toward Sudong. Apparently they were the same Chinese who fired upon the Army officers in the morning. A roadblock established by the enemy had a platoon of Marine engineers pinned down around a hydroelectric power plant there. The Chinese occupied the ridge above the Marines and were delivering plunging fire (fire from above at short range) into their camp. The Marine commander, Lieutenant Thomas Glendinning, radioed for help. The Chinese shot down the American flag that the lieutenant had flown from his command post. Glendinning crawled out and replaced it.

Schmuck dispatched a patrol from "C" Company with a forward artillery observer. When shells poured into the enemy positions, the engineers came out carrying their wounded and driving their trucks, tractors, and heavy equipment. The last thing out was a bulldozer, its blade held high as if executing a right-hand salute. Artillery fire continued until dusk. Silence fell on the ridge. Darkness came shortly thereafter and with it the top officers of the battalion gathered to chat at the CP.

A friendly, healthy rivalry existed between the rifle company commanders. Each officer admired the soldiering qualities in the other too much to permit jealousy to divide their friendship. Thus far in the war, all companies had performed well. But Bob Barrow's "A" Company had achieved spectacular success since the Inchon landing and had led a charmed life in the process. In evaluating the officers, the NCOs, and the men of each unit, I would give very high marks to all in each category. I'd tip the scales in "A" Company's favor if asked to select the best, primarily because of its commander.

Through a series of battle tests, Bob had emerged as an outstanding leader. Was there some secret formula for his success? I think not. Barrow wasn't a complex person. He was patently unslick. He had a strong knowledge base; that is, he knew his own job, the job of the men above him, as well as the men below. He was friendly, straightforward, confident, talking in terms that all could understand. He knew every man in his company and the strengths and weaknesses of each, and he would listen to what they had to say.

Barrow understood the enemy, neither underestimating nor overestimating its strength. He knew how to give orders as well as carry them out. In battle, he acted only on solid information. Once he made his estimate of the situation, he acted quickly and forcefully. While engaged in a firefight, Barrow exhibited admirable creativity in the application of what he knew. He embodied the rare combination of ambition and courage. Whatever secrets he held pertained to his private life; his worth as a Marine officer was visible to all who knew him. Where then should Barrow fit into Schmuck's plan for the attack north? Schmuck would soon be faced with this decision.

In attacking a defended beach, men in the first waves are often expended. They move inland as far as they can go before being cut down, thereby paving the way for others to succeed. Those who first attacked the entrenched Chinese on the Big Hill would likely suffer this same fate. Which company then should be designated to catch the brunt of enemy fire? Schmuck's decision was not an easy one. When he retired for the night on December 6, he knew this decision must be made the following day.

On the previous day, we had learned that the main body of the 1st Marine Division would begin moving from Hagaru to Koto-ri on December 6. The move began with the 2nd Battalion, 5th Marines, under Lieutenant Colonel Roise attacking the Chinese on East Hill simultaneously with the jump-off south. After a heavy artillery barrage, Roise's men swept the Chinese off the hill with astonishing ease—a hill held tenaciously by the enemy for eight days. Roise's Marines then dug in. There they would wait until the division cleared Hagaru.

After dusk, Sung sent his men on one of the most futile onslaughts of the Chosin Reservoir campaign. Thousands of Chinese soldiers shuffled through the snow to retake East Hill, now skillfully defended in strength and backed up by every variety of supporting arms. The defense was not a struggle; it was simple slaughter.

The main body of the 7th Regiment had not gone far at 0500 the next morning when Lieutenant Colonel William F. Harris directed the deployment of his troops to beat off an enemy attack on the division column. Shortly thereafter, he was missing in action. Later in the day he was reported felled by enemy fire. His father, Major General Field Harris, learned of his son's death in late afternoon. General Harris left Yonpo Airfield;

went aboard Admiral Doyle's flag ship in Hungnam harbor; took a shower; ate dinner in Doyle's wardroom; sat in silence; then returned to Yonpo Airfield to direct his planes against the Chinese.

Heavy concentrations of air power assisted ground troops in removing the Chinese from the mountain ridges along the route south to Koto-ri. Puller directed that hot food and warming tents be provided for all troops from Hagaru upon arrival. The last unit entered the Koto-ri perimeter at 1500 on December 7. Again, the Chinese had suffered heavy casualties in their efforts to stop the Marines.

General Smith realized his troops could not tarry in Koto-ri. Air spotters had seen numerous enemy reinforcements rushing to the battle zone. It was time now for Smith to order our attack north.

A few days earlier, Smith had concluded that an air drop of a treadway bridge was necessary to span the gap at Funchilin Pass. Unknown to us, prospects for a successful bridge drop appeared dim. A bridge section was badly damaged on December 6 after being test-dropped at Yonpo Airfield by an Air Force C-109. The section simply plummeted to earth too fast. After the causes of the unsuccessful test drop were analyzed, larger parachutes were flown to Yonpo from Japan with a special crew of Army parachute riggers. It was decided to go ahead with the drop to Koto-ri. In order to have a 100 percent margin of safety in case of damage, eight sections were dropped.

Late on the morning of December 7, three of the 2,500-pound bridge sections landed unharmed inside the Koto-ri perimeter. The remaining five sections were delivered by noon. One fell into the hands of the Chinese; one was damaged. Plywood center sections were dropped so that the bridge could accommodate any kind of Marine wheel or track vehicle. Tanks could cross on the metal span only, while the trucks could manage with one wheel on the metal span and the other on the plywood center. The engineers at Koto-ri assembled all necessary equipment for the bridge by late afternoon.

At Chinhung-ni, we never worried about the problems connected with the bridge's erection. We assumed that the question had been solved long before orders came for our attack north.

Shortly after sunrise on December 7, Marines at the road checkpoint spotted a lone figure moving through the valley. A fire team crept forward to investigate. The figure in question was Wu'Ting Kun, a Chinese soldier. He was the regimental librarian in the 60th Division, Political Section. Wu was captured without a struggle. During his interrogation, Wu verified that the Chinese 60th Division was charged with the duty of blocking the 1st Marine Division's move south from Koto-ri, and that the 59th and 58th Divisions were assisting the 60th.

He said that the 178th Regiment of the 60th Division was charged with attacking the American unit that moved north to Koto-ri, meaning us. Wu further added that the 179th Regiment of his division was located in a railroad tunnel and was expected to establish roadblocks to the south. He did not know the exact location or disposition of the Chinese troops, but said some battalions had been reduced to as low as 500 men due to the cold and lack of food. According to Wu, there was no food left in the Korean homes and all the Chinese were hungry. He expressed pity for the poor farmers who had nothing; he had been searching for food when captured.

Wu stated that Lin Piao's 4th Field Army would advance on the west side of Korea. The mission of the four corps of the 9th Army group was to "annihilate the 1st Marine Division," considered to be "the best in the U.S." After dispatching the 1st Marine Division, they would move south and take Hamhung.

The defense of the bridge site now came into better focus. The Chinese Communists' 178th Regiment had the responsibility for its protection. Part of this regiment occupied the Big Hill and the road south of the chasm. The remainder held defensive positions across the narrow valley to the west. During the day, returning patrols brought back three more Chinese prisoners, another from the 60th Division, two from the 87th. One prisoner reported the Chinese had again occupied the valley on our west.

Before noon, General Mead's Task Force Dog, consisting of the 3rd Battalion, 7th Infantry, the 92nd Armored Field Artillery Battalion, plus detachments of engineers, signalmen, and anti-aircraft troops, began arriving at Chinhung-ni. By mid-afternoon, the entire force entered our perimeter and relieved us. It brushed aside some Chinese roadblocks en route.

An atmosphere of excitement escalated as everyone made last minute preparations for battle. Near dusk, Jim Adair came into our tent. He was laughing.

"I've just come from 'A' Company. That's the damnedest bunch you ever saw!"

"Have a tuna fish sandwich," Fritz offered.

After sitting down, Jim began. "Well, a few men have mouth harps, one a jew's harp. A big group is gathered around that tall staff sergeant's tent—the one from the Midwest."

"You mean Thatenhurst?"

"No, he's the gunnery sergeant. Not him."

"You mean Umbaugh?"

"Yeah, that's the one."

"Ernest Umbaugh," Fritz added.

"A lot of men are clapping hands and some southern boys are in the middle doing some of the damnedest steps you ever saw."

"They must be clogging, Jim. Or maybe flat-footing—it's about the same thing."

"How should I know the names of the dances you rebels do?" Jim laughed. "And that machine gunner from West Virginia is a sight! You ought to see the way he throws his feet down and around. The men shout, 'Go at it, Tucker!' and that really turns him on."

"Is Umbaugh dancing?"

"Nope. He's in the middle clapping his hands, egging them on, and laughing like crazy."

"I'd like to see that, but they'll probably quit by the time I get there," I said.

Adair took a few bites of his sandwich and continued, "And that isn't all! A reporter from Chicago, Ned Sparks, came in with the Army and he's over there in Captain Barrow's tent writing a story for his paper about the 'magnificent battle-hardened Marines on the eve of battle'! I looked over his shoulder as he wrote. I never read such bullshit in my life." He broke out laughing. "Hell, Captain, we're heroes already! Every damn one of us."

Everyone laughed as we munched the last of Pruitt's delicacies. Adair left for the CP tent. A few minutes later, he returned to say Colonel Schmuck wanted all company commanders to meet with him and his staff in thirty minutes. Somehow the mere announcement settled us into a more serious frame of mind.

Bob Barrow was the last to arrive at Schmuck's meeting. He had been helping the Army captain who relieved him get his men in place. The captain had arrived with a totally inexperienced unit, half of whom were Americans hastily assembled from noncombat units throughout the Pacific and Far East. The other half were non-English-speaking South Koreans conscripted off the streets of Pusan.

"The problems of discipline and control seem insurmountable," Barrow remarked. "I wouldn't have that captain's job for all the tea in China."

Schmuck's meeting began with an intelligence report. The numbers of Chinese occupying the Big Hill could not be easily assessed. Air spotters and Korean civilians reported it heavily defended, but we were unable to estimate the exact size. The force appeared to be a battalion. We knew it occupied well-camouflaged bunkers on and around the Big Hill extending to the road, with the balance of the regiment dug in across the narrow valley. No comparisons were made with our size; everyone knew our numbers were less than the Chinese defenders. We did not discuss the division's estimate of the situation: "The nature of the terrain through which the MSR [main supply route] passes will make necessary the literal driving out of the enemy from his favorable position. Simultaneous with such a defense he may be expected to launch large-scale attacks against our troops from all sides."

The weather forecast reported earlier in the day "multiple layers of clouds lowest at 4,000 feet, tops at 9,000 to 10,000 feet, visibility six to ten miles, ceiling lowering tonight to 1,500 feet in light snow showers; visibility lowering to one to three miles in showers; clouds dissipating tomorrow morning to scattered lowered clouds at 5,000 feet, visibility improving to ten to 15 miles." Although this weather was not the best, it did not preclude the use of artillery and airplanes.

After Major Bridges reviewed the details of the battle plan, Colonel Schmuck enthusiastically discussed our assignment. The 11th Marine Artillery would move forward about a mile in the valley so as to have a better field of fire against the enemy. They would be accompanied by the 92nd Armored Field Artillery Battalion. All available artillery would concentrate fire on the Big Hill. Our air force would strafe and drop napalm bombs on the mountain crest before we approached. With this concentration of fire, our task should not be too difficult. Experience had taught us, however, that the elimination of half the Chinese by preliminary bombing would be the most we could hope for.

According to Schmuck's battle plan, the companies would proceed in column formation in predawn darkness prior to the bombardment. Since we planned to attack at 0800 on December 8, all company units would start for the assembly area, a designated place in the valley, at 2400. A 0200 start was considered necessary to make the six-mile approach up the mountain.

In spite of Schmuck's apparent enthusiasm, a tense look showed on every face in the command tent. As the final details were discussed, I found myself pulling out my wallet to look at the picture of my wife and child, then returning it, then pulling it out again.

Schmuck ordered Wray's "C" Company to lead and take the first objective, the southeastern nose of Hill 1081. The 81-millimeter and 4.2 mortars would then be moved inside Wray's perimeter. With good observation, it would give support for the remainder of the attack. Barrow's "A" Company would pass through Wray's "C" Company. It would fight its way to the summit of Hill 1081. Noren's "B" Company would advance along the right flank on the road and clear the slopes to the left of Barrow and Wray. The battalion command post would follow closely behind "B" Company.

It was apparent that Wray, Noren, and Barrow all had tough

assignments as none of them had drawn the short straw. Schmuck's choice made sense. After Wray had engaged the enemy, Barrow would be available to complete the assignment. Sung's block on the Big Hill now became the focal point of our attack as well as of his annihilation strategy.

The deployment of Sung's troops took the shape of a long four-mile bottle. Thick layers of Chinese northwest of Koto-ri formed the bottom of the bottle. Funchilin Pass became the bottle's neck. The Chinese on the heights and mountainsides to both the left and right of the road formed the sides. The blown-out bridge over the chasm plus Chinese defenders on the Big Hill and across the narrow valley gave Sung a double cork to contain the bottle's ingredients: the 1st Marine Division. Smith's plan for uncorking Sung's bottle called for our battalion to knock the Chinese off the Big Hill and neutralize the enemy dug in across the valley. Smith's engineers would then erect a bridge over the deep chasm.

One regiment from the 60th Chinese Division had been broken up into units of battalion, company, and platoon size. They were directed by Sung to place roadblocks along the road between Majon-dong and Chinhung-ni. These Chinese could harass, but were not sufficient to stop the flow of Marines once Sung's double cork had been extracted.

After Schmuck's meeting ended, the company commanders returned to their CPs. Bob Barrow found his platoon leaders waiting when he arrived.

"What's our job, Skipper?" one asked.

Quickly he briefed them on "A" Company's mission while assigning specific tasks to each.

"Damn, Skipper!" one said dejectedly. "We're gonna be in reserve for the most important operation of the war."

Disappointment showed on the faces of the others as they stood around chatting about their assignment. However, enthusiasm readily replaced frustration as Barrow explained "A" Company's complete role.

Immediately after Schmuck's meeting, I called a conference in my tent of the senior officers and NCOs in charge of the various sections of H&S. I explained we were to take only three jeeps up the mountain, one for communications and two as ambulances.

"Keep the motors running," I emphasized. "Take along extra gas for this purpose. Whatever you do, don't let those motors in the ambulance jeeps stop turning. We'll play hell getting them started again in this cold!"

Two day's rations would be issued. The C rations would be taken inside the parka; they would freeze if left in the pack. The canteen had to be worn on the belt under the parka. The water would surely freeze and burst the canteen if worn on the outside. Everyone was ordered to take at least two pairs of extra socks and shoe pacs to prevent frostbite of the feet.

Because of the steep terrain, every available man would be needed to carry the wounded. Only one tent would be taken up the mountain: the first-aid tent. It would be pitched on the flattest ground we could find. The medical unit would follow the CP as closely as possible; it would be difficult to get the wounded to the aid station.

Turning to the battalion surgeon, I said, "You and all corpsmen except one will come up the mountain; we need to keep the sick bay here intact. Your assistant and one corpsman will stay. Contact the Army medical unit tonight; let them know that we will need help tomorrow with the wounded."

"Wouldn't it be better to keep two corpsmen at this sick bay? One will be needed for record-keeping and to tag medical instructions on the wounded before evacuation to the coast."

"O.K." I nodded agreement. "What about blood plasma?"

"We'll keep it here. It'll freeze on the mountain."

"Do you have enough?"

"Who knows, Captain? I'm sure the Army brought some we can use. When should I tell the Army doc to expect the first wounded?"

"Tell him to keep his men at full alert from 0800 on."

All units were ordered to start for the assembly area at 2345. There we would make our final check. This would be a sleepless night. We needed the time to check weapons, pack gear and attend to a multitude of minor details—little details that might save a life. The tents were left standing for Task Force Dog. All unneeded equipment would stay at Chinhung-ni.

H&S had no malingerers when roll call was taken at midnight. With only one exception, all other companies in the battalion had the same experience; one rifleman shot himself through the foot to avoid going up the mountain. There was an air of confidence among the officers and men as we readied for our climb. Barrow showed his optimism by issuing extra hand grenades to all his riflemen. The hand grenade becomes useful only when engaged in close combat with the enemy.

Sung's block on the mountain was deeply entrenched, with orders to hold its ground at all costs. Smith's block had orders to occupy the same ground. To accommodate the demands of both Smith and Sung, one block had to give way. In the language of Nathan Bedford Forrest, Sung's block had got there "fustest with the mostest."

In the late afternoon, after all his command was concentrated on Koto-ri, General Smith was enthusiastic about his chances for success. But after nightfall, he began to worry. His study of tactics told him that Schmuck's attacking force might be too small. Smith stayed awake in his tent at Koto-ri. For the first time since his men had been surrounded, his optimism ebbed.

Settled in his tent, Puller had the same concern, but he knew there was no alternative. He knew the division could not come out of the trap until the Chinese had been removed from the Big Hill. If every man in his regiment had to be expended in this effort, that was the price he was willing to pay.

Shortly after 2200 a group of Olin Beall's truck drivers gathered in a tent near Smith's. A rowdy, noisy bunch, they began singing the Marine Corps Hymn verse by verse—when finished, they sang it again. Smith propped himself up on his cot. He listened as they continued singing. His confidence restored, he dozed to sleep.

Smith's and Puller's fears were not shared by the Marines in the valley. We knew which block was going to survive.

13

The Attack

Company commanders and platoon leaders made final inspection. Food, ammunition, and clothing—the essentials—were checked with each man. For lack of an extra pair of socks, a man could get frostbitten feet. No one seemed to notice he'd not slept since the previous night.

Major Bridges spoke softly on the radio. "We will now have a report for all companies. 'A' Company."

"'A' Company all present or accounted for."

"'B' Company."

"'B' Company all present or accounted for."

"'C' Company."

"'C' Company all present or accounted for."

"Weapons Company."

"Weapons Company present or accounted for."

"H&S."

"H&S present or accounted for."

"We will now synchronize watches. When I say 'now,' it will be exactly H hour minus 25 minutes, or 0135. Now."

Schmuck made his report to Puller at Koto-ri. "The 1st Battalion, 1st Marines, is ready to move."

Puller replied, "The weather forecast is bad. The airplanes can't get off the ground in the morning at Yonpo Airfield. With no observation, there will be no artillery fire. Move out as ordered."

Weather is a most important factor in battle. Why had our

previous forecast been wrong? It was simply because the prevailing wind currents move from west to east. All territory
west of us for 8,000 miles lay in Communist hands.

Puller continued, "Notify me when you begin your move,
then maintain radio silence. Don't break the silence unless
absolutely necessary."

The snow began to fall. One Marine spoke up, "All right,
men. Put your white side out now." A small wave of nervous
laughter followed. (The helmet cover had two sides, green for
summer and brown and white for winter.)

Someone called out, "Hey! How many Chinese hordes are
there in one platoon?" Again, forced laughter.

As the minute hand approached twelve, the tense mood of
the men reminded me of ball players before a championship
game—only here the stakes were life or death. The valley was
dark, very dark. A low buzz of chatter could be heard in each
company area. Everyone had been ordered to cease talking
when we moved out.

"It is now H Hour, 0200," Major Bridges announced. His
words silenced the battalion, the same as a cut-off knob on the
radio. In a soft firm voice he continued, "'C' Company report."

"'C' Company is moving out."

"'B' Company report."

"'B' Company is moving out."

"'A' Company report."

"'A' Company is ready to move out following 'C' Company."

The sections of Weapons Company and H&S Company were
attached to the rifle companies or the battalion CP. Thus, neither made a further report.

Schmuck radioed Koto-ri headquarters that we were on our
way. We hadn't planned for snow or heavy overcast skies. The
attacking force now lacked artillery or air support. The Chinese guarding the bridge site had superior numbers. We had
thought it was going to be tough with supporting fire; now it
would be tougher.

The valley was black and silent, the sound of footsteps muffled by the snow. This time it was different—the most important mission ever for the participants. Every Marine had at
least one battle star; many had more than could be counted on

one hand, some more than two hands, yet none had been involved in this kind of start. Predawn white flashes followed by crackling, whistling, booming artillery usually announced a Marine's attack up a mountain. The full-throated roar of the big Navy guns always preceded his arrival on a defended beach. This was different—somewhat like the Roanoke Marines' march down Jefferson Street, no noise, no drums, no applause, but with one added ingredient. Here the risks were known, the danger great, yet all moved forward. Each knew that in the hours ahead a single man could make a difference, a rare occurrence in the lives of most.

By 0400 we had advanced a third of the way up the mountain. This was good progress. Now the climb became steeper. The new snow was two inches deep. Visibility was at best 25 to 30 feet, even though our eyes were accustomed to the darkness. Everyone remained silent.

The snow came down harder; the wind blew colder. Bob Wray's men climbed, crawled, crept up the steep, slippery mountainside. Wes Noren's men on the slopes and the road could move faster, but Wes held them back. He did not want to get ahead of Wray. There were stops and starts, then more stops and starts. Normally this causes men to become impatient, but not this time. With each stop men unbuckled their parkas to cool off. Everyone knew what would happen to anyone who became overheated in this kind of cold. The delays were useful. Many a Marine found that his pack needed adjusting or his ammo load needed shifting.

At daybreak, the powdery snow swirled in the wind. We were more than halfway up the mountain. Everyone remained silent. Daylight did not bring the expected visibility. Thick cloud layers on the mountain further inhibited sight. Occasionally the snow would let up, but the break was always short-lived. Progress could not be measured by looking back towards one's starting point. The clouds and snow sealed off the view. They also prevented an accurate judgment as to the height of our climb. Silence. Deafening silence spawned periods where one's mind dreamed of better times. The intense cold and physical strain repeatedly rocked it back to reality. At 0800, the silence was broken for the first time.

"This is Captain Wray reporting to Colonel Schmuck. We have reached our objective, the southeastern nose of Hill 1081. There are no enemy in sight."

Schmuck directed the 81-millimeter and the 4.2 mortars to proceed into Wray's perimeter. He ordered Wray to report back when this had been accomplished. Again he said, "Report when 'A' Company has passed through your area. Maintain silence."

Wray reported "A" Company's clearance to Schmuck an hour later.

At 1000 we reached the place where we expected a Chinese outpost on the road; none was in sight. The Chinese defense pattern usually called for defended roadblocks and small unit outposts at varying distances in front of the main body's stronghold. These troops would fire upon an approaching enemy, then fade back to the main line of resistance.

"A" Company progressed very slowly now. In places the incline was nearly vertical. The rest of the battalion moved slowly so that it would not get ahead of Barrow's men. Only light snow continued to fall, but the fog was too thick for one to see far ahead. The snow had stuck to the outside of each man's helmet and parka. The parka hood covered the helmet. The white-headed, no-neck figures moving up the mountain looked like snowmen from another planet. Each silhouette faded into the white background at a distance of 25 to 30 paces.

General Sung Shih-lun knew that for centuries Chinese warlords had taught "Annihilation of the enemy must always be the final goal of strategy." This he understood. Thus far, Sung's strategy of separation and annihilation had failed. The Marines had consolidated forces at Yudam-ni, again at Hagaru, and again at Koto-ri. Now the division moved south. Sung had not yet failed, although the Marines were neither separated nor annihilated.

Smith's troops could still be playing Sung's tune. They were concentrating into a smaller and smaller area. Only three and one-half miles separated the rear guard at Koto-ri from the abyss at Funchilin Pass where all had to halt. The Marines were surrounded. Sung's troops blocked every avenue of escape. True, his losses had been extremely heavy, but with the Marines locked in Funchilin Pass, he could then apply Mao's strategy: "Guerrillas should be as cautious as virgins and as quick as rabbits. . . . [They] are like innumerable gnats which by biting a giant in front and in rear, ultimately exhaust him."

Sung held reserves across the valley to the west that could bite away at the Marines with impunity. Our mission was to prevent this annihilation.

Marines continued to inch up the mountainside. Here and there an icy figure fell, picked itself up, then fell again, slowly and surely edging its way up the steep, treacherous cliffs In unison with other icy figures that found the going equally hard. Those who carried the light machine guns, machine-gun belts, extra hand grenades, or radio gear suffered greatly from the extra load. They resisted the temptation to lighten their burden; each knew he carried equipment essential to success.

On the Koto-ri side of Funchilin Pass, Colonel Litzenberg's 7th Regiment was assigned the task of leading the attack to the south. His plan called for two of his four battalions (the fourth being the Provisional Battalion of Army troops) to clear the high ground on either side of the road. The third battalion would advance astride the main supply route, followed by the reserve battalion and regimental train.

His attack began at 0800. The battalion on the south side of the road made slow progress against Chinese small arms fire. The Army Provisional Battalion took its objective on the north side without opposition. The battalion advancing down the main supply route made gains of 2,000 yards in short order against no enemy opposition. But overall progress was slow.

By noon, Murray's 5th Regiment began moving out from Koto-ri to attack Hill 1457, the highest peak north of Funchilin Pass, two and one-half miles from Koto-ri. It drove a small enemy force off the hill by midafternoon, and repulsed a weak counterattack later in the day.

Marines at Koto-ri received scattered small arms fire around the perimeter. On the road north to Hagaru, a roadblock held back a human torrent of Korean refugees. Cruel as this may seem, the refugees could not be admitted. There was a probability of Chinese soldiers infiltrating among them, each watching for an opportunity to use a hidden weapon. The homeless men, women, and children huddled without shelter in the snowstorm. The Marines could do little else, but in some instances gave medical care. Navy medics assisted two women giving birth in the bitter cold.

At midday on our side of the Funchilin Pass, the snow continued to fall; the wind increased in velocity. The slow climb, now reduced to a crawl, continued up the steep mountainside. More than six inches of snow had fallen, with drifts up to two or three feet in places.

For the next few hundred feet, Barrow's men faced a cliff that was almost vertical. Professional mountain climbers would have used ropes to scale the heights and bring the needed ammunition to the top. Barrow's men had none. Luckily, scrub trees jutting out from the cliffside gave them needed support to scale the heights. There had been no break in the silence since Wray's last message.

The mortars were brought into Wray's perimeter. Placement had been difficult. After removing the snow, the frozen topsoil had to be penetrated. By 1400 the mortars were ready for support. The men of Able Company continued to make slow progress.

Beginning at 1430 Noren's men came upon hundreds of enemy footprints in the snow, but no Chinese. All footprints looked like the makers wore a size five or six shoe. Wes Noren motioned his men to advance more carefully. Schmuck directed the communications jeep to park on one side of the road with its motor idling. We had now traveled more than five miles on the road from the communications center at Chinhung-ni. Telephone wire had been laid along the ground from two rolls at the back of the jeep. Our moving CP kept an open line with the artillery placed in the valley and Task Force Dog CP, which in turn maintained telephone contact with our planes at Yonpo Airfield. "A," "B," and "C" Companies had lines connecting to the communications jeep.

For the next half hour, Noren's Marines moved stealthily—slowly—deliberately—along the mountain slopes and the road like innumerable cheetahs stalking their prey. They continued this calculated advance until each crouched motionless along the snowy mountainside.

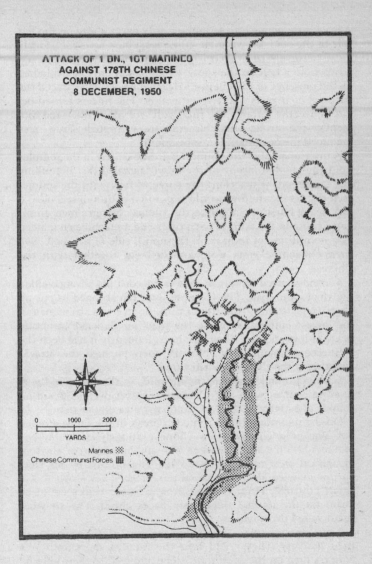

ATTACK OF 1 BN., 1ST MARINES
AGAINST 178TH CHINESE
COMMUNIST REGIMENT
8 DECEMBER, 1950

0   1000   2000
YARDS

Marines ▧
Chinese Communist Forces ▦

Eyes froze on a Chinese bunker only paces ahead on the left side of the road. Brown eyes, gray eyes, blue eyes—cold, steely eyes—were affixed to a curl of light steam lazily spiraling upwards from a hole in the snow, which could only be explained by the presence of the enemy. Trigger fingers lightly traced the outlines of triggers and trigger guards. The fingers tensed before squeezing through the final pull. For moments—and moments—the strong wind blowing snow through scrub trees produced the only sound or movement.

A dry throat, plus the pounding drumbeat felt in the temples from the rapid pumping of the heart, signaled that life-taking and its attendant reaction, the surge of fury with the unforeseen results that follow, would begin in a matter of seconds.

A heavy burst of fire broke the silence. Noren's men eliminated those in the bunker with rifles and a machine gun, aided by a 60-millimeter mortar on the uphill side of the road. Two enemy machine guns were knocked out together with the Chinese.

Marines moved rapidly as Noren speeded his advance along the slopes and road. The Chinese were too stunned to put up effective resistance. A kettle of cooking rice was abandoned in the largest bunker alongside the road, an elaborate structure made of logs and dirt-filled rice bags. Evidently it had been the Chinese command post. Noren's men pursued the attack, shooting at the Chinese as they fled.

Schmuck quickly moved us forward, so that we could stay in close contact with "B" Company. As yet, we had heard no sounds of activity in the "A" Company area on our right.

On the mountain ridge, a sudden break in the snow afforded Bob Barrow a glimpse of a Chinese stronghold. Numerous bunkers lay on a knob between him and his objective, the topographical crest of Hill 1081. With Thatenhurst by his side, Barrow crawled along the mountain ridge. They stopped at a small pinnacle. From this position Chinese voices could be heard on the reverse slope only paces ahead. The snowfall again veiled the ridge.

The Chinese knew something was up. Many were out of their bunkers. They could hear the muffled shots from Wes Noren's men on the mountain slope and road to their left and

left front. Fortunately, snow and fog obstructed their vision.
Barrow sent Thatenhurst back to assemble his platoon leaders.
In the meantime, he moved nearer to survey the area before
returning with his plan of attack.

Although handicapped by reduced visibility, Barrow saw that
the ridge formed a narrow razorback piece of ground with both
sides dropping off sharply. A small defending force could raise
havoc with the attacker; the approach on the narrow front afforded little opportunity for maneuver. Only part of a platoon
could be accommodated on the ridge itself. The men could go
forward or backward no other way. Barrow observed that on
the knob occupied by the enemy, the ridge widened considerably; enough to accommodate many bunkers. On the north
end of the knob, the ridge again narrowed, sloping slightly upward.

Barrow directed Sergeant Myers to lay in 4.2 mortar fire. He
reasoned that mortar fire would suggest no one was nearby. The
mortars began to fire to his immediate right at a 90° angle from
the ridge. Myers plotted its path due north a few hundred yards,
then brought it due west until the shells exploded on the
mountain ridge ahead. He then carefully edged the shells south
down the ridge until the impact shook the ground around him.

Upon completion of mortar fire, Barrow directed Lieutenant
Don Jones to execute a limited enveloping movement on the
left face of the ridge. Before moving out, Jones's men stacked
bedrolls and packs in a pile. All faces had a stern look. Everyone knew that within the hour they would be locked in hand-
to-hand combat with the enemy. Red blood would color the
fresh, white snow. Each was determined the crimson that
flowed would be an enemy's, not his own. Each carefully fixed
his bayonet to his rifle barrel without orders.

Two squads moved forward on the left slope of the ridge.
Jones's third squad came forward in crouched position, single
file on the crest. Lieutenant Bill McClelland was given a similar mission on the right. Barrow accompanied Staff Sergeant
Roach's 3rd Platoon following Jones's third squad. The next 30
minutes were spent getting all the men in place for a frontal
assault on the bunker complex.

Many defenders on the knob had remained out of their foxholes and bunkers when Barrow's men began their attack. One Chinese spotted Jones at close range coming up on the left, then fired in his direction. Jones's men returned fire, felling the Chinese plus many more in the open. Jones quickly moved his men forward, taking casualties as a result. When closed with the enemy, each man yelled as if on signal. All of "A" Company joined in the assault as they pounced upon the stunned Chinese.

Most of the Chinese seemed too confused to fire back. The Marines had erupted with maximum violence out of the snowstorm, shouting while they rushed forward to engage in close combat. The enemy ran in every direction, many toward the Marines, and there they were immediately bayoneted or gunned down. Barrow's men methodically eliminated those in the bunkers using rifle fire and hand grenades. Although the Chinese fired from every bunker, it soon became apparent that many shot blindly into the falling snow, unable to discern the direction from which the Marines had come. The most effective resistance came from a Chinese machine-gun nest. It caused the majority of our casualties. In the final assault, Corporal Joe Leeds led his fire team around to one side and knocked it out, killing nine Chinese in the process. Just as he completed his mission, enemy fire caught him; never again would Leeds feel the need to prove his worth.

A silence fell over the ridge—an eerie silence. Occasional groans distinguished the wounded from the dead. All platoons quickly formed a defense of the captured area. Now came the dangerous job of recovering the wounded. A corpsman becomes an easy target when advancing to a wounded Marine.

We could find no level ground near the road for the first-aid tent. In addition, we occupied territory less than 400 yards from the enemy, not normal for the placement of a battalion first-aid station. Schmuck decided to use the large Chinese bunker on the roadside, just abandoned, as his command post. I walked into Wes Noren's area, looking for a plot of flat ground, but found none. Approximately 50 yards behind Schmuck's CP at a hairpin curve in the road, the hillside was less steep than the surrounding terrain. There we pitched the medical tent.

The ground was frozen hard. When we tried to drive in

stakes, they split. After many unsuccessful attempts, we decided the tent would have to be held up by guide ropes tied to
nearby tree limbs and scrub bushes. This sufficed long enough
for the oil stove to warm the inside area. Later, when the earth
became soft, stakes were driven around the bottom to keep out
the wind. Near dusk, the first of the wounded arrived at the
aid station.

Although we neared Barrow's position, the mountain was so
steep that litter bearers took three to five hours in daylight to
struggle down the mountainside with each man. When news
came of the first man hit by enemy fire, a team of six was
dispatched to retrieve him. Rank held no privilege in care for
the wounded. Every man available, including top-ranking
NCOs, joined to bring the casualties as quickly as possible to
the first-aid tent. When darkness came, many of the guard platoon were still bringing in Barrow's wounded. Luckily we had
only 17 injured this first day. They were given first aid, then
rushed six miles down the mountainside to Chinhung-ni.

The Chinese defensive plan now became apparent. They
commanded the road to the north and south for a distance of
1,500 yards. The skillful placement of bunkers and foxholes
kept them immune from artillery. The shell trajectory would
carry it into the mountain ridge before damaging the bunker.
Tall mountains on the north side of Funchilin Pass also
blocked the path of artillery shells aimed at Hill 1081. Bunkers
and foxholes had been dug from two to five feet in depth. Most
were covered with logs and rice bags filled with dirt—some
only with logs and dirt. All were well camouflaged with brush
to keep them unidentifiable from the air.

Each series of bunker configurations had the same deficiency
as the French Maginot Line. Their construction did not take
into account attack from the rear. A slit in the front permitted
rifles and automatic weapons to fire toward the bridge site and
the road. There was no slit in the rear. Most bunkers had one
side entrance, but these also would accommodate only one
man to pass to and fro at any given time. In close combat, all
were highly vulnerable to hand grenades, for each had a blind
side.

The Chinese had not planned for an attack in a snowstorm,

believing that attack by large numbers from the rear was impossible. Although there were some shelf areas along the ridge on most of the crests, men at best could only advance in double file. This accounted for the Chinese failure to place outposts to the rear.

Barrow's men cleared the bunkers of enemy dead before darkness arrived, to provide protection against a counterattack and the cold. Sending one squad at a time, platoon leaders had the men retrieve bedrolls and packs which had been stacked in three separate piles on the ridge before the attack. Don Jones was the last of his platoon to pick up his gear.

"Damn! I hate to see those unclaimed packs and bedrolls!" he thought as he returned to the now empty bunkers.

Barrow ordered everyone to change socks and felt insoles. Those on foot were wet from perspiration and snow. He realized that the cold had numbed the energy and senses of his men. Immediately he directed his officers and NCOs to take a personal view to ensure that all socks and insoles were changed. He ordered his men to work their hands and fingers as much as possible to keep the blood circulating. These precautions saved many from frostbite.

Across the narrow valley to the west, the balance of the enemy regiment was entrenched below us. Noren's men on the slopes came plainly into view when the fog lifted near dusk. Automatic rifle fire from this direction continued until nightfall. Half of Noren's casualties came from this source. Most of H&S was not visible to these nearby Chinese. A slanted ridge from the mountaintop to the valley obscured the view. The guard platoon was deployed on the lower side of the road to prevent attack from this direction. When a squad was placed on the roadside around the first Chinese bunker to be overrun, enemy small arms fire peppered the area. Before anyone was hit the squad was redeployed on the lower side of the road out of sight of the Chinese riflemen.

By nightfall, Wes Noren's men had cleared the hillside and road of Chinese. Barrow was now entrenched on the mountain near the enemy, holding the topographical crest of Hill 1081. Noren had suffered amazingly few casualties in driving the Chinese off the mountain slope: three killed, six wounded. Barrow achieved a more spectacular success, with light losses of ten killed and eleven wounded.

At the end of the first day's fighting, our success exceeded our most optimistic hopes. We shared the mountain with the Chinese. Our casualties were very light under the circumstances. The enemy had suffered heavy losses—many had run away, we held good position to continue the fight.

We were afforded three benefits not anticipated the previous day when we planned our attack. The swirling snowstorm gave us the greatest of all offensive advantages, the element of complete surprise. Complete surprise temporarily reduces a military unit to a mob; without orders or directions, each man operates on his own. His mind is controlled by the instinct for survival—most often he runs. The snowstorm covered our penetration into the Chinese stronghold. Once inside the defensive network the arrangement and design of the bunkers left the enemy vulnerable to an attack from our direction. Without the snow this day would have been a disaster for us. No amount of supporting fire could have helped as much as the snowstorm.

As Noren's men bedded down for the night, a Chinese soldier from the Big Hill came down the slope through "B" Company, apparently carrying a message to the dug-in enemy across the valley. He was dropped before he reached the road. Wes again sent out patrols to ensure that his area was cleared. Jim Adair, with a squad composed of clerks and supply men, took positions on the upper side of the road to guard against infiltration of the CP from above. On the mountain ridge soon after dark, a Chinese platoon counterattacked Bob's front, and was annihilated.

At dusk, the sky cleared. Snow covered the ground. The temperature dropped and dropped fast, reaching 25° below zero, made worse by steady 30- to 40-knot icy winds howling through Funchilin Pass. It was the coldest night we would see in Korea, the coldest that I have ever experienced. Our mutual enemy, the cold, began to take its toll.

After dark, one of my men began swearing, cursing, and yelling so loudly I thought he had gone berserk. He was a member

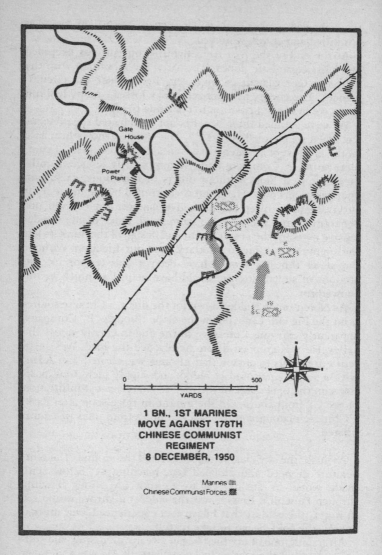

Gate
House

Power
Plant

0 ————————————— 500
YARDS

**1 BN., 1ST MARINES
MOVE AGAINST 178TH
CHINESE COMMUNIST
REGIMENT
8 DECEMBER, 1950**

Marines ▦
Chinese Communist Forces ▦

of the guard platoon occupying a position on the lower side of the road. He came to where I stood.

"What'll I do, Captain? What'll I do?" he exclaimed in obvious anguish.

"Tell me first what the hell's wrong."

"There's a hole in my sleeping bag!"

Everyone knew what this meant. The nylon bag could no longer function as a thermos, and had lost most of its protection against the cold.

"It's useless to stay here," I said. "You'll be frozen stiff by morning. Go down the mountain to Chinhung-ni. Be careful as you approach; a soldier may shoot you in the dark. That's your only hope."

"Goddamn, Captain! I'll be killed for sure!"

"Go ahead," I repeated. "It's your only hope!"

Off he went into the darkness.

Barrow put the captured Chinese bunkers to good use for protection against the cold. Nevertheless, some of his and Noren's men suffered severe frostbite.

The clear night air promised air and artillery support the next day. The extreme cold prevented the enemy from mounting a major counterattack until morning. But there was a negative side. The Chinese still outnumbered Barrow's men on Hill 1081; the element of complete surprise had been eliminated, and the dug-in enemy across the valley had not been hurt. Throughout the night, Chinese and Marines anticipated the coming bloody battle.

On the north side of Funchilin Pass, the weather and terrain had done more than the enemy to prevent assault units from securing their assigned objectives. Casualties had not been heavy. The troops were in a position to renew their efforts in the morning.

I got no sleep that night. I crawled into my sleeping bag, and ate my K ration chocolate bar. Chocolate converts quickly to heat energy. The wind blew so hard that snow invariably got into my bag, then melted. I tried burying myself in the snow, but this did not help. Snow came inside the bag at the neck. To prevent freezing, I walked up and down the road. I frequently sat in the snow. As soon as my feet turned cold to the point of freezing, I got up and walked. I repeated this procedure many times before morning. I worked my hands and fingers at short intervals. I changed socks and felt insoles. I thought my feet would freeze in the process, but the extra socks and insoles saved me.

Each time I got up to walk, I realized that frostbite, with its spreading takeover of the body, was dangerously near—once begun, there can be no reversal of the freezing process in 25° below zero cold. All senses were numbed. My mind contracted, and focused only on the immediate. The minute ahead was the only one that mattered.

A young Marine walking south with the division column aptly expressed my thoughts when asked by a war correspondent, "If you had one wish to be granted, what would you wish for more than anything else in the world?"

"I'd wish for tomorrow." He paused, then repeated, "Yes, I'd wish for tomorrow."

14

The Battle for the Big Hill

As I paced the road to escape freezing, more than anything else I yearned to see the sun rise again, although I knew that by day's end there would be no more tomorrows for many on the mountaintop.

When predawn twilight arrived, I was walking up and down the road near the aid station. Men were stamping about in circles to avoid freezing. Others were dragging one foot or leg, giving the appearance of being crippled.

One man walked up beside me. He blurted, "Captain, I can't stand this anymore."

"The hell you can't! The sun'll be rising soon."

"The sun won't help this," he choked, as he held up his left hand. The fingers, thumb, and edges of the hand had frozen a solid white. The palm of his hand, a dark red, had swollen large.

"Serves you right, goddamn it! Why didn't you wear your gloves and work your fingers like I told you?"

"Captain, my gloves got soaking wet from carrying a wounded man off the mountaintop last night."

"Well, that fur-lined parka has pockets."

"Yes, but they got wet too, from falling in the snow."

"Come on, we've got to get you off this mountain right now," I said. "Let's see a corpsman."

The jeep motors had been kept running; I doubt if we could have started them again in such severe cold.

As sunrise neared, it became obvious that we had sustained numerous severe frostbite casualties. Some had frozen hands. Others had frozen feet. A few had both. I never again want to see that pained, shocked look on the faces of those with frozen parts. Most of the men who carried Barrow's wounded suffered frostbite. All who had brought wounded to the aid tent after dark became serious frostbite casualties.

Once the freezing process begins, there is no abatement until relief is given. This means warm water over the frozen limb. But warm water in sufficient quantities to treat even one man was not available on the mountain. Numerous canteens froze and burst during the night, creating a drinking water shortage for many. The temperature might rise as much as 35° during the day, but once frozen, a limb won't thaw in temperature that is still 20° to 30° below the freezing point.

Fritz and Pruitt came to the aid station. Fritz began accounting for each man to be evacuated. Pruitt dispatched the jeeps to Chinhung-ni with as many men as possible on each trip. The worst cases went first. For the next few hours the ambulance jeeps were kept busy carrying frostbite cases to Chinhung-ni. After additional first aid, helicopters evacuated them to the coast. No one was sent south unless tagged by a corpsman. As I turned to visit Schmuck, Pruitt admonished the jeep drivers, "No man gets on one of these jeeps unless he's wearing a doctor's tag, do you hear?"

"Yeah, Gunny, but suppose a man without a tag gets on the jeep anyhow?" one driver asked.

"Kick the bastard off and let the yellow son-of-a-bitch freeze!" Pruitt snapped back. "It'll be your ass if I see you taking any man on that jeep without a tag!"

I walked to the CP and called on Schmuck. "Colonel, it looks like you've lost half your men from freezing."

"Goddamn you, I don't need you to tell me it's freezing up here!" Schmuck snapped. "Major Bridges, get a report from all companies." Everyone seemed to have a short fuse as the day began.

Bill Bridges first called "C" Company. Bob Wray reported that his men were suffering from the cold, but he had only a few frostbite cases. He needed to bring additional mortar ammunition into his perimeter to give Barrow the support he needed.

Noren reported he had made a reconnaissance and determined that his company had stopped one ridge short of its assigned objective. He was in the process of moving his men forward. He, too, had a few serious frostbite cases that required evacuation. Bridges then called Barrow.

At daybreak, Bob Barrow had stood, field glasses in hand, quickly yet thoroughly surveying the terrain ahead. Five hundred yards due north lay the dome of Hill 1081, the Big Hill.

"A tough 500 yards," Barrow thought to himself as he made his assessment before formulating his plan of attack. He started by looking at the ground to his immediate front. Approximately 100 yards ahead, the ridge widened on the left and right, although on the right-hand side, the cliff was decidedly steeper than on the left. As his view moved closer to the Big Hill, the ridge continued to widen, forming a shelf area on both the left and right. At a point approximately 200 yards from the Big Hill dome, the ridge line took a slight drop that continued downward until it reached a point about 100 yards from the foot of the dome. From there it moved sharply upward, making a saddle-like formation on the mountain ridge. The dome itself was the saddle's pommel. He looked for Chinese bunkers between himself and his final destination. None could be seen. "That doesn't mean they aren't there," he thought as he continued to survey his front.

As he forced his field glasses upward, Barrow watched Chinese pour out of the honeycomb of bunkers encircling the Big Hill near the top of its dome. They looked like bees immediately prior to swarming. The Chinese had come outside to determine the origin of fire the previous afternoon and night. Barrow tried to approximate their number; they were too many to count. For moments he watched them go in and out of their bunkers.

As he shifted his sight to the top of the dome, a dual high-tension line pole of Japanese make—two poles connected by a crossbar—caught his eye. He turned again to the Chinese and bunkers. A thought flashed through his mind. Immediately he focused again on the dual powerline pole.

"I'll be damned! It's there all right! Hum-m-m, side by side, right in the middle of that Chinese beehive. Those poles will come in handy later in the day," Barrow mused, as he returned his field glasses to their case.

Barrow now found himself in that position where a thin line separates success from failure. He knew that final victory hinged upon full utilization of all resources at his disposal. These included mortars, machine guns, tactical air support, and the fire team, squad, and platoon blocks of "A" Company. Artillery fire could not be used; the shells' trajectory would force them into the mountainside or into his own troops more often than into the enemy. He knew that supporting arms, air power, and brave men are not enough. He needed men who "knew what to do when they got there," for untrained brave men, faced with his problem, often succumb to that first law—survival.

On the defense, a Marine may fire from his foxhole at what appears to be overwhelming odds because he knows that remaining under cover offers him his best chance of survival. On the attack, the situation is different. Each move forward exposes one to the fire of an entrenched enemy. This pulls against his basic instinct. How then does he advance? He must carefully calculate each forward move in coordination with others so that he exposes himself as little as possible. Pinning the enemy down with a base of BAR or machine-gun fire, diverting his attention by fire from many directions, and communication by silent arm and hand signals are tools the leader must combine to advance.

Before the actual event, intense practice on principles of fire and movement greatly increases the chances for success. In battle, every situation is different, but troops previously drilled in attack principles will adapt to the exigencies of the occasion where others will fail.

While Barrow studied the terrain, his men breakfasted on the dry components of their rations. Most of the C rations had frozen. Barrow's men had learned that acute gastritis is the certain and immediate result of consuming food in this condition.

Barrow ordered his men to test-fire all weapons before

mounting his attack on the Big Hill. Many of the mechanisms had frozen, primarily the BARs and carbines. When they heard the shots, the Chinese rushed back into the bunkers. Even while test-firing weapons, Marine rifles were aimed at the enemy. It was at this point that Bridges phoned.

"Bob, I hear shots. Are the Chinese counterattacking?"

"No," he replied. He explained that he was test-firing weapons. The Chinese bunkers had been put to good use during the night; he had only a few serious frostbite cases. After thawing out the weapons by manually working the frozen parts, he would direct his attack.

An hour after sunrise, with the new snow sparkling in the sun, Wes Noren phoned the CP. He reported completion of the move forward to his new position on the northwest slope of Hill 1081, which covered the approach to the bridge site. The move was made without opposition. Upon arriving at his new position, Wes saw Chinese soldiers gathering across the valley. Then they began to come forward in attack. They were numerous—more enemy than he had ever seen before.

"Now I know what they mean by Chinese hordes," he thought, watching them come nearer.

Some days earlier, a disabled Marine helicopter had been abandoned near the road on the east side of the valley. By the hundreds, the curious peasant soldiers advanced toward the downed helicopter. This was probably the first and, indeed, the last helicopter they would ever see.

Wes ordered artillery fire. Cold weather caused the howitzers to fire sporadically. The shells hit on target but were not fully effective. The 155s from the 92nd Armored Field Artillery Battalion joined in to lay down a heavy barrage. Explosive shells rained upon the enemy for more than an hour. A professional job of bracketing the area continued until there was no motion in the silent, frozen white valley. For the remainder of our stay on the mountain no more small arms fire came from this direction.

Air power and mortar fire were used extensively on both sides of Funchilin Pass to clear the Chinese off the high ground. Barrow realized early that the bunkers on the Big Hill were too well constructed and camouflaged to remove the Chinese by these methods. He knew many would remain until eliminated by his men. He directed Jones's second platoon to advance on the right. It was pinned down by heavy rifle and automatic fire after moving forward only a few yards.

Jones immediately deployed his men along the right face of the ridge near the crest. From this position Jones could get the maximum number of trigger fingers to fire at the entrenched Chinese, thereby forming a base of fire for McClelland's move on the west slope.

Barrow placed a light machine-gun section on the ridge crest itself, to give additional covering fire to McClelland's forward move. A red tracer in every fourth round showed when the gunners were on target. Before firing, one gunner gave Barrow a cigar. The cold had dehydrated the leaves to the point the cigar crumbled like a cracker as he raised it to his mouth.

Each time a Chinese fired, riflemen and gunners poured bullets back into the bunker honeycomb. When an enemy bullet came near machine gunner Guy Tucker, he contemptuously spat to the side, then settled his machine-gun tripod deeper into the snow. After carefully adjusting his aim, Tucker fired away with renewed determination.

Barrow next ordered fire from the heavy mortars. During the mortar bombardment, both McClelland and Jones made significant advances. By midmorning, however, McClelland's platoon was hit hard by Chinese fire. It had advanced to within 200 yards of the topographical crest of Hill 1081. On one move, the enemy spotted Sergeant Gordon as he gave a silent hand signal. He was hit and instantly killed. His new baby pictures were among the personal effects recovered when his body was brought to the aid station.

Jones continued on the right, although his men were not as far advanced as McClelland's. He, too, lost men with each forward move. As McClelland reached a point about 200 yards from the Big Hill, he sighted two large enemy bunkers tucked in a small shelf area approximately 30 yards ahead. Two squads firing at the embrasures kept the Chinese pinned down. Staff Sergeant Umbaugh took this opportunity to lead a squad forward. He was shielded from view of both the Chinese on the

Big Hill and those in the bunkers. Approaching each bunker from its blind side, Umbaugh wiped out the Chinese with hand grenades and lost no men in the process.

Now a stretch of only 175 yards swept bare in places by the icy wind lay between McClelland's men and the final knob. At this point, he observed a wooded section extending horizontally along the mountainside, which could conceal his men from enemy view. He elected to move through these woods.

Again Barrow called upon the heavy mortars to plaster the Chinese stronghold. During this second mortar attack, McClelland's men advanced to within 150 yards downhill from the enemy. Jones's platoon closed to within 200 yards on the right. "A" Company now formed an arc-like formation south of the Big Hill, with Jones on the right, Roach in the center, and McClelland on the left. Between the heavy mortar bombardments, Barrow used 60-millimeter mortars. Although the smaller shells could not penetrate the bunker rooftops to the same degree as the heavy mortars, the bursting shells kept the Chinese pinned down while Marines advanced.

Near noon, Barrow realized the time had arrived for use of his most potent weapon. He motioned Robbie Robinson forward. Rather than expose his entire team, Robinson arrived alone with his 40-pound MAW radio on his back.

Bob began, "Robbie, I've got a present for you."

"Well, it's about time—what is it?"

"Look straight ahead."

"I don't see anything special."

"Do you see that dual high-tension line pole atop that hill?"

"Yep."

"Perfect aiming stakes," Barrow replied. "This is the first time in Korea you've had perfect aiming stakes! The Chinks have crowded their bunkers around the bottom of those poles."

Before transmitting directions to the eight aviators circling above, Barrow directed his 81-millimeter mortars to fire a white phosphorus smoke shell at the target area. The shell landed approximately 25 yards north of the power line poles. After all aviators acknowledged seeing the smoke shell, Robinson radioed, "The enemy has dug in around the dual power-line poles on the peak, 25 yards south of the smoke, and about

200 yards ahead of us. All planes should identify the dual powerline poles on the peak before making the first run. The
enemy occupies ground beneath those poles. I repeat, the
enemy occupies ground beneath those poles."

First the Corsairs made a dry run, each plane flying low
enough to spot the poles. Robinson confirmed they were on
target. On the second dive, the Corsairs came screaming out
of the air with 50-caliber machine guns spitting fire into the
enemy. Three more runs were made with the Corsairs discharg-
ing 50-caliber machine-gun bullets. On the fifth run, each
plane dropped a 265-pound frag bomb into the middle of the
Chinese. The debris from the explosions rained upon Mc-
Clelland's men only 150 yards down hill. On the last run, each
Corsair dropped its belly tanks of napalm. The napalm exploded and burned atop the bunkers, sucking up oxygen as it
burned.

Immediately after the smoke lifted, one Chinese jumped up
out of his bunker in clear silhouette, then turned to run down
the hill. He was cut down before taking a second step. With
the Chinese still stunned from the strafing and bombing, Barrow's men sidled closer. McClelland's men continued through
the woods, then shifted right so that they approached the Big
Hill from the northwest or Koto-ri side, a distance of only 100
yards from the enemy.

After the planes finished, Barrow gave Schmuck a firsthand
account, concluding that he'd never seen a better job. Everyone
on the road, including the doctor and corpsmen, watched the
strafing. As the Corsairs flew back to Yonpo Airfield, I decided
to check on supplies.

Approximately two miles down the road toward Chinhung-
ni, John Coffey had established an auxiliary supply dump on
the roadside. From there, men of Wray's "C" Company formed
teams to carry ammunition and supplies to the top of the
mountain. Rifle ammunition and mortar shells composed the
largest portion of supplies at this site. The ambulance jeeps did
double duty, carrying wounded to Chinhung-ni and bringing
back ammunition to this spot on each return trip.

I walked south to inspect the supply-handling to and from
the road to the mountaintop. When I reached the first bunker

overrun the previous day, I looked across the valley. Enemy small arms fire no longer peppered the area. The still, silent snow-covered valley looked like the perfect picture of peace.

Continuing down the road, I heard sporadic rifle fire from the mountaintop. This told me Barrow's men were again exchanging shots with the enemy. When I arrived at the auxiliary supply dump, men were unloading mortar ammo from one of the jeeps. As I watched, a combat correspondent came walking up the road.

"How much farther is it to the 1st Battalion CP?" he asked.

"About two miles," I answered.

"Oh my god!" he replied. "I thought I was nearly there! This is the most demoralizing situation I've ever see. How in hell does anyone survive under these conditions? I'm freezing."

"Keeping alive isn't easy, that's for sure."

"I've got to get back," he said. "Can that jeep take me back to Chinhung-ni?"

"No way," I replied, shaking my head. "That jeep's needed to pick up wounded at the aid station."

"I can't make it back. My feet are freezing."

"You'll make it all right. Just keep walking, but not so fast that you work up a sweat. That jeep's got to be used for wounded."

That combat correspondent came closer than any other newsman for an on-the-spot view of the battle scene.

When I got back to the CP, the wounded began to arrive at the aid station. I cautioned the litter bearers—many had fallen in the snow—to change the felt insoles in their shoe pacs. One sitting on the side of the road looked up.

"Captain, I hope I never go through anything like these past few hours. No man should suffer like these wounded suffer. The man we was carryin' was hurtin' something awful an' he'd done pissed all over hisself. When the piss got to the outside of his britches, it just froze there."

"Do the best you can, that's all you can do," I said as I turned away. The Marine on the roadside finished smoking his cigarette, then joined a litter-bearing crew to pick up another wounded.

On the Koto-ri side of Funchilin Pass, the division made

slow yet determined progress. Resistance on the mountain overlooking the road was light to moderate. Korean refugees preceded the forward echelon of the division's move south toward the pass. At the bridge site, the refugees bypassed the chasm by a slow climb above the gatehouse, then returning to the road. From there they continued south. By noon some refugees carrying only a few belongings passed the CP.

Shortly after my return from the auxiliary supply dump, a little girl with her much younger brother passed by. Somehow they became separated, and the little girl came back up the road looking for him. She had long hair that covered her ears and bangs cut across her forehead in a manner that reminded me of my sister at 10 to 12 years of age. She was crying and shaking. Just as she reached the turn in the road near the aid station, she passed out in the snow. Her clothing was insufficient to combat the cold.

We took her inside the aid tent and warmed her frostbitten hands, ears, and nose. She seemed calmer as she ate warm C rations and drank hot tea. After reviving her, we regretfully sent her back into the cold. We told her to go down the mountain and stay with other refugees. Bravely she went on her way.

By midafternoon, the wounded were stacked along the road outside the aid tent. The corpsmen had more than they could handle for the remainder of the day. Jeep drivers rushed down the mountain with a load of wounded, then back again without picking up any more ammunition. The CP and the hillside around it were bare except for corpsmen and wounded. In the meantime, Wray moved a platoon forward to occupy the ground that had been captured the previous day.

Soon after the artillery barrage on the Chinese in the valley, Wes Noren dispatched squad patrols in all directions to make sure that the mountainside was clear of the enemy. Most patrols moved out shortly after noon. An hour later, while trudging along the snowy mountain slope, one patrol came into view of the Chinese on the Big Hill. The enemy failed to fire at it. Sung's defenders were too heavily engaged with Barrow's men. When the day began, the Chinese enjoyed a numerical advantage of more than two to one. Now their ranks were so reduced that they no longer outnumbered Barrow.

The Chinese concentrated all eyes and trigger fingers in the direction of Barrow's Marines, who crawled along the frozen rocky ground. The Marines now approached hand grenade range; with unbelievable determination each moved closer as if drawn by a magnet. Mortars, machine guns, and close air support had been used to reduce the enemy. Now Barrow's men were too close for supporting fire. The likelihood of killing his troops was too great. One resource remained—the same he possessed when starting up the mountain though now halved in number—trained foot soldiers with guts!

An hour after the air attack, Jones's and Roach's men reached positions that joined McClelland, surrounding the Chinese. Now Marines fired at short range and threw hand grenades toward the enemy. In return, hand grenades and rifle fire came from the bunkers. Every man was involved in the fight. Marines and Chinese traded lives as the fighting raged, with neither taking an obvious advantage.

Then came the most dramatic event of the day. In the heat of battle, one Marine looked down at the road where he saw the nose of the division column approach the bridge site. He shouted, "The division is coming!" Momentarily, every Marine took time to look. The sight served each like a shot of adrenaline. This was what the battle was all about.

Caution was thrown to the winds. With fixed bayonets, shouting rebel yells and battle cries, they rushed the Chinese. Some threw grenades frontally into the embrasures. Not one Chinese made an attempt to surrender. Twenty or more were killed when they came into the open from among the rocks in a last-ditch effort to break the charge.

A sniper's bullet caught Staff Sergeant Ernest Umbaugh at the moment of victory. He died before reaching the aid station.

As Barrow's men cleaned out the bunkers, rifle fire came from the north. He located the source; four Chinese bunkers near the ridge crest about 75 to 100 yards north of the Big Hill. His men had exhausted their ammunition, but from the captured bunkers they were able to replenish their supply of hand grenades and carbine and rifle bullets. After pinning down the enemy, they threw hand grenades into the embrasures.

The final phase of battle was a mop-up operation. Corporal

Billy Webb and others wiped out the Chinese with grenades in scattered bunkers around the hill. One achieved the nickname "Hand Grenade Reilly."

The Chinese followed Sung's orders by resisting to the last gasp. Near 1500 all resistance on the Big Hill ceased. Sung's block no longer existed. Smith's block survived. The next hour was spent in eliminating snipers from around the mountain. Silence then shrouded the area. Barrow's exhausted victors inherited the painful job of caring for the dead and wounded.

Compared to the previous day, we had sustained heavy casualties. Every available man, including top NCOs, carried the wounded. On the lower side of the road, the mountain lay bare. Our CP was unprotected from this direction. Care of the wounded took precedence over defense against a possible Chinese attack up the mountainside. It was unlikely in any event, since Sung's men from across the valley no longer posed a threat.

Somebody standing on the road at Wes Noren's CP facing due north could see the gatehouse over the blown-out bridge at a distance of about 200 yards. Near the foot of the deep chasm stood the power plant, its generators activated by water from the penstocks that plunged vertically down the mountainside. Previous to our coming, a cable pulled rail cars up to the crest. The downed helicopter appeared at 10 o'clock, approximately 400 yards away. To Noren's right the road made a deep cut into the mountainside, then back again to the bridge site, forming the largest hairpin curve on the route to Koto-ri. This indention suggested that eons ago Nature's fist had landed a body blow at this point, from which the mountain had yet to recover. Schmuck's CP and first-aid tent were directly south, roughly 75 to 125 yards respectively, but neither could be seen due to a fold jutting from the mountainside about 25 paces behind Noren's CP.

Across the narrow valley, the top of the ridge paralleling Noren's position appeared a few hundred feet below our elevation, a distance of 500 yards. The dome of the Big Hill, towering 400 feet above us at four o'clock, could not be seen as the mountain was almost vertical. It did not slope back until near its peak.

The M2 replacement bridge was brought to the pass, and erection began. During the three hours it took the engineers to put the bridge in place, Chinese enemy hunters became the hunted. Those shifting south were fired upon by Noren's men. When they attempted to move north, they ran into men of the 5th and 7th Marines. Many attempted to escape by running up the mountainside along the rail tracks using the cross-ties to accelerate their move. They were easy targets for our riflemen. Only a few made it to the crest, then dropped out of sight.

Some enemy soldiers came into view at the foot of the chasm near the power station. They attempted to avoid a 7th Regiment patrol in the valley that moved parallel to the mountain. At one point, a Chinese might come into view of Noren's men with a Marine occupying the same spot moments later. Noren ordered his men to hold fire for fear of shooting friendly troops. Many times his men shouted at the Marines below so as to give directions on the whereabouts of the enemy. However, the Chinese were more interested in escape than in returning fire.

One patrol found more than 50 Chinese in foxholes on the lower side of the road. They were so badly frozen the Marines simply lifted them from their holes and sat them on the road. There they stayed until the guards took them south. They came through our area a few hours later while I was climbing up the mountainside. Jim Adair recalled that many had developed gangrene, and "the stench was almost as bad as the Chigyong prison." Some died before reaching Chinhung-ni. They were part of the group that had run across the mountainside the day before. The sudden drop in temperature caused them to freeze in their own sweat. Approximately 300 others were brought down the next day. By 1800, the division column was ready to move south toward Hamhung.

Sung's plan for annihilation had been rent asunder. He could not visualize the dropping of a tank-bearing bridge from the air and its erection over the deep Funchilin Pass in only three hours. Simultaneously with the extraction of Sung's double cork from his annihilation plan came the shattering of the plan itself. Marines in front of the column walked across the new bridge.

The attack against an entrenched enemy is the most difficult of all operations in battle. It demands expertise at every level A break in the telephone line to Chinhung-ni would have prohibited use of artillery when the Chinese enemy began crossing the valley. Faulty radio communications would have precluded the use of planes. Improper maintenance of jeeps would have prevented the evacuation of wounded. Without trained, dedicated soldiers at every level, Murphy's Law takes over in the attack situation. That is, "If anything can go wrong, it will."

Only a few vehicles had reached the south side of the pass when an accident threatened to undo everything that had been accomplished. A tractor towing an earth-moving pan broke through the plywood center panel of the bridge, rendering it useless. This incident closed the bridge for wheeled vehicles. An expert tractor driver backed the machine off the wrecked bridge. The treadways were then placed as far apart as possible, thus giving the bridge a total width of 136 inches. In early darkness, the first jeep crossed. The convoy got underway again as engineers guided vehicles across with flashlights.

An endless stream poured across the span, which at that moment in history was without a doubt the most vital bridge in the world.

15

The Return

Shortly after sunset on December 9 Bob Barrow called the command post to give Colonel Schmuck a status report. He had checked with all platoons. He now had 111 men left of the 225 that started up the mountain with him two days before. His men were exhausted; he had five seriously wounded that had to be taken down the mountain as soon as possible.

All platoons were low on ammunition, especially machine-gun belts. He didn't have enough on hand to sustain a Chinese counterattack. Barrow knew it was dangerous to move at night, because his men shot at anything or anybody moving outside a foxhole, but he needed the ammo now. He would warn all platoon leaders to be especially wachful for Marines coming up the mountain with ammunition. The Big Hill was solidly in our possession.

Schmuck turned to me. "Get the ammunition to Bob and bring the wounded back."

I knew I could not delegate this chore, so I took charge of the party myself. Already the cold had claimed more than half of H&S Company as severe frostbite casualties. When collected, our party included the remnants of the guard platoon, cooks, supply men, and those communicators who had finished stringing wire—40 men in all.

We began our climb in almost total darkness. At first our task seemed impossible. Each man would slip and fall with his boxes after climbing only a few yards up the mountainside.

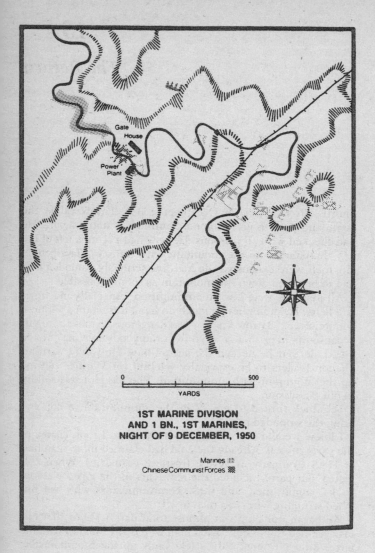

Gate
House

Power
Plant

0 ——————————— 500
YARDS

**1ST MARINE DIVISION
AND 1 BN., 1ST MARINES,
NIGHT OF 9 DECEMBER, 1950**

Marines ▦
Chinese Communist Forces ▨

Man, ammunition boxes, helmet, all came tumbling down, until each hit the road. After numerous unsuccessful attempts, I decided on another plan.

"First, leave all ammunition on the road. We'll form a chain up the mountainside. Then we'll pass the ammo from one man to the other until it reaches the man at the head of the chain. Each man will hold and assist the man above. We will then make the human chain again and stretch it up the side of the mountain in caterpillar style."

After forming the chain, we stacked the boxes of ammunition at a plot on the side of the mountain. The snow had a hard crust on its surface. Once the boxes were shoved to the ground, this crust prevented them from slipping. A man or two would fall as we made each chain length. In a few instances, the man rolled to the road and did not return.

The thermometer showed the temperature to be below zero, but not nearly as cold or windy as the previous night. A communications team had laid a phone wire to the "A" Company CP. I decided to follow the wire, for I knew someone had successfully climbed the route before us. Five hours later we were still struggling up the mountainside with the boxes of ammunition.

Roughly 40 feet from the crest, I could see that we were near the end of our climb. The sky had cleared. The half-moon's reflections upon the snow gave us good visibility, especially since our eyes had become accustomed to the darkness. At this point, I moved to the head of the chain. The last few feet rose almost straight up. This part of our climb was negotiated by clutching scrub trees and relying on toe holds in the rocks to support us.

When I neared the top, I looked up and was so startled that I almost fell over backwards. About three feet away were the frozen eyes of a dead soldier staring straight at me. The intense cold had misshaped his face. With eyelids and mouth open, his eyes looked like two round white stones. The teeth appeared out of proportion to his shrunken cheeks. Only after looking at his cotton-quilted uniform could I see that he was Chinese rather than American. I moved to one side, then stood up on the mountain crest to receive the boxes of ammunition from below.

It was shortly after midnight before we could walk to our final destination. I stayed in front, fearful that someone from "A" Company might mistake us for Chinese infiltrators. On our way across the mountain crest, numerous Chinese bodies lay in our path—more enemy dead than I had ever seen. The look on some of the frozen faces reminded me of pictures usually seen in horror films. We were not challenged as we walked among the dead to find our way to the CP.

We could see the Chinese had constructed a network of strong, well-camouflaged bunkers. The numerous dead showed that many had occupied each bunker. The ground was frozen hard, making it impossible to bury anyone on the mountaintop. Again, the Chinese dead had American weapons beside them, mostly 1903 Springfield rifles, a few carbines, and Thompson submachine guns. Barrow's men now slept in the bunkers. The ordeal of the last two days had left them so exhausted they were unable to stay awake for adequate sentry duty.

The combination of wind, napalm bombs, Chinese, and Marines had removed most of the snow from the mountaintop. After we deposited our ammunition at the command post, the telephone operator directed us to the company aid station nearby where our wounded and dead were stretched out on the icy ground. There we formed into five groups to take the wounded back down the mountain.

"Cap'n, this man's dead. He's frozen stiff," one said.

"This one is too," said another.

"Leave them here," I said. "We can get the dead tomorrow in daylight. It's the living we need to get to the battalion aid station."

There were five Marines living when we started our trip down the mountain. I assigned six to eight men to each wounded Marine. A litter crew consisted of five bearers; the extra men were used as relief. Each litter crew took a different route back down the mountainside. I knew there had to be a better route down than the one we came up. Unfortunately, I was wrong. The trip down was worse.

Although the trip back was rough on us, it was even harder for the wounded. Often the litter bearers were unable to maintain footing; many times the wounded man was thrown out of the stretcher. When I reached the aid station at daybreak, the man we were carrying was dead.

A strapping, broad-shouldered corporal from the guard platoon cried: "I done nearly busted every goddamned gut in my body comin' down 'at mountain and the son of a bitch done went an' died on us!" Lowering his voice, he continued, "You goddamned, heavy bastard, why'd you go and up an' die on us? You heavy bastard . . . you heavy bastard . . . you heavy bastard!" he sobbed. Completely exhausted, he sat in the snow beside the dead Marine, lying with numerous other dead near the aid tent.

I had difficulty suppressing my own emotions as I turned to report completion of our mission to Schmuck. Three of the wounded survived the night's ordeal; one other had died on the way.

At sunrise, the men of "A" Company slowly came out of the Chinese dugouts to greet the new dawn. Barrow had slept sitting up with his feet and legs in a partially caved-in bunker. When he began to stir, Thatenhurst spoke: "Sleep well, Skipper?"

"I'll say! My feet were as warm as toast!"

"Who's your friend, Skipper?" Thatenhurst asked as he pointed downward.

Sometime during the evening, a critically wounded soldier in cotton-quilted uniform and canvas shoes had crawled across Barrow's feet and legs. There he collapsed and lay unconscious for the remainder of the night. He breathed heavily while being lifted from the bunker. His eyes opened momentarily, then closed forever—before anyone had time to summon the aid of a corpsman.

Soon thereafter, Barrow reorganized his company, dividing the survivors of his third platoon between the first and second platoons. He collected his dead, and with the aid of men from "C" Company began moving them to the road beside the battalion aid station.

Throughout the morning no more shots were heard. The bridge had been built, and the men from the 1st Marine Division were coming down the road in column formation. Often a column of refugees was on one side of the road, while the Marines were on the other. Jeeps, trucks, and tanks were interspersed with the people. The trucks were always filled with dead or wounded.

For most of the morning I stood beside the road. I slept for only brief periods, even though this was my third day in a row without sleep. I looked for officers and men I knew. Each time I saw someone whose face was familiar, I would ask if he had knowledge of an acquaintance. In most cases, he did not.

Most of the men had their heads down. Thankful to be alive and safe, their faces showed dejection nonetheless. The knowledge that each would never again see one or more of his closest friends could not be erased. Moreover, they were moving in a direction away from the Chosin Reservoir—meaning retreat, regardless of what General Smith might call it. It was a steady stream of depressed humanity.

General Sung had failed in his mission to annihilate the 1st Marine Division. His trap had been broken. The Marines were coming out with their wounded, dead, arms, and equipment with them. The Chinese 9th Army had been severely battered—as captured documents and enemy prisoners would reveal later, much worse than we suspected at the time. But worse yet, Sung had lost the greatest battle of all when fighting on foreign soil—the hearts and minds of the Korean people. His soldiers had abused those they were sent to protect.

Had our airplanes bombed the homes of the civilians at the beginning of the campaign, we too would have incurred their enmity. But this we failed to do until it was well established that Chinese occupied most of the huts near the Chosin Reservoir. Marine aviators worked in three-plane teams. One would burn a house while the other two strafed the Chinese soldiers as they came out.

In the latter part of the campaign, airmen saw numerous Chinese returning to Manchuria. With no aid stations nearby for medical care, a wounded soldier's chance for survival rested on his ability to drag himself back across the Yalu. More astonishing was the number of groups, some platoon size and even larger, which were seen trudging north along the snowy mountains. They appeared in good health. It was believed that these Chinese had expended their ammunition and had to retreat back to Manchuria for resupply. Each time I talked with someone about what had happened up north, he would tell about the masses of Chinese dead and the large numbers of Chinese soldiers who tried to give up near the end of the fight.

In the cities and towns around the world, the news media heralded the escape of the 1st Marine Division and attachments. *Time* magazine's cover pictured Air Force General William H. Tunner, with the caption "Air Lifter." On the inside it said, "The retreat of the 20,000 in Korea would not have been possible without the ultra modern air lift which supplied them with all the ammunition and food they could use and even with bridging equipment. . . . The world's first air drop of a bridge . . ." General Tunner was quoted as saying, "We can fly anything, anywhere, anytime!"

In conclusion, *Time* noted, "What happened in northeast Korea was proof that even in disaster and defeat the most significant element of U.S. power was mobility."

Omitted were the names or any mention of the men who scaled the mountain in a blinding snowstorm, removed a Chinese force of superior numbers, and made the erection of the bridge possible.

To the living, the sight of the Marines coming out of the trap on their march to safety was compensation enough for their deeds. To those who gave their all, it probably did not matter that after going through the maze of paperwork and notification of next of kin, their names would appear only in the obituary columns of the local newspapers as killed in action in Korea. In small-town America, the obituary might make the front page of the paper, but in large cities it would appear somewhere on the inside in a space less conspicuous than a used-car-for-sale ad.

The United States Marine Corps is a closed society, with a set of values of its own, separate and apart from those of the average American. The opinions that count most come from those inside its ranks. The individual Marine draws strength from an undying allegiance to the American flag, and an unswerving faith in the Corps itself. Here again the faith had been kept. Someday a monument may be erected on the mountain beside the road in commemoration of the dead. A simple stone would be appropriate, inscribed with a message similar to the one at Thermopylae: "Fellow Marines, we who died on this mountain performed as you would have wished us. December 1950."

As the day wore on, I sat in the snow and dozed from time to time, but could not sleep. The unfolding narrative on the road made sleep impossible. The plight of the refugees was the most dismal sight of all. The stream of refugees had started long before the battles. They had been thrown out of their homes, some for as long as a dozen days.

Initially the family unit would stay together. As time passed, however, in the cold weather without food, many succumbed in the fight against the elements. It became a battle of everyone for himself. In many cases, the family unit disintegrated; the man went one way, the wife another, and the children still another. Each became reduced to possessing only one basic instinct, the animal instinct for survival, nothing more.

The refugee stream moved like a sullen, brown river, moiling toward the sea, for somehow each felt that life would be better in Hamhung or Hungnam. Orders forbidding the refugees to infiltrate our lines were not carried out, for it was evident that the North Korean women, children, fathers, mothers, and old people were suffering, and mutual suffering molds bonds of mutual friendship. A cow or an ox at the end of a rope occasionally passed by. A baby's cry was often heard.

On the heels of the disillusioned column, Wes Noren's men continued active patrolling. Near noon, one patrol spotted two Chinese bunkers overlooking the bridge. His men eliminated the occupants with a hand-carried bazooka. At approximately the same time, Barrow's men on the mountaintop spotted enemy troops advancing toward Funchilin Pass from the north and northwest. Their numbers suggested division strength.

The Chinese were bunched together in long columns on the

ridge crests instead of the hillsides; others moved forward in the valley. The ridge crests and valley floor gave the Chinese the fastest route available. Yet it left them easily visible. They were hurrying to engage in battle.

Bob called for a heavy concentration of air strikes. The Corsairs, joined by Navy planes from the aircraft carriers, eliminated these Chinese from view long before darkness arrived. Sung's last desperate attempt to stop the Marines had ended in tactical suicide.

Under stress, people find ingenious ways to survive. The North Koreans' clothing was totally inadequate for long periods of exposure to this cold. They found, however, that by hovering closely together in large groups each person's body heat helped warm the others. In numerous places about the road, large groups assembled, lying very close together with their blankets and straw over the snow on the ground. This helped many to escape freezing. If the group stayed stationary too long, however, some part of the body, the most exposed part, inevitably froze.

As the endless column of Marines and refugees kept passing by, I became increasingly concerned about what had happened up north. After walking up and down the column and asking about persons I knew, I realized I had seen none of the Roanoke Marines. Their absence told a story I didn't want to hear.

Logan Bowman came walking near the end of the 5th Regiment column. He had been in Yudam-ni and had been part of the rear guard on a number of occasions. When I saw him, we both yelled.

"Logan, I thought you were dead! Damn, I'm glad to see you alive," I exclaimed.

"Did someone say I'd been killed?" he asked.

"No, but I asked about you a dozen times at least and no one seemed to know whether you had made it. I knew you were at Yudam-ni." I explained that we had knocked the Chinese off the Big Hill.

"We wouldn't be here if you hadn't." He paused. "Bill, it was tough back there, real tough." He named a number of Marines killed in action who had been with us on the *U.S.S. General Walker*, then added, "Both Cooke and McGregor were killed."

"Logan, you remember how they were that last night at the Carlsbad—how blue and despondent they were?"

"Yes."

"How did they know?"

"I don't know how they knew, but they knew. Somehow, Bill, they knew then. They knew that night at the Carlsbad."

I changed the subject. "Logan, could we have stayed?"

"I don't know, Bill. There were so many and they kept coming." He then looked down the road. "Bill, I'm getting behind. I have to catch up. See you at Hungnam."

"Goodbye—I'll see you," I said as he departed.

Bowman and others indicated that numerous Chinese had tried to give themselves up all along the way in the last stages of battle; they too had had enough. In our area, both along the road and on the mountain, there was no indication of any more surrender until near the end. Aside from those who escaped by running when the initial attack was launched, the Chinese lost because they were annihilated. The dead bodies were there in mute testimony.

During this time, I developed an intense hatred for the Chinese Communist soldiers who had caused so much grief to the Marines and the civilian population of North Korea. Then a group of almost 300 Chinese prisoners came by. They had retreated south ahead of the 1st Marine Division and upon reaching the bridge site, now defended by Marines, found their escape route had been cut off. They were being herded down the mountain like animals. About half did not wear hats. Most wore canvas shoes, but no gloves. They did have quilted uniforms. Most, if not all, were in various stages of severe frostbite; white ears, white noses, white cheeks, and, in some instances, white hands and feet. Many soldiers' hands and feet were swollen large; blood-clogging is the last stage of frostbite before the parts turn white. It was impossible not to have compassion for any living creature so obviously in pain.

Combatants and refugees were all faced with terrible suffering, but the Chinese were the most wretched-looking of all. As I watched them being marched down the hill to Chinhung-ni, I wondered how many would survive. It was obvious that to escape death many a man would have to have a foot or hand amputated. I hadn't realized until then that the Chinese couldn't combat the cold as well as we could. Of the North Koreans, Chinese, and Marines, the Marines were easily the best prepared to survive the cold.

A tank passed by. Its crew had written on the rear, "Only fourteen more shooting days 'til Xmas!"

The 1st Regiment began coming through. Jones and Bodey drove by in Colonel Puller's jeep. A dead tank commander was strapped to the hood, another dead Marine was strapped to the top, a third one on the back. Wounded Marines sat in the back seat. Only in combat and mutual danger can men rise above their own selfish interest to that brotherhood of man that is usually associated with peace but seldom found there.

Chesty Puller walked some distance behind the jeep, checking on abandoned vehicles. He insisted we were going to take out everything we came in with, if it would still move. Furthermore, he was going to bring all the stuff the Army had abandoned. He was astonished to find many vehicles with their keys in the ignition on the roadside. As a result, the 1st Regiment acquired more trucks and jeeps than it could use.

When night arrived, most of the division had cleared the bridge. There were not many travelers along the road. Only the units engaged in the rear guard action remained north of us. I got into my sleeping bag and dozed sitting beside the road. At 0200 on December 11, I was awakened by a loud explosion nearby. After the last of the division crossed into safety, Colonel Partridge's engineers destroyed the treadway bridge with explosives. This reestablished the gap over the deep chasm. An hour later, all of Barrow's men came to the roadside from the Big Hill, bringing the remainder of their dead with them.

At daybreak we were ready to move south. Schmuck had a checkoff list of all units, to make sure that everyone had passed through our ranks. We followed the column down the mountain as the rear guard, but even with these precautions we moved before a Recon company had passed us. It was the final unit to come down the mountain.

Our trucks were brought up from the valley. The wounded who died in, or on the way to, the first-aid station were placed outside in the snow. A blanket covered their bodies. They were placed aboard the trucks and brought down the mountain. Later the photographer David Duncan took a photo for *Life* magazine that was captioned "The living walk and the dead ride."

Gus Geisert and other members of my company were shown following the truck. I was on the opposite side, out of view of the camera lens, when the picture was taken.

About two-thirds of the way down the mountain, the little girl with my sister's haircut was lying at the side of the road, frozen in the snow. As we proceeded, we saw the bodies of other refugees who had succumbed scattered beside the road.

Marshal Foch once said, "La victoire, c'est la volonté" (victory is a matter of willpower). As we neared the valley, I had the gnawing, aching feeling deep down inside that the Chinese had been handed an unearned victory. This thought saddened me more than any other as we walked.

The absolute determination of the individual Marine contrasted greatly with the physical and emotional condition of the captured Chinese as well as with their overall performance for the past few days. The availability of supplies to us, the harsh weather, and a favorable civilian attitude gave us advantages that were being abandoned.

When we reached Chinhung-ni, we felt safe, although we learned that company- and platoon-size Chinese units had placed roadblocks en route to Sudong and Majon-dong. After a temporary rest and, unfortunately, no food, we proceeded on. From there, we rode in trucks. Even though there was food available at the railhead at Chinhung-ni, no one had the presence of mind to replenish his supply. We didn't think of food despite the fact most men had finished their supply of C and K rations perhaps a day or a day and a half before.

The trucks moved slowly until we reached Sudong, where we heard distant rifle fire from our left. The trucks stopped. The shots were probably aimed in our direction, but from a distance. A Puerto Rican second lieutenant moved his platoon in the direction of the enemy. I admired the way he performed his job. He showed no fear of the Chinese.

From Sudong, we rode the rest of the way to Hungnam without incident. When we arrived at Hungnam, large tents had

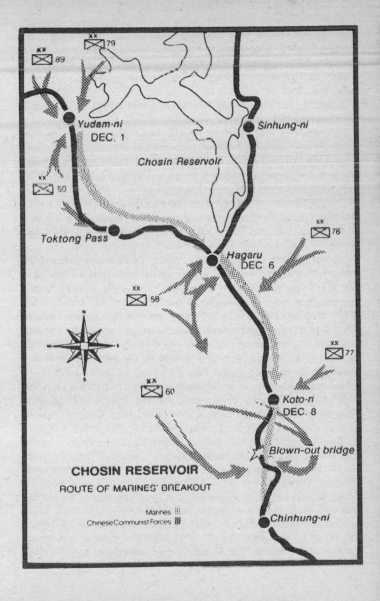

CHOSIN RESERVOIR

ROUTE OF MARINES' BREAKOUT

Marines
Chinese Communist Forces

been erected. Straw was available to place on the ground. The Marine service troops had yet to erect our tents since we were the last group to arrive. The news cameraman Yoder met us.

"Smile, Captain," he said. "The whole world has its eyes upon you. Smile!"

"I could care less about what the whole world thinks right now," I replied.

The weather was warmer on the coast than in the mountains, though still cold. Because there was a drizzle of rain, we were told to delay bedding down until our tent had been pitched. I was too exhausted to wait. I spread some straw on the ground and got into my sleeping bag.

Through a sleepy haze I heard someone shout, "Mail call!" Normally nothing could prevent me from running for a letter from home. On this occasion I was too tired to get up. I fell asleep.

Sometime late in the night I awoke. I felt water coming up through the straw, wetting my sleeping bag. When I got up I saw that I was sleeping on the ground by myself. Everyone else was inside a tent. Although the rain had stopped, the bottom of my sleeping bag was wet. I found my way to the tent where H&S was bunked, got some more straw, put it on the ground and immediately went back to sleep. My wet sleeping bag was not of my choosing, but it was not so uncomfortable that I could not go to sleep again. I awoke about 12 hours later.

I had missed first chow call and Gus Geisert decided I needed some food. Fritz and Pruitt gave me my letters. There were numerous letters from Ginny, my father, and friends. After I ate two canteen cupfuls of stew, with bread and coffee, I started reading. I would read two letters from Ginny, one from a friend or relative, and then go back to Ginny's again. Ginny's letters I kept and read over and over; the others I destroyed after reading a second or maybe a third time.

The letters revealed a new enemy upon the scene, an enemy that had lain dormant until now, the American public. Time and again I was bombarded with such expressions as "Why are you there in the first place?"—"All the Chinese and Koreans there are not worth the blood of one American boy!"—"We should use the atomic bomb and blow them up, then you could come home."

U.S. News and World Report stated, "A wave of demand for dropping atom bombs on Chinese troops swept the United States after these troops moved into Korea in force." In the same issue it said, "[The atom bomb] can strike terror, destroy thousands of cities. It can't knock out Communist armies. They're too scattered. There are no big mobilization centers; no concentration of war industry or transportation, few other good atom targets."

The men of our battalion were exhausted physically, mentally, and emotionally. We received word we were going aboard ship. Everyone was instructed to clean weapons and all other gear before boarding. We used fish oil and rags to get the weapons in shape. This was in keeping with our basic training. The rifle, its care, and its use are as much a part of each training phase as are the more complex maneuvers.

Although we had abandoned none of our disabled, bulldozers made mass graves for hundreds in the early and last phases of fighting. Before departing, General Smith held a memorial service at the 1st Marine Division Cemetery at Hamhung, with only a few of his command in attendance. Neat crosses covered the small field, each bearing the name of a Marine who had been brought back with us. The American flag, lowered to half-mast, drooped downward as if hugging the pole.

Chaplains of three faiths said prayers. General Smith uttered a brief tribute. The contingent of grimy, gaunt, battle-scarred Marines stood rigid at "Present arms." A rifle salute rang out . . . a lone bugler sounded taps.

16

Back to the Bean Patch

The bosun's pipe sounded. "Now hear this! Now hear this! Water is to be used for drinking purposes only. Water is not to be used for washing. Water is not to be used for washing."

Shortly thereafter our ship weighed anchor and headed south. But it would be somewhere below the 38th Parallel. Before we had moved very far the bosun's pipe sounded again. The same announcement was made. "Ain't that a useless announcement?" somebody commented. "This ship would have to sink to get enough water to wash this dirty bunch."

The ship was literally stuffed to the gunwales. There was no way to hold an abandon-ship drill. There were too few life jackets for the passengers; none were distributed. Men slept on deck, in many cases in the open—any way to get the most men possible aboard. Only majors and above were assigned bunk space. A lower-ranking officer had to curl up on the deck in any space he could find. After we had gotten underway, we were told we were going to Pusan, and from there we would be trucked to a tent camp near Mason.

En route, it was announced that only one meal would be served during the 36-hour trip. The ship's galley crew stretched itself to the limit to serve us at all. It was the only time I had been aboard a U.S. Navy ship when the coffee gave out in the officers' wardroom. Even so, the voyage was relaxing. It was the first time in weeks any of us could sit and chat in comfort while wearing only one layer of clothing.

All of us had received mail at Hungnam. Each read and re-read his letters. Bob Barrow opened a Christmas card: "Dear Captain Barrow   Merry Christmas! Look after the big lug for me. Mrs. Ernest Umbaugh." He sat in silence, then carefully placed the card in the pocket of his utility jacket.

Midway through the trip, most of our battalion officers gathered in the wardroom. It was evident that all had received the same type of letters from home I had received. For the first time many wondered, "Why are we here?" or "Why should we be here?"

Paul Vnencak spoke: "I know why I'm here! I'm an officer in the Regular Marine Corps. Being here is my job. I want to hear what Captain Hopkins has to say. He's a Reserve. Cap'n, do you think we belong here?"

"Yes, I do," I said. "I feel it's right for our country to be in Korea. No one argued this point while we were winning. The fact that the Chinese took the first round doesn't change the picture. After what Truman said about the Marine Corps, I don't like to side with him on anything, but I think he has the right concept about this war. It *is* a police action. A hell of a big one, I admit. But a police action. We had an iron-clad agreement with Russia about a free and independent Korea. They didn't live up to it, then tried to take over the country by force. If there's ever going to be any semblance of world order, we've got to have a military police force capable of protecting our interests and carrying out our commitments. The United States can have no effective foreign policy without such a force."

Wes Noren and others joined in the discussion. All wanted to feel that our participation in the Korean War was worthwhile and in the best interest of our country. Obviously, many had doubts.

We were still worn-out and tired. Everyone had lost weight, anywhere from 15 to 30 pounds or more. Pruitt announced he was going to have a picture taken the minute we got to Mason. "My wife won't believe how thin I am," he said. "If nothing else good came out of the Chosin Reservoir campaign, it was the best program for reducing I ever saw!"

When the ship docked, trucks were waiting to take us to

Mason, 45 miles away. Tents were pitched on the outskirts of the city in the same bean patch the Marine brigade had used when it first arrived in South Korea. Our battalion kitchen was established, and within a few hours we were served a hot meal of stew and coffee.

General Smith reported to the 8th Army Command that his Marines had received fresh rations on only three days since landing in Korea. It was important to build up the physical strength of his men; they had lost too much weight during the Chosin operation. He sent a copy of his report to the commander of Naval Forces Far East, who reacted promptly by sending a refrigeration ship to Mason with 50,000 rations of turkey. The 8th Army also responded with fresh produce. So we did have good food at every meal.

On the second day in camp, we erected a make-shift shower for the battalion. It consisted of six 50-gallon oil drums on a stand about seven feet high, with small nail holes punched in the bottom of each drum. When the water became hot on the oil stoves nearby, a bucket brigade poured it into each drum. By the time the water came out the bottom, the temperature was about right for a good hot shower. The shower was always filled to capacity, operating each day from 1000 till noon.

Though the climate at Mason was cold, it was much warmer than in North Korea. The men played softball, touch football, or volleyball on every open field around camp. The troops recuperated rapidly from fatigue and nervous tension.

Bob Barrow bought a radio in Pusan. Each day at noon we gathered in his tent for 30 minutes of country music on "Stars and Stripes." Wes Noren couldn't understand why Barrow and I enjoyed listening to Little Jimmy Dickens sing "Take a Cold Tater and Wait," or "Sleeping at the Foot of the Bed."

"It's nostalgia," we said. "Some people where we come from would rather hear country music than eat." New Orleans jazz was Bob's favorite; the Glen Miller sound was mine.

While gathered together, we compared notes about skin peeling off our hands and feet due to the severe cold in North Korea. All had experienced this in varying degrees. "You know, during the spring of the year I used to walk along the creek banks back home," I commented. "Oftentimes, I came upon a moccasin snake shedding its old layer of skin. From the way my hands and feet are peeling, I feel the same way."

Near the end of our first week in Mason, S. L. A. Marshall, the Army historian, began interviewing us about the battle of the Big Hill. He stayed a few days taking statements for a manuscript he was writing on the campaign in northeast Korea. (See the Appendix.) Afterwards he made his candid appraisal in a letter to a Marine friend.

"This past month I have been with 1st Marine Division, making a study of its operations up north. I have collected about 80,000 words on this subject. It will probably be the main basis for the official history of it in future.

"The show was extraordinarily good; probably the best yet.

"I had previously completed a similar study of 2nd Infantry Division.

"Now let me say that I cannot stop the voice of slander nor reform all of my half-assed brethren in the American press. Most of what you have heard is in error.

"At least one tragic mistake was made by the command.

"There were critical shortages which inveighed against the defense. There were not enough grenades. No pyrotechnics. Some of the positions had been too loosely organized. The communications were definitely bad.

"But, for all that, 2nd Division behaved like men—I'm speaking of the line. Perhaps a few ran—but not many. I exaggerated nothing in my statement.

"Further, anyone who tells you that '12,000 men ran back to Seoul' is a lying son-of-a-bitch. . . . By the time this Div. lost 4,200 killed and wounded in the first four days of battle it only had 6,700 men left.

"One shouldn't traduce Americans who fight. The regrettable thing is that our press sometimes takes the lead in this and the country is never wiser.

"On the other hand, I am not defending the Army—its training, disciplines, morale programs or anything else. I think we need reform until hell won't have it. The system directly contributes to the breakdown of men.

"Higher commanders are either too blind or indifferent to recognize this and to do something about it.

"But if a few of our generals would start specifying and quit their damned generalizing, there might be hope!

"I think we could take over your methods and make them work in the Army on a broad scale. In fact, I have no doubt of it.

"Men are men. At base, the average American is still good; he wears testicles, though you would never think so, judging by what the Army does to condition him.

"It isn't necessary—nor has it ever been so—to tell a Marine to have faith in his service.

"But today, the average American just holds on and hopes that his Army is better than it looks—which it isn't.

"Even the ranks are aware of the dry rot in the system.

"You might judge from this letter that I am clean fed up. If so, you judge rightly. I had not thought it possible that we could do so many things so badly.

"Thank you for writing. I will preserve your letter. 1st Marine Div. is still heads up and I have never met finer men anywhere."

Marshall made a study of the 2nd Infantry Division as well as of the 1st Marine Division. When he submitted his manuscripts on the war in North Korea to his superiors, they contained material unacceptable at the time. He prepared two findings, "Chinese Communist Forces I," featuring the 2nd Infantry Division, and "Chinese Forces II," on the 1st Marine Division. Although Marshall disavowed any intent of a broad comparison between the two operations, when the accounts are read together, conclusions highly favorable to the Marines readily emerge. Both manuscripts were classified Secret by the U.S. Army. Their inclusion in the Appendix of this book constitutes the first time they have been published.

The 2nd Infantry Division's mistakes that Marshall pointed out in his first manuscript should have been immediately published throughout the 8th Army, just as the news of the Marines bayoneted in their sleeping bags at Kojo was spread throughout the 1st Marine Division.

Many of the errors made by the 2nd Division Command could be attributed to the officers' apparent belief in the nightly intelligence summaries emanating from MacArthur's headquarters. There was little use of flankers while on the march, as well as an insufficient interval between the point and the main body while in movement. This made the moving columns vulnerable to the Chinese military's favorite tactics, "Hochi Shiki."

The lack of outposts beyond the perimeter and of strong and persistent patrolling kept the command further in the dark. In many instances, there was a breakdown of lateral communication between company units. When the radio failed, companies did not resort to runners to inform others of their situation. In consequence, companies with theoretically joined flanks would be totally surprised by a Chinese attack even though neighbors had been heavily engaged for sometimes as long as three hours.

Marshall made no mention of what I consider the worst mistake of all: abandonment of the fire team concept of squad organization that had proved so successful in World War II, and which was especially adapted to the kind of fighting experienced in Korea.

At night, the 14,000 men of the 1st Marine Division became 14,000 generals. Everyone had his strategy for defeating the Chinese. With all Marines now living in the bean patch, frequent visits were made between friends of different units. "Where were you when the shit hit the fan?" was the standard invitation for one to relate his personal experience up north. Most often, he responded with a humorous story.

The friendliness of the North Korean civilians was not a subject of conversation. We took their hospitality for granted. We were the good guys, the Chinese the bad. Newsmen did not write about these good relations, so that outside the combat area the North Korean people were erroneously looked upon as enemy. Yet 1st Marine Division Intelligence did not point to a single instance where a North Korean civilian planted a booby trap, destroyed a bridge, or acted in any manner other than to help the Marines in the Chosin Reservoir Campaign.

In conformity with the wishes of the Joint Chiefs, MacArthur reluctantly placed Almond under Walker's command, yielding to the overriding wisdom of consolidating our strength in Korea. As a first step toward marshaling forces in the south, MacArthur notified the Department of the Army on December 12 that the ROK 3rd Division was already en route by water to Pusan. The plan for the remainder of the evacuation provided for the contraction of the 10th Corps defense perimeter around Hamhung-Hungnam as the Corps units departed in phases. As the Corps perimeter contracted, rifle, artillery, and heavy gun support were intensified against the possibility of an enemy build-up. The 3rd Army Division provided the last defensive forces for the perimeter. On Christmas Eve it, too, successfully executed the final withdrawal from the Hungnam beachhead.

The Chinese made no concerted effort to overrun the beachhead. As prisoners and captured documents revealed later, they were unable to do so. Unlike Dunkirk, this evacuation called for the removal of all equipment, supplies, and personnel. Altogether 193 shiploads of men and materiel were moved out of Hungnam harbor aboard Navy transports. Approximately 105,000 fighting men, 17,000 vehicles, and 350,000 tons bulk cargo were removed from the beachhead. In addition, 98,000 Korean civilians who were displaced from their homes by the Chinese were brought south. Unfortunately, many thousands more were left on the docks at Hungnam.

Admiral Doyle said, "We could have completely evacuated the entire area, for they all wanted to leave. As we left, in fact, refugees with bundles under their arms were still pouring in for a sea lift south. The Army did a magnificent job ashore with the refugees. Since Hungnam was wrecked and there was little shelter and was terribly cold, I ordered all ships with baking capacity to bake extra bread and cook rice. Every ship with a bake shop baked to capacity. We distributed rice to all the ships to help keep the people alive."

He continued, "Later, two civilian representatives of the ROK government came to thank Admiral [Turner] Joy and me, with tears in their eyes, for the compassion toward their fellow countrymen during the Hungnam withdrawal."

This successful evacuation was the Navy's Christmas present to the land troops and their families in the States.

On our first Sunday in Mason, a notice tacked on the bulletin board announced communion services at the Regimental Chapel tent for all Episcopalians. Having been raised in the Episcopal Church, I decided to attend. Only 15 to 20 Marines showed up, among them Chesty Puller.

After the service, Puller spoke: "Hey, Roanoke! I'm glad you made it."

"I'm glad for both of us, Colonel," I replied.

He invited me for a visit that afternoon. When I arrived at Puller's tent, Lieutenant Colonel Olin Beall was describing how he and his truck drivers rescued the Army wounded of the Faith Task Force. At age 53, Beall had a tough, leathery face. He was a mustang who had served more than 30 years in the Marine Corps. For most of that time he was a master sergeant. Those serving under him claimed he was still a master sergeant, but with silver oak leaves.

As our Intelligence Summaries had previously noted: "Throughout the campaign, the Chinese soldiers' attitude toward American wounded remained inscrutable and in major respects contradictory. During the evacuation of the wounded, Chinese riflemen stood on the bank and did not fire at the wounded, only at the rescue team. Friendly North Korean agents went into huts where they found our wounded in common quarters with the Communists. The Chinese made no effort to feed or otherwise serve these casualties, but if they reached for food for themselves, they did not interfere. Native agents delivered notes to these men in full sight of the enemy soldiers, telling them what steps to take toward rescue. The Chinese neither molested the agents, nor attempted to stop the wounded. Yet, in repeated instances during attacks upon a road column, the Chinese centered their fire upon the ambulances wearing the Red Cross marker."

Beall's story confirmed the Intelligence reports in many respects. He said that some of the wounded were used as bait to get the Marines out on the ice, where the Chinese had a clear shot at them. This fascinated Puller. He plied Beall with questions, wanting to know every detail, especially about the wounded who were abandoned in the trucks.

"Are you sure you didn't leave any living soldier in those trucks?" Chesty repeated.

"I'm certain," Beall insisted.

Puller had deep feelings about anybody or anything necessary to wage war. He constitutionally opposed wasting either.

After almost two hours of conversation, Chesty turned to me; by then it was time to leave. I told him I had enjoyed the visit, but I had to get back to my company.

The most damaging morale factor was the news concerning the 8th Army. We knew that thousands of tons of military supplies had been abandoned to the enemy when the Army retreated south. Now war correspondents reported that "bug out" was used extensively by these troops, without shame. The route to the rear was known as "haul asbestos route." Gasoline was hoarded by motor transport units. This reserve supply could not be touched because it was "bug out" gas. *Life* magazine reported: "The expression 'bug out'—taking it on the lam—was used some in the last war, but in Korea it is spoken by many thousands of times a day. Until recently, the expression had a pleasant sound, for it was applied to gooks and Chinese. Now it is a nasty word. The most dangerous 'bug out' in American military history is in progress."

At home Americans read about this attitude; by the end of December the Korean War had become a most unpopular war. For a totally different reason, my own morale took a nosedive. I learned that a full report of Marine casualties had been posted at Regimental Headquarters. I ran to see the list even though I dreaded every step of the way. I read the names of eight Roanoke Marines on the "Killed in Action" pages. Corporal Paul Martin's name appeared near the top of one page. The picture of him, his pretty wife, and baby at the N&W Railway Station flashed vividly into mind. Numerous Roanokers appeared on the wounded roster, two to three times the number on the "Killed in Action" list. I knew that many more must have suffered serious frostbite. I later learned that two Roanoke Marines had had feet amputated; one lost both feet. My morale sank to its lowest level while in South Korea.

A few days afterwards, a friend from the Marine Air Corps gave me two fifths of bourbon. I invited Major Glenn Martin and Logan Bowman to join my tentmates for drinks. Pruitt volunteered to serve. Ice and an assortment of cheeses, cold cuts, and crackers were obtained from the battalion mess hall. We spent the evening talking about the Chosin Reservoir campaign, rehashing all the moves that had been made. It was a joyous occasion. Before the first bottle was consumed we agreed that the Chinese had taken one hell of a beating. I asked Logan and Glenn to stay around; I had another bottle and Pruitt would get it for us. But Pruitt could not be found. Neither could the bottle. While he was serving the first bottle, Pruitt, with some friends, had consumed the second.

"Captain, I don't think Pruitt'll show his head around here again tonight," Fritz advised. "He's ashamed to come back."

When we met at noon the next day, I began in a loud voice, "Pruitt, you're one hell of a gunnery sergeant! You've been griping about confiscating officers' whiskey the whole time you've been here. You finally succeeded. Why did it have to be my bottle?"

"It was your fault, Captain," Pruitt replied, shaking his head. "It's like you southerners say—you shouldn't have put the fox in charge of the hen house."

"Oh, my gosh, what'll I hear next. You're a fox, all right, Pruitt! But I didn't put you in charge of any hen house. I put you in charge of my whiskey and gave you some to boot."

"Cap'n, the Good Book says, 'Lead them not into temptation.'"

"Now, that's a good one, Pruitt! I never read that—and when did you ever read the Bible, anyhow?" Before he could answer, I continued. "Look, Pruitt, last night I was mad as hell. I felt better when I woke up. All morning long I've been waiting for you to show up. I've been anxious to hear what you were going to say. And let me tell you this, you didn't disappoint me! I thought you'd come up with something like that hen house bit. I've got to admit, I didn't expect you to fall back on the Bible! I'll tell you one thing, though. You'll never get another drop of my whiskey."

With or without whiskey, each time we compared notes with other Marines it became apparent the Chinese were being overrated, in spite of MacArthur's pessimistic communiqués to the contrary. Unfortunately, his views extended to our chief planners in Washington. Had MacArthur and the Joint Chiefs known the actual state of Sung's 9th Army group, both would have changed their viewpoint about our future. The official battle summaries from the 20th, 26th, and 27th Chinese Armies would certainly have encouraged our side.

The Chinese 26th Army reported that more than 90 percent of its personnel had suffered from frostbite. It said further: "The coordination between the enemy infantry, tanks, artillery and airplanes is surprisingly close. Besides using heavy weapons for depth, the enemy carries with him automatic light firearms which, coordinated with rockets, launchers and recoilless guns are disposed at the front line. The characteristic of their employment is to stay quietly under cover and open fire suddenly when we come to between 70 and 100 meters from them, making it difficult for our troops to deploy and thus inflicting casualties upon us."

This comment would have pleased Chesty Puller especially, for he always maintained, "You've got to punish the enemy to beat him," and, "The best way to punish the Commies is to let them get in close, then open fire. Wait for good targets before you shoot."

The Chinese 27th Army complained of more than 10,000 noncombat frostbite casualties out of its strength of four divisions. Part of its report said: "The troops did not have enough food, they did not have enough houses to live in. They could not stand the bitter cold, which was the reason for the excessive noncombat reduction in personnel (more than 10,000 persons). The weapons were not used effectively. When the fighters bivouacked in snow-covered ground during combat, their feet, socks and hands were frozen together in one ice ball; they could not unscrew the caps on the hand grenades; the fuses would not ignite; the hands were not supple; the mortar tubes shrank on account of the cold; 70 percent of the shells failed to detonate; skin from the hands stuck on the shells and mortar tubes."

The Chinese 20th Army, which included the 60th Division that opposed us on the Big Hill, was probably battered worst of all. Parts of the 27th Chinese Army group had recuperated by the middle of March 1951. No division of the 20th Chinese Army returned to action until late April. The Chinese battle summaries clearly established why Sung's troops failed to attack the Hungnam redeployment. They were too riddled by battle and nonbattle casualties to make the effort.

From prisoners' interviews we learned that the 125th and 126th Chinese Divisions, neither of which took part in the fighting at the Chosin Reservoir, suffered heavy noncombat casualties. Both had been in the Chosin area on November 15, then moved south to the 8th Army sector. Neither division was committed to action during the November-December fighting. Their heavy casualties were the result of frostbite.

Chinese prisoners confirmed civilian reports that Sung's greatest defeat came as a result of his soldier's treatment of the North Korean civilians. Although they were indoctrinated not to take or steal food or to take over the North Korean homes, they did just the opposite. Their supply system failed to provide the food, clothes, and housing necessary to survive the cold. Months later, Chinese prisoners complained bitterly about the North Koreans' resentment against them. When questioned about the attitudes of the civilian population toward the soldiers, Sung's men evaluated the relationship in China as good, but in North Korea as very bad. Our indiscriminate use of air power later neutralized, then turned these civilians toward the Communists.

On Christmas Eve, a large group of schoolchildren came with their teacher to our camp to sing Christmas carols. First, they sang Korean, then American tunes. The men delighted in hearing "Jingle Bells," "Dreaming of a White Christmas," and many others sung in the Korean language. At the Post Exchange, Jim Adair handed out to the children cookies and candy, now available to us for the first time in Korea. He gave a carton of cigarettes to the teacher, who bowed low in deep appreciation.

This Christmas season was among the best I had spent. I received many presents from home, including cans of sardines, fruit cake, boxes of candy, Brunswick stew, and pictures of Ginny and Dabney and members of my family. Other Marines received similar gifts. We decorated a Christmas tree in the battalion mess hall. The cooks delighted in serving good meals daily. Everyone recognized that being alive and healthy was a lot to be thankful for; then, too, the contrast between us and the Koreans represented the difference between the haves and have nots. Living daily with this evident contrast made us appreciate our heritage.

On Christmas Eve, Morse Holliday phoned he was sending a jeep to pick me up for noonday Christmas dinner at Division Headquarters in Mason. Morse was an excellent junior officer in World War II; he received a number of medals for bravery and was now a major. He and I had served in the 21st Marine Regiment at tent camp, Camp Lejeune, in 1942. We were together until after the Bougainville Campaign. On one occasion, we hiked ten miles into the mountains of Guadalcanal to visit an Australian gold mining camp which had been abandoned after the Japanese occupied the island. We panned for gold for a couple of days before returning to our tents in Coconut Grove.

Morse was a member of the Mormon Church. He didn't drink or smoke, but knew that I did on occasion. When I arrived he gave me a drink of Scotch whiskey, later a second. We reminisced about old times—Camp Lejeune, the West Coast, New Zealand, and the Solomon Islands. We spent more than two hours talking about what we had done since the summer of 1944 when we parted.

For dinner we had steak, fresh potatoes, fresh broccoli, hot rolls with butter, and delicious pumpkin pie à la mode for desert. After the meal, Morse brought in a box of cigars. I felt relaxed and content as I puffed away. We then talked about our plans for after the war. I said I intended to return to Roanoke to practice law. Morse hesitated. He had been a contractor in Tucson during the five-year interval between World War II and Korea. He said he had been thinking seriously of staying in the Marine Corps, then retiring after 20 years' service, since he had already accumulated nine years.

"About six weeks ago, I started thinking differently." He explained he had the responsibility of getting Division Headquarters' supplies, including winter clothing, from Wonsan to Hungnam. "I placed guards on a boxcar containing our fur-lined parkas. Some sons-of-bitches stole those parkas somehow. The guards couldn't give an explanation how it happened! We did without parkas for more than a week! I got blamed by top brass. That kind of guff I don't have to take on the outside," he concluded.

Before he had finished, I choked on my cigar. "The smoke went the wrong way," I insisted. Moments later I told Morse I had to get back to camp. "My men need me," I said. "You know we're being sent to the front in a few days." Nothing dampens the spirit on a festive occasion like a guilty conscience. Nevertheless, I felt it was neither the time nor the place to tell Morse who got those parkas.

When I arrived back at camp, I learned that General Walker had been killed. The next day it was announced that General Matthew Ridgeway would be the new commander-in-chief of the 8th Army in Korea. Shortly thereafter our battalion received orders to move to the front. I took a shower each day because I didn't know when I would have the opportunity to bathe again after leaving Mason. We were ordered to take only necessary equipment. In the event of evacuation no equipment should be left which the Chinese could use.

On December 31, 1950, we boarded trucks and headed north toward Uisong. Slow progress was made over the dirt and gravel roads. About five miles north of camp we met the first group of young South Korean men who were coming to the Pusan-Mason area for military training in the ROK Army. Many times during the day our trucks had to stop because of the great number of men on the road. I cannot give an accurate estimate of how many, but there must have been more than 50,000.

We bivouacked in late afternoon about 25 miles south of our destination. Our morale had been greatly enhanced by what we had seen. We reasoned that if the South Koreans had the determination to win, so did we. Tents were pitched and fires were made. I ate a can of Brunswick stew which had been sent as a Christmas present from Ginny's uncle, Dr. Charles Tennant. Afterwards, I joined the company commanders at Schmuck's tent.

He told us that when we arrived at Uisong the next morning we would establish a defensive perimeter on the outskirts of the city. From there, we would immediately contact village and town officials in our designated territory, covering approximately 15 miles in all directions. Our assignment was to destroy the North Korean 10th Division, which operated in small units as saboteurs behind the UN forces' main line of resistance. Each day fire team, squad, platoon, and even company patrols would be on the move to seek out and destroy the enemy. This would be ideal combat training for the many new recruits added to our ranks at Mason.

Before returning to my tent, I joined a group gathered around the radio jeep. For an hour we listened to the latest tunes on "Stars and Stripes." "Good Night, Irene," still a popular hit, was among those played.

I looked forward to the next day. There is something about war that causes a Marine to hash over and rehash the latest battle until a new mission comes along. Then he thinks about tomorrow, but never more than one day ahead—except to the day when he returns home.

When in a battle zone, it is dangerous, psychologically dangerous, to permit oneself to dwell on past encounters where heavy casualties have been sustained. Thus, even before darkness came, the Chosin Reservoir Campaign had been moved to a special locker in my memory bank. It would not be opened again for examination until I came back safely to Virginia.

17

Reflections

At Uisong, Korea, near daybreak on January 30, 1951, I was seriously wounded. A bullet severed the bone in my left leg about four inches from the hip joint. My left hand was also badly injured. I was taken to a MASH unit at Andong, then flown to Japan, where I received four blood transfusions. For the next year I was a patient at Portsmouth Naval Hospital, in Virginia, the Navy hospital nearest my home. In April 1952 I returned to my law practice.

When my Marine company left Roanoke in the summer of 1950 there had been very little fanfare, and none upon my return twenty months later. Now, when I reflect upon the Korean War, I have mixed feelings. I remain deeply impressed with the performance of the Marines at Chosin, yet the war itself is a case history of our country's having "had the experience, but missed its meaning."

The tremendous efforts made by the Republic of Korea in its own defense have never been fully appreciated by the American public. The war demonstrated that the United States should send troops to defend nations only when those nations are willing to defend themselves. It was the Korean people who carried the heaviest load in saving their country from a Communist takeover. We had support from other western nations, although not as much as we desired and perhaps deserved. However, the help of our allies was important.

Not enough recognition has been accorded General Matthew

W. Ridgeway for his part in saving the day for the UN troops in Korea. He took a defeated and dispirited 8th Army and molded it into a fighting force of which all Americans could be proud. With no more divisions than were available to Douglas MacArthur in November-December 1950, Ridgeway's troops defeated and turned back the Chinese Communists in the spring of 1951. His performance demonstrated that sound generalship would have denied victory to Mao's army in the first instance. Why such a turnaround? The answer: outstanding leadership. Moreover, "the coach was there where the game was being played."

The resounding defeat of our 8th Army in November 1950 caused MacArthur to chart a course detrimental to both himself and his country. Thereafter, a wounded ego dominated the man. When Ridgeway met MacArthur in Tokyo immediately prior to taking command of the 8th Army, MacArthur had decried the value of tactical air support. "It could not," he flatly stated, "isolate the battlefield or stop the flow of hostile troops and supplies." For the remainder of his life MacArthur refused to come clean on this subject with the American public. His refusal to take responsibility for mistakes clearly his own, and the methods employed to extricate himself from all blame for the debacle in North Korea, rightfully caused his dismissal by President Truman in April 1951.

Nevertheless, the American public gave MacArthur an unprecedented hero's welcome upon his return to the United States. He was granted the unusual privilege of addressing a joint session of Congress where he eloquently defended his conduct. His hands had been tied in North Korea, he claimed, and he went on to assert that we were denied victory by the politicians in Washington. His solution was to use unrestricted military power: ". . . once war is forced upon us there is no other alternative than to apply every available means to bring it to a swift end. War's very object is victory, not prolonged indecision. . . . In war indeed there can be no substitute for victory . . ."

Congress scheduled hearings, which proved to be its lengthiest. MacArthur took the stand early. After claiming he was interested in victory, he said the Korean War could be terminated by bombing Manchurian bases, blockading the Chinese coast and utilizing Chiang Kai-shek's army on Formosa against the Reds. When asked about the ground forces needed, MacArthur replied, "As far as our ground forces are concerned, I don't believe there would be any appreciable increase necessary. As far as the air, it might be advisable to start with an increment of two additional B-29 or B-36 groups."

These were magic words to the American public. We could bomb Manchuria, punish the Chinese, and win the war without having to use any more foot soldiers, the ones who had suffered the heaviest casualties. But what about targets in Manchuria? As for North Korea, there were few if any worthwhile targets for strategic bombing. In answer to questions by Senator William Fulbright of Arkansas, MacArthur replied, "They have practically no indigenous products they can manufacture; they have no great manufacturing centers whatsoever." Such admissions made no impression on the American public. It heard what it wanted to hear. Victory had been denied by the politicians.

Repeat a fable often enough and it takes on the status of fact. Sadly, many in high places in the United States, both in the military and in political office, accepted MacArthur's explanation as genuine, and today they still do.

At the root of much of our problem in the Korean War was the fact that to Douglas MacArthur and numerous other American political and military leaders, the Communist world was a monolith, taking its every cue from Moscow. Many, if not most, American voters also shared this misapprehension. We did not realize that there were differences among the various Communist regimes—that while the Soviet Union had close ties with Mao Tse-tung, Communist China's leaders were not Joseph Stalin's lackeys, any more than was Marshal Tito of Yugoslavia.

Thus when the North Koreans came down on South Korea in 1950 and when later the Chinese threatened to intervene in the war if UN forces moved near the Manchurian border, they were not necessarily acting as parts of a concerted blueprint for world conquest drawn up in Moscow. The Russians supported both of them. No doubt they encouraged the North Koreans to make their attempt to take over the Korean peninsula. But when the Chinese acted, they were on their own.

Had the independence of Communist China been recognized for what it was, we might have seen that they were genuinely perturbed by the threat to their border and that for all Mao's hostility to the United States, China's intervention was not so much part of a monolithic Soviet blueprint for conquest as a move to protect what its leaders saw as a menace to their own country. Had we understood that, we might have restrained MacArthur in his desire to plunge ahead and occupy all of North Korea by UN forces without regard for the consequences. But as it was, and because he represented powerful segments of American public opinion, we allowed him to send the UN forces northward without restraint.

We did not understand what President Truman and Secretary of Defense Marshall were beginning to grasp: that our task was to *police* the borders of the free world, not to proceed as if each attempt by a Communist country to take over neighboring territory was part of a concerted, calculated program of aggression by the Soviet Union. And in order to conduct that policing effectively, our armed services had to be ready to fight local, limited wars. Nuclear strategy was not sufficient; it was necessary to maintain a military strength and presence that could intervene decisively whenever and wherever needed, in order to stop aggression when it occurred. A strategic air force and an arsenal of nuclear weapons were not practical deterrents to aggression along the perimeters of the free world. Conventional weapons and the trained, combat-ready troops that could use them quickly and decisively were essential to the defense against Communist adventuring.

The war continued in stalemate for two more years. Once the Chinese entered North Korea, strategic bombing of non-strategic targets became the order of the day. At the MacArthur hearings, Major General Emmett O'Donnell of the Far East Bomber Command asserted, "I would say that the entire, almost the entire, Korean peninsula is just a terrible mess. Everything is destroyed . . ." In spite of his testimony, all restrictions were lifted on bombing North Korean targets, and with this continued destruction North Korean civilians turned to the Chinese. Accordingly, the enemy's supply system was greatly improved. The number of rounds of enemy artillery and mortar fire received by UN forces rose from an average of 150,000 to 200,000 rounds per month in the last six months of 1951 to more than 700,000 rounds in October 1952, the average per month in 1952 being approximately 350,000 rounds per month.

This increased movement of supplies caused the deputy commander of the Far East Air Force to comment, "It has frequently been stated by commanders in Korea that the one man they'd like to meet when the war is over is the C-4 of the Communist forces. How he has kept supplies moving in the face of all obstacles is a real mystery."

A look into the mirror would have revealed the answer. True, our planes disabled tremendous numbers of enemy trucks and trains bringing supplies to the front, and these were legitimate military targets. But we also conducted air missions against population centers. At the start of the war Pyongyang, the capital, had a population of 400,000, at the end 80,000. Other cities in North Korea shared similar fates. Being human, the survivors reacted as one would expect of humans—they sought vengeance. The surprising tenacity and determination of North Korean civilians in keeping their rail and highway networks in operation answered the question as to why isolation of the battlefield could not be achieved with naval and air power.

The North Korean Department of Military Highway Administration numbered some 20,000 personnel, and was divided into two regiments of three or more battalions each. Their equipment was simple but effective—shovels, sand bags, wicker baskets, picks, axes, and other hand tools. In time of emergency, local labor was drafted to repair important bridges and tunnels. Sometimes as many as 1,000 laborers, including women and children, would be used to repair a single bridge or tunnel. The North Korean Railroad Recovery Bureau, numbering some 26,000 personnel, was similarly organized for railroad repair. In all, hundreds of thousands of civilians joined in the effort to keep supplies moving southward to the front.

Such local support for the enemy had not been available at

the Chosin Reservoir, nor could it have been mustered. In 1985, John Y. Lee, a former ROK lieutenant assigned to the Marines, wrote an article for *The Korea Herald* about the Chosin Reservoir Campaign. In it he said, "Thousands of families were caught in the battle and suffered miserably. Although they were not participants in the action, they helped us in many respects. They were friendly to us; no instances of sabotage or hostile action were reported. They carried our wounded soldiers in their ox carts on the frozen reservoir and they shared their food with us. I am sure that there are many people now living in Seoul who came out of the reservoir with us." And I am convinced the methodical bombing of North Korean noncombatants to the point that they turned to the Communists was one of the most senseless actions of the war.

"There is a right kind and a wrong kind of victory just as there are wars for the right thing and wars that are wrong from every standpoint. . . . The kind of victory MacArthur had in mind—victory by bombing of Chinese cities, victory by expanding the conflict to all of China—would have been the wrong kind of victory." So said Harry Truman in his memoirs. But even he missed the point. The case against MacArthur's plan does not rest on moral or political grounds, nor would the plan have produced victory. The history of war, before, during, and after Korea, shows that the massive bombing and killing of Chinese would have had the same negative effect, militarily, as the indiscriminate bombing of the civilians in North Korea. Our next war would reaffirm this axiom. In Vietnam our air force dropped twice the tonnage of bombs used in all theaters of war during World War II. Yet this tremendous display of power did not importantly assist our soldiers on the battlefield. The bitter lesson, that military victory is foolhardy if political defeat is the end result, was borne in by subsequent events.

In retrospect, leaders in both North and South Vietnam have recognized the error of indiscriminate bombing. South Vietnamese General Lu Mong Lan, commandant of the Command and General Staff College at Da Lat, has said, "At the U.S. Army War College today, people look back at Vietnam and ask

the question, 'What should we have done?' Now they realize
that they should have used the Vietnamese forces on a territo-
rial mission, and U.S. forces on the DMZ and Ho Chi Minh
Trail to stop resupply from the north. This way the U.S. forces
would have had no conflict with civilians and no confusion.

"I used to tell my soldiers, the minute you harm an innocent
person you put the whole family in the hands of the Communists. . . . Our job must be to win over the hearts and minds of
the people. And that should be kept in mind all the time. You
should always respect the villagers."

Truong Nhu Tang, the most senior Viet Cong functionary to
desert to the west, explains how the Communists were helped
immeasurably in Cambodia by U.S. B-52 air strikes. In *A Vietcong Memoir* he writes, "To the Cambodian villagers these
bombings brought an incomprehensible terror, precipitating
the more militant into the ranks of the Khmer Rouge and leaving the rest increasingly sympathetic toward America's ene-
mies." And to other people around the globe they demonstrated that the United States, with all its good qualities, had
a broad ugly side.

If unrestricted military force, especially indiscriminate
bombing, is wrong, then what is the alternative? An objective
study of the Chosin Reservoir Campaign may supply some
needed answers on the proper use of force.

Even though heavily outnumbered, the 1st Marine Division
was not defeated in North Korea—which evokes some obvious
conclusions. The art of war, especially land battle, has changed
very little since the days of Sun-tzu; there is no substitute for
thorough training and determination. This campaign reaf-
firmed the age-old principle that performance of men is more
important than performance of equipment, though both are essential.

In no way is this statement meant to depreciate the value of
superior technology. The Marines at Chosin could not have
coped with the Chinese mass had they not possessed far better
equipment and air cover. But use of the highest levels of military technology should not blind one to the virtues of what is
adequate, less sophisticated, and simple, present at the right

place and time. For example, pack animals, as Chesty Puller later suggested, would have been invaluable had we determined to stay in the mountains, or had we formed a defense line at the narrow waist in North Korea, as recommended by the Joint Chiefs. These animals, coupled with air drops, would have enabled us to maintain adequate supply to strong defense points and outposts where there were no roads.

A less obvious lesson concerns the importance of weather and terrain in battle. The skilled commander should make both work to his advantage, rather than the enemy's. The sub-zero temperature and the mountains posed formidable logistical and fighting problems for General Smith, but even worse for Sung Shih-lun. He was denied the use of his artillery, and the cold disabled a far greater proportion of Sung's command than Smith's.

The most important military principle exemplified by the Chosin Reservoir Campaign was smothered by the rhetoric of MacArthur and his "unrestricted military force" adherents. People power outweighs military power. In short, local civilian support can contribute more than guns to those engaged in battle on foreign soil. Military efforts will fail unless the commander in the field demands that his soldiers treat the inhabitants with a sense of human dignity. No small part of General Smith's success can be attributed to the fact that he made his Marines respect the property and human rights of the North Koreans, as well as honor their culture. A devastating defeat of the Chinese Communist 9th Army group and the survival of 14,000 Marines and soldiers who lived to fight again justly compensated our country for his ingenuity. As one of the survivors, I am forever grateful that Oliver P. Smith commanded UN troops at Chosin. He embodied all of the features required by Sun-tzu: "By command I mean the general's qualities of wisdom, sincerity, humanity, courage and strictness."

Now, more than 35 years after the Chosin Reservoir Campaign, I consider myself fortunate to have been a part of the 1st Marine Division and to have witnessed American troops perform at their very highest level of competence. The verdicts of Chesty Puller and S. L. A. Marshall have merged in my memory like a telescope and made me see that what they said and

I sensed was there. Still with me is the picture of the Marines coming down the mountain at the close of fighting in north-central Korea. To me the memory is as vivid as, for other Americans, the famous photograph of the Marines raising the flag at Iwo Jima. I hope this book explains why.

CCF in the Attack
by S. L. A. Marshall

PART ONE: *A Study based upon the Operations of 2nd Infantry Division Rifle Companies in the Battle of Kunu-ri, November 1950*

1. *Assault on a Perimeter*

In operations against 2nd Infantry Division rifle companies, the Chinese did not attempt a general envelopment of a defensive perimeter at any stage. The focus of initial attack was usually the rear of the company perimeter. The full weight of the attack would fall on one platoon position, or occasionally two, particularly if they were closely joined. After breaking the perimeter, and consolidating the ground, the enemy would then press on against the open flank of the next hill position. This is a general but not invariable pattern. In attacking Company F, 38th Infantry, all platoons were brought under heavy fire in an attack which continued through the night. All of the defenders became close-pressed within a two-hour period, as the attack developed. However, the weapons platoon and CP, on the rear, were not invested by enemy infantry, though hard hit by mortar and machine gun fire from the flanks. The enemy did not attack in a long skirmish line, nor did he come on in successive waves against 2nd Division's infantry company perimeters. About 60 to 70 skirmishers was the maximum which would be seen at any time in the attacking line. Usually the group would be 30 to 40.

Written in 1951, the two parts of this report on Chinese Communist Forces in Korea were classified under U.S. Espionage Laws as secret documents. After twelve years, they were declassified. They have not been published before.

2.   *Pattern of Movement*

These men usually came forward standing straight, but were sometimes seen crouched. Usually they advanced at the walk, though they occasionally moved at a trot or run. When stopped, they did not crawl or wriggle forward to take advantage of accident in ground. When prone, they moved only sufficiently to find the first cover which would put them in defilade. This is characteristic of their action in night attack; there is no far reaching deployment of men covering, for example, an entire flank and rear of a platoon position in the initial rush. The Chinese find what seems to be a favorable portal of entry into the immediate position; it may be a draw, or ravine or footpath; if the defender is closed around high ground, the enemy will usually avoid the sharp hill facings and attack up the gentlest slope. The first group moves straight up, sometimes in a fairly well spaced skirmish line, sometimes in file columns, sometimes in an uneven group.

3.   *Use of Marching Fire*

They advance with marching fire, almost invariably, irrespective of whether they are walking or running. This is the characteristic beginning of their fire engagement and it usually precedes any firing with machine guns or mortars. The marching fire, however, is erratic and ineffective. Our troops have suffered few losses from it and they say, almost to a man, that they do not find it demoralizing and it does not pin them down to the point where it checks their return of fire. CCF's tactical object in advancing this way seems to be to close within infighting distance so that they can build up the attack with hand grenades at close range while machine guns and mortars work over the defenders at ranges varying from 50 to 800 yards. These assault waves never seem to attempt to close on the US line until our forces have nearly exhausted their ammunition supply and show it by their fire rate. *In fact, there is not one single instance in which the enemy assault line came right on over the top to overwhelm so much as a platoon by storm and force the remnants to flee in terror.* They do not crack positions by unusual valor or fanaticism, or by main weight quickly applied. They squeeze them by a gradual build-up of numbers and fire pressure, and by patiently waiting for them to disintegrate, as the defenders run out of weapons, ammunition and the men to use them.

4.   *Nature of Target*

As soon as CCf's first skirmishers are engaged with fire (this usually occurs at less than 50 yards range) they go to ground. If the fire lifts temporarily, they will arise and come on until they are engaged once more. Then they go to ground again. But once they have committed themselves to an avenue of advance they do not relinquish it, even though tactical developments would seem to make it unprofitable. They simply continue the build-up behind those who made the first rush. As they die or are wounded, others come forward to take their places. The burp gun, rifle and grenade are the weapons of this forward element. This element never presents a very broad target to our automatic fire power; four or five Chinese at a time are the most that a machine gun or BAR is likely to get. This latter weapon and the fragmentation grenade are the basic means for keeping the CCF attack in check. Any kind of illumination put on the rear of these Chinese in-fighters works havoc upon them and forces recoil, sometimes verging on near panic.

5. *Use of Cover*

In daylight fighting, these tactical groups try to fight from entrenched works and, when forced from them, continue to engage while using underbrush, trees or similar cover. In attack at night, under a bright moon, they make utmost use of shadows cast by boulders, overhangs and ledges. Anything that would burn out their natural cover during daylight or put them under light at night would reduce the effectiveness of these furtive tactics. 2nd Division's infantry used no flamethrowers in the attack and had no flares, starshells or other pyrotechnics. However, in three instances, inadvertently, our gunfire started conflagrations in the rear of the enemy assault line. The results were startlingly good; in one case the enemy quit attacking and fought the grass fire for 1½ hours. Our machine guns cut down scores of CCF men in this period.

6. *The Defense Under Pressure*

When brought in check by our fire, the enemy assault line moves forward spasmodically, as temporary slowing or cessation of our fire, because of casualties, or for any other cause such as ammunition shortage or stoppage of a machine gun or BAR, affords the opportunity. They will come with a rush only when our forces have had to pull up stakes and yield the ground immediately in contest.

The record of 2nd Infantry Division in the battle north of Kunu-ri in defense under pressure is most impressive; of the 16 infantry company actions which were checked in detail, there is only one instance of a unit of platoon-size yielding its ground for any reason other than exhaustion of ammunition supply, or some cause of similar nature. In the one exception, the platoon had no central leadership, did not reconsolidate its ground toward the direction of the attack and was ripped apart and beaten back squad by squad. Even so, it evacuated its wounded, and there were only 11 whole bodied men when the platoon at last withdrew.

Company B, 9th Infantry Regiment, had a strength of 126 when engaged by a strong force of enemy at the base of Hill 219 at 1000 on 25 November. Twenty-five hours later it was still fighting and still holding ground when ordered to withdraw. There remained only 34 able-bodied men in the position, some of whom had been hit by grenade fragments. These are not notable exceptions. They are characteristic of the 2nd Division's infantry reaction as a whole.

7. *Emphasis on Grenades*

In a well-set local attack, the enemy seems frequently to prefer to move in first with grenadiers. On occasion, these files carry no other weapon. The grenades are carried in a pouch around the waist. They are used prolifically. In consequence, as the supply becomes exhausted, our men see the enemy pushing towards their lines seemingly empty-handed. Little rifle fire is used in support of the grenade attack, but a great deal of submachine gun fire. The men on these weapons move right up among the grenadiers. From further back, machine guns in numbers from one to three (but not more than that in an attack on a company perimeter) are used to graze the high ground and other areas being defended. On a percentage basis, our heaviest losses appear to be due to the accuracy of the machine gun fire. In an attack in which, for any reason, CCF rifle groups form the initial wave, the intent appears to be to push grenadiers through the ranks of riflemen as quickly as possible and at every opportunity, in order to be available when the lines have closed to within a distance which offers prospects for grenade use. Not all grenadiers are riflemen but most riflemen carry at least 5 grenades of the small potato-masher concussion type. (None of these CCF troops carry the bayonet.) All of their close-in tactics seem disposed to put final reliance on the grenade as the weapon which will force UN troops to vacate ground.

As to the effect on US forces in particular, the grenade attack, in itself, misses the mark, despite the fact that CCF impresses upon its people the idea that Americans are peculiarly vulnerable to grenade assault. Our troops who have been under steady attacks by CCF grenades for hours at a stretch still express contempt for the weapon. Their attitude can be attributed to two main factors:

1. The Chinese are inept and weak-armed throwers.
2. The grenade itself has little lethal potential.

On the first point, there are no conspicuous exceptions to be found in a review of more than a score of closely joined grenade actions. On level ground the maximum range attained by the CCF fighter, who uses an underhand looping throw, is between 20 and 25 yards. On an uphill throw, it is considerably less, depending on the grade. In one action uphill, in which the enemy was disposed less than 20 yards below our position at the crest, their throwers tried vainly for an hour to get a grenade over the embankment. In another action, when engaging seven Americans closely packed together on a small knoll, they placed 50 to 60 grenades on the knoll within one and one-half hours. This was at about 15 yards range. About 30 or 40 of these grenades were thrown out, or kicked out, by our men; the others exploded within the position. Practically all men received fragment injuries. None was killed or even seriously wounded. In yet another action involving a platoon, about 30 men were lightly wounded by grenade, without any man being so seriously hit that he had to leave the action. Wounds from the CCF grenade are commonplace in all these company fights; KIA's from the same cause are extremely rare. It seems to be the case that the body or head must be in almost direct contact with the grenade for a serious wounding to result from the explosion. Our troops have become familiar with these effects, and in consequence, the CCF grenade is not a demoralizer.

When our own grenade is in good supply during the defense, the CCF grenade attack is invariably neutralized or driven off. This was rarely the case in the Kunu-ri actions. None of our infantry carried more than two grenades and some riflemen had none. In most instances, local re supply was either impossible or most difficult after the fighting was begun. But where grenades could be brought up, and the fighting was continued by the defenders with resolute use of this weapon, the enemy was held.

8. *Range of CCF Grenade Action*

To keep grenade re-supply at maximum during engagement would seem to be a main object of the CCF infantry system. In all of the close encounters brought under study, there is not an instance of their tactical groups running out of grenades, except in chance-meeting engagements by small groups, when the enemy was not prepared. On the other hand, when taken at close quarters, with full surprise, they are seemingly unable to make impromptu use of this valuable in-fighting weapon.

There are two examples of this, one occurring in 1st Battalion, 23 Infantry at night, and the other in 2nd Battalion, 9th Infantry in day-light. The unit of 23 Infantry was in bivouac, and not set up for de-fense. After breaking into its position, numbers of the enemy sought ground cover within the camp, and then remained inactive although armed with grenades and rifles. When the unit formed a skirmish line and swept forward to eliminate these infiltrators with grenade and rifle fire, the enemy made no reply; not one grenade was used by CCF in this phase of the action. Similarly when one column of about 120 Chinese walked in broad daylight into a defile where they were cov-ered by G Company, 9th Infantry, they did not use the grenade, though possessing it, and after ineffective rifle fire for a few minutes, they all were destroyed or made prisoners. Only the small (potato-masher) concussion grenade was used in grenade actions by CCF. If they have other types, they were not used in the battle.

9. Problem of Recognition

Averaging out the various actions, it appears that the mean distance at which recognition occurred and our men in the infantry positions became certain they were dealing with CCF enemy, was somewhere between 15 and 50 yards in night engagement, and between 50 and 200 yards in daylight. This was partly, but only partly, because of the method of the enemy approach in which fire is rarely used as a cover and partly because of the normal difficulty of distinguishing friend from enemy.

Other factors limiting quick recognition at longer ranges were these:

1. Little use of flankers while on the march.
2. Insufficient interval between the point and the main body while in movement, particularly in the ascent to high ground.
3. Absence of outposts beyond the perimeter and at warning distance from the general body.
4. Lack of any devices such as trip wires, etcetera, which might facil-itate warning and recognition.
5. Breakdown of lateral communications between company and com-pany. When radio failed, companies did not then resort to runners to inform others of their situation. In consequence, companies with theoretically joined flanks would be totally surprised by the CCF

attack one at a time, though the neighbor had been heavily engaged for one and a half to three hours. The same condition existed within the several platoons of a company perimeter.

6. The lack of strong and persistent patrolling.

10.   *CCF's Weapons Effects*

In degree of effectiveness during the Kunu-ri battle, the CCF weapons used against our own infantry forces could be approximately evaluated on the basis of casualties suffered, effect on fighting morale, and impairment of the general position. Order of effectiveness of the weapons was found to be as follows:

1. Machine gun, light.
2. Mortar, (usually 60mm).
3. Grenade.
4. Submachine gun, hand carried, usually a Thompson.
5. Rifle.

CCF's machine gun fire is almost universally accurate and persistent, and they will keep the gun firing until it is knocked out, pushing it forward to very short range as cover affords. There does not seem to be a surplus of these weapons; almost never are more than two guns used in attacking a company position. The main tactical object appears to be to deliver a pinning fire on the defender.

The mortar was not employed in batteries in the average situation. There were instances in which two or three mortars were used to effect a concentration but these were exceptions. Usually, CCF fired a single tube, and it was put to work only after the attack was well begun. Fire was of two main types; general area, and concentration against main installations, such as defending machine guns, mortar positions, CP's and supply points. Their area fire was not distressing and troops were not greatly harassed by it. On the other hand, in concentration fire, their mortar comes down so quickly and accurately on specific targets as to suggest that they are employing some method of rapid battlefield triangulation. The tactical situations in which this extreme accuracy was noted were such as to permit on-the-spot triangulation for the determination of range, though it may be that they had occupied the ground for some time and knew the range, and thus needed only to follow the flash.

As with their rifle fire, their burp-gun fire during daylight skirmishing or in the night attack is not markedly accurate, and they tend to employ the submachine gun from too far back. However, CCF has an abundant supply of the Thompson Gun, as judged by reports of its use in the Kunu-ri battle and by the number of them collected from their dead and prisoners.

CCF made limited use of the bazooka during the Kunu-ri battle, not against infantry positions as a rule, but against the covering armor. In the few cases when this occurred, they engaged our tanks at extremely close range (20–40 yds) and their marksmanship was excellent. In these situations in which CCF was engaged at favorable range by our tank fire, with their elements in full view, the enemy broke and fled. Whether FA fire would have the same effect is unascertainable, there being no examples of FA action under close observation. This was not a situation in which FA could do its best work because the two sides were too closely joined.

11. *Manner of Deployment*

In the general movement toward the area of engagement, CCF columns appear to advance by the easiest avenues of approach and the most negotiable—the MSR's, the feeder roads, stream beds and valleys. While defending along high ground, they do not come forward by way of the ridgelines. The deployment of combat groups occurs as they encounter resistance; the groups then peel off one at a time until the tactical column has evaporated. The view is put forward, tentatively, that CCF's success in striking so many CP's, artillery positions, and similar sensitive installations in our rear, was fortuitous rather than the consequence of detailed reconnaissance and planning. Our field army structure tends to hug the arteries and intersections, and if the enemy advances by the most natural route, he can scarcely miss us.

12. *Disengagement*

At dawn, in the opening stage of the Kunu-ri battle, CCF sought to disengage where this was possible. Following disengagement, at about 0700, these troops began as usual to mess, feeding from a common kettle. At this time of day, litter parties, sometimes covered by rifle groups, are sent forth to collect the wounded and bring in the dead. First-aid stations operate at the assembly point where the men are feeding. The dead are given a superficial burial nearby. It seems that during this interval CCF takes few security precautions close in. The troops generally are in a relaxed attitude, and when encountered by any of our forces are not disposed to fight.

13. *Supply at Company Level*

During the Kunu-ri battle, our typical infantryman carried around 90 to 110 rounds for the carbine, 2 bandoliers and full belt for the M1, and between 0 and 2 grenades. Few companies carried rations forward on the man. In most companies, sleeping bags were man-carried as well as light packs. With these loads, tactical disunity developed because of straggling, when the march was in excess of 3½ airline miles, which would be roughly equivalent to perhaps seven miles overland, considering the nature of the country.

14. *Conservation Problem*

During the action, particularly at night, the reloading of carbine magazines and M1 clips was a problem of some magnitude. There was in most cases an over-expenditure of automatic ammunition in the first stage of engagement in most companies, despite a dearth of visible targets. On the other hand, good conservation of grenades was marked in all companies, possibly because of short supply, and certain companies were conspicuously successful in getting the line to hold bullet fire until crises occurred in which good targets could be seen. In the average situation, during the hilltop actions, automatic fire could do little to hold back or destroy enemy skirmishers after they had closed on the position. The CCF men used rock and ledge cover. To get at them, our men had to risk undue exposure against the skyline. Even so, it is remarkable that in many of these situations intrepid use of the BAR became the pivotal factor in the defense. After the enemy had closed and taken cover, the grenade became the most valuable weapon in the close-in defensive fighting. But because of the grenade shortage, automatic fire was also further expended on targets, which were in the main, unprofitable, thus additionally depleting our defense power. Largely in this manner, as casualties mounted, possibilities of continued resistance became exhausted. Nearly every position was without grenades before the action was two-thirds complete. In the semi-final stand of B Company, 9th Infantry, there was a noteworthy scene in which part of one platoon, led by the CC, stood up in the morning light and grenaded the Chinese with rocks and C-rations so that the others could withdraw to new ground. As indicative of the gravity of the immediate situation, five of their number were KIA and two wounded at this juncture.

In four other episodes, when fighting supply was used up, our men engaged CCF with their fists and rifle butts, as the enemy closed in. The Chinese do not show well when met on these terms.

15. *Other Weapons*

CCF fired no artillery anywhere along the Kunu-ri front. One new weapon made one brief appearance—a small rocket, not of the bazooka type. It was used against B Company, of the 9th Infantry, and skidded off their positions, exploding into the embankment beyond them with only a moderate bang.

16. *Maintenance Problems*

Various kinds of trouble were reported by men armed with carbines; misfires, jamming, sluggish response of the weapon. Some part of this trouble has been traced to insufficient maintenance, principally lack of lubrication because of shortage of oil within the unit. However, experience indicates that in cold weather the weapon sometimes has to be warmed before it will fire as an automatic, this being required because of hardening of the oil by the cold. Fifteen or so rounds fired single shot will usually restore operation. Performance by the M1 was up to expected standards, with relatively few failures reported by the men of the infantry line. The survey further shows that the companies which make a practice of testing their weapons and inspecting their pieces prior to possible engagement have the best record of successful weapons-operation during battle.

PART TWO: *A Study based on the Operations of 1st Marine Division in the Koto-ri, Hagaru-ri, Yudam-ni Area, 20 November–10 December 1950*

Introduction

Detailed study of the operations of 1st Mar Div against CCF in the Koto-ri, Hagaru-ri, Yudam-ni area 20 Nov to 10 Dec 1950 substantiates in nearly all major particulars the conclusions drawn in the paper, "CCF in the Attack," published on 5 Jan 1951, ORO–S–26 (EUSAK), wherein CCF tactical methods and weapons employment were evaluated on the basis of the experience of 2nd Inf Div in the Battle of Kunu-ri, 24 Nov to 1 Dec 1950.

In its onfall against 1st Mar Div, CCF did not at any time succeed in enveloping and fractionizing any major element of the command, or in overrunning more than a minor outwork of a general defensive perimeter. Hence its tactical elements were at no time as fully extended in the attack against local positions as occurred during the enemy assault against 2nd Inf Div's line east of the Chongchon River. There was thus far less chance to observe CCF characteristics in the fire fight under wholly fluid conditions.

Since the circumstances of the fighting around Kunu-ri by 2nd Inf Div and north of Koto-ri by 1st Mar Div were wholly unlike, not only as to the character of the countryside, but as to the manner of initial employment by our forces and initial deployment by CCF, there is no warrant for any broad comparison between the two operations. Where that is done hereinafter, it is solely with the object of emphasizing CCF characteristics and capabilities.

Weapons and Works

In general, the CCF Divisions engaged by 1st Mar Div appear to have been no better armed than those engaged by 2nd Inf Div at about the same time. The major material difference was that the CCF divs engaged by 1st Mar Div appear to have been critically in short supply, both as to food and ammunition. Whereas the persistence of CCF fire from fixed positions, the circumstance that the machine gunners and grenadiers seemed never to run short of munitions, and the observation that troops in the rifle line were backed up by an ample train of bearers, were noteworthy in CCF operations against 2nd Inf Div, the situation was quite the reverse among CCF operating in the Chosin Reservoir area. CCF divs committed to the battle seem quickly to have exhausted such stocks as they had brought forward. Their effectiveness ceased at this point, since resupply had not overtaken them. When they withdrew because of ammunition failure, fresh divisions came forward into that part of the line, and the supply-exhausted division then disappeared from the front.

This phenomenon was remarked upon by Maj Gen Oliver P. Smith, commanding, and was confirmed by regimental and battalion commanders. PW interrogations showed that the great body of these troops had crossed the Yalu River between 13 and 16 Nov, concurrently with 1st Mar Div's first advance from the base ports northward, and had then pressed on toward the battle area as rapidly as possible. It seems probable that all other major considerations, such as competent supply arrangements, were subordinated to the necessity for getting these troops forwarded in time to intercept 1st Mar Div's column and cut the MSR after the preponderant strength of the Div had been committed to the attack in the Reservoir area.

Consistent with this hypothesis, it was also noted by all forces within 1st Mar Div that the CCF enemy were invariably committed to the attack on one line, with no options. This held true of divisions, as of battalion and company formations. Each had been given one set task. Each appeared to persist in this task so long as any cohesive fighting strength remained. When at last beaten back from it, the CCF appeared planless and aimless, incapable of rallying toward some alternative object. The troops withdrew and sat on the countryside.

Even so, prisoner interrogations indicated a high order of average intelligence. Not alone among officers, but in the rank-and-file, the average interrogee could name his company, regiment, division, army and army group, and was knowledgeable of the plans and intentions of higher headquarters. Thus it was from enlisted PW's that 1st Mar Div first learned that the CCF plan was to attack in main against the MSR "after two regiments had passed to the northward." This intelligence was gained while the advance was still in progress. But what was particularly puzzling was that PW's had little or no consciousness of rank. The prisoner would identify himself as a "soldier" or "officer" but could not state his grade. If there were CCF NCO's, they could not identify themselves as such.

During 1st Mar Div's campaign, there were six instances in which the CCF attack was supported by light artillery pieces. Not more than two or three guns were employed at any one time, and the shelling was limited as to rounds. In the main, enemy offensive power was based upon automatic weapons, chiefly the .30 caliber machine gun (including Lewis and Hotchkiss types), with the submachine gun, the rifle and the light potato-masher grenade being the principal other arms used by CCF infantry, both in defense and during the enemy attacks on 1st Mar Div's defensive perimeters. There were no novel or eccentric employments of any of these weapons, other than ineffective attempts to string grenades so that they could be used to booby-trap the facings of physical roadblocks, with a lanyard leading back to a roadside pit. This device usually failed because the Chinese soldier in the pit was dead before the time came to pull the string. In one instance the failure was due to the grenade pins freezing.

On the defense, these CCF furnished their hilltop positions with artillery-resistant bunkers, walled with heavy logs wired together in double thickness, with timbered ceilings and a two-foot-thick rock and earth covering. These works resisted air attack except under a direct hit by rockets. Their materials had been moved to the high ground on horseback, and after the CCF deployment through the general area, the horses had then been withdrawn into the back country, away from the MSR. There were few horses to be seen in the area by the time that the US air began to work it over.

In cutting 1st Mar Div's MSR north of Koto-ri and west of Hagaru-ri, with the object of isolating and destroying the division, CCF used both roadblocks (physical) in substantial number, and demolitions in lesser number. The explosives were properly employed in the most sensitive spots along the withdrawal route, a notable example being the blowing of the apron bridge across the penstocks not far from the base of Hill 1081, south of Koto-ri. This bridge was directly above the facing of a 1500-foot-deep gorge. Unreplaced, it meant that the road south was blocked to all vehicles. The division had foreseen the problem and was prepared to span the gap without loss of vital time to the column. A treadway bridge had been flown in to move with the column. Even so, CCF had accomplished this block with some expertness, getting a maximum of impairment with a minimum of explosive. The whole road was replete with opportunities of this sort had the enemy been well fixed with explosives. The MSR was a narrow track cut into the side of a mountain. A few heavy rockslides would have completed its ruin. But though CCF was in possession of this part of the countryside for more than one week, no major demolitions of this type were attempted. There, and farther to the north, between Hagaru-ri and Yudam-ni, CCF appears to have had only enough explosives at hand to wreck a few minor bridges which could be unhinged with small charges.

The usual physical road block was accomplished by the piling-up of rock, earth, and rubble so as to form a not-too resistant barrier averaging between 2½ and 3½ feet in height. About half the time, these road blocks were given some supporting fire from the flanks—usually one or two machine guns, and perhaps a mortar, firing from the ridgelines off the flanks. In other cases, the block was not given active support, even though the high ground off flank had not been swept by friendly skirmishers, and readily pushed aside by the dozers moving in the van of the infantry column.

However, there are also examples in which the road block was supported strongly and persistently by automatic fire from the high ground, and snipers closing in at practical small arms distance. There then ensued the knocking-out of vehicles by bullet fire, the temporary blocking of the column, and a steady attrition in men and materiel along the road, until at last the CCF were brought in check by superior fire and movement.

Discipline in the Column

Among the incidents of this character, the most instructive is the experience of TF Drysdale, on the road from Koto-ri to Hagaru-ri on the night of 27–28 Nov. This small TF of British Commandos, one company of Marines and one company of infantry, was sent north from Koto-ri, to open the MSR to Hagaru-ri after receipt of the first report that CCF had cut the road. It moved in trucks after having first swept the ridges immediately north of Koto-ri—the one area where there were commanding ridgelines right next to the MSR. A supply convoy was supposed to follow in its wake, moving under its protection. In the forefront of the TF moved one platoon of medium tanks. Another platoon was assigned to follow after the truck convoy, serving as rearguard for the column as a whole.

The subsequent breakdown of this column, as it ran into an ambush installed by CCF (the force was estimated at less than 3 battalions of enemy) in the open country beyond the Koto-ri ridges can be attributed largely to the manner in which the armor was handled. On a small scale, the action and reaction were almost identical with the misfortunes of 2nd Inf Div's column on the road between Kunu-ri and Sunchon, three days later. Whereas the safety of the thin-skinned vehicles, once they came into the fire gauntlet, depended almost wholly on rapidity of movement, the armor stopped to engage as soon as CCF fire began to rattle against its sides. This in turn blocked the road and subjected the motorized elements to a punishing fire from the flanks, which they were in no position amply to return. Argument and pleading with the tankers proved largely futile. They had not been placed under direct command of the TF leader, and they were largely insensible to the effects which their tactics were having on the friendly elements to their rear.

In an effort to save the TF from total ruin, the officers with the infantry elements (and the Air FO as well) sought to intervene with the armor, and to persuade it to desist from fire and keep moving. Those farthest to the rear could not even understand what was happening and did not realize that it was the armor, more than the enemy, which had produced the paralysis. About half of TF Drysdale's personnel got through this ambush finally; fifty percent of its vehicles had been lost. The supply convoy was lost altogether; the personnel were either killed or captured. Notably, the tanks, which by their fire had brought the other elements into jeopardy, escaped without loss.

Those who were in best position to observe the ambush and breakdown of this small column, agreed that the losses had been due less to the direct effects of CCF fire than to lack of control within the armored force, lack of communication between it and the motorized element, and the failure of the tankers to understand what their halt-and-fire tactics were doing to the train behind them.

This is a relatively new problem for US armor and motorization in joint movement via the road. Its common denominators are emphasized by the identicality of experience between TF Drysdale and 2nd Inf Div's column. They should perhaps be given rather close study in common, since there are several major lessons to be emphasized, and the problem is likely to be a recurrent one for so long as enemy tactics are directed toward crossing the rear and closing the escape route. What is plainly indicated is that short of a clear appraisal of the problem, and the determination of SOP's which will assure tactical unity within the column, the presence of armor does not of itself assure additional protection to a motorized column moving through enemy country over narrow roads, and may vastly increase its vulnerability. What is intended as a shield becomes in fact a drag upon all movement, in a situation where mobility is requisite to safety.

In the case of 2nd Inf Div, the armor was interspersed through the length of the column. With TF Drysdale, it was used as a covering force front and rear. The results were alike dismal, because in both cases the means of control and communication had not been made firm prior to movement.

CCF's Grand Object

TF Drysdale's experience has here been stressed out of all proportion to its significance, in the general operations of 1st Mar Div, because it illuminates the one point at which CCF's general object in the attack upon 1st Mar Div achieved a measure of local tactical success. Here, once again, as in CCF's operations against 2nd Inf Div south on Kunu-ri, the main purpose of the Chinese enemy was to entice and permit a maximum extension of the forces in the attack, then close across the MSR, and undertake the general envelopment and destruction of the main column as it responded to the mounting pressure against its rear.

This effort was beaten down in detail at every point by 1st Mar Div which, throughout its advance to the Chosin Reservoir and westward to Yudam-ni, and subsequently during its withdrawal southward to Chinghung-ni, put uppermost the principle of firmness within its own lines, both during the attack and when on defense. After the one sally by TF Drysdale, made with the object of reopening the MSR between Koto-ri and Hagaru-ri, 1st Mar Div did not again employ minor forces in any attempt to shake CCF's hold on the MSR, though the enemy had closed across the road, both between Koto-ri and Hagaru-ri (1st Mar Div's CP) and between Hagaru-ri and Yudam-ni, where 5th and 7th RCT's were operating. Temporarily, 1st Mar Div accepted this situation. At all points its forces operated fortress fashion within their own perimeters, counter-attacking in such measure as was necessary to keep CCF off balance, and to deny the enemy any undue advantage in ground. In effect, 1st Mar Div stood in column on a line of strong points within enemy country. Supply of critical materials to these strong points, and the evacuation of the wounded from them, was maintained by air. The construction of airstrips had been undertaken immediately, and the construction was in process even before the strength of CCF in the Reservoir area had been felt.

As will be discussed later, 1st Mar Div at its four main positions—Yudam-ni, Hagaru-ri, Koto-ri, and Chinghung-ni—put depth of organization, and unity within the local force, above all else, and occasionally with deliberate intent foreswore certain of the higher ridges in the immediate vicinity to the enemy, for the sake of greater tightness within its own lines. This choice paid phenomenal dividends and in no instance invoked any inordinate cost. CCF proceeded to impale itself upon this line of strong points. In all four areas, as the days and nights wore on, its attacks, at first pressed in full fury, gradually diminished in violence, until finally the enemy pulled off, having had enough. Though they continued in great numbers in the countryside and swarmed among the ridges during the daylight hours, their role was strictly passive and they did not resume the organized attack.

Perhaps the most startling example of the effect of a resolute defense upon CCF's moral aggressiveness was provided by Fox Company, 7th Marines, which for five days and nights preserved a perimeter defense in isolation, holding the pass between the division force at Hagaru-ri and the 7th and 5th RCT's at Yudam-ni. During this period the Company was wholly surrounded by CCF troops in aggregate strength of perhaps two battalions. The perimeter was close invested and broken at one point on the first night, though the ground was regained and CCF driven off before morning came. The enemy attacked along the same line and in about the same strength on the second night, but was again repulsed. On the third night, CCF came on less surely, though by that time Fox Company had taken heavy losses. Then came the respite; though CCF forces in large number remained within seeing distance during the next two days, there was no further assault. On the fifth morning, a battalion of 7th Regt, moving cross-country to the relief of Fox Company, was temporarily halted by strong CCF resistance within less than 1000 yards of the latter's lines. Such was the morale of Fox Company, after its successful defense of the position for five days that it offered by radio to send a patrol out and bring the relieving battalion in.

The incident was not the rare exception; it was typical of the spirit which activated 1st Mar Div's operations as a whole. "We had the feeling at all times that we had the upper hand and that we were giving the enemy a beating whenever he chose to fight," said General Smith of the operations of his forces. This estimate is supported by the detailed study of what occurred to companies and platoons in 1st Mar Div main areas of engagement, and of what was seen, by men in the fighting line, of CCF's losses and reactions. They believed, on the basis of what they saw and felt, that they had been victor on every field. They were confident that they had achieved these results mainly with their own fighting power. They were indignant that what they had done had been in past discounted by those press reports which said by inference that 1st Mar Div, having become overextended in enemy-held country, had to be extricated by the intervention of other than Marine Forces.

It suffices to add that on the record, 1st Mar Div was fully confident of its own situation and power to contend against such further pressures as CCF might put upon it from the hour that 5th and 7th RCT's, withdrawing from Yudam-ni to the westward, closed upon Hagaru-ri at the southern tip of the Chosin Reservoir, where the division CP and defensive perimeter were established. Thenceforward, it was a question of how best to conserve force and drive CCF from the ridges flanking the MSR to the southward, with minimal loss in personnel and vehicles to the column.

Attrition and Concealment Within CCF

Apart from those enemy forces which had become broken or neutralized in the attempt to destroy, by direct assault, 1st Mar Div's defensive perimeters at Yudam-ni (a two-RCT position), Hagaru-ri (a reenforced battalion position), and Koto-ri (a reenforced battalion position), the effort of CCF during the period 27 Nov to 2 Dec had been directed toward deploying other maneuver bodies against the corridors connecting these focal points in the battle. These CCF, though out of range of the infantry weapons in the defensive bases, were not left unmolested. From Chinghung-ni to Koto-ri was 12 miles, from Koto-ri to Hagaru-ri 9 miles, from Hagaru-ri to Yudam-ni 13 miles. Such targets as were brought under observation by air or by road patrols were thus usually within range of 1st Mar Div artillery in one or two of the four defensive bases. Weather, for the most part, was favorable for air strikes.

Early in the campaign, 1st Mar Div G2 had become convinced, on the basis of reports from civilian sources, that CCF was moving through the countryside in columns of substantial size, and that these bodies were harboring in native villages, and in mineshafts which were common in the Koto-ri, Yudam-ni area. These views were reported to the air arm; it was thought that the enemy's disappearance during daylight hours could be accounted for in this manner, rather than because any considerable number was dug-in and concealed along the high ground. Initially, the air arm discounted this theory because daylight reconnaissance failed to show any number of troops active within the villages, but the civilian reports persisted, and North Korean natives besought the command to attack the villages in order to destroy the Chinese invaders.

Following the cutting of the MSR, air bombardment of villages adjacent to the road and in the back country was undertaken on a large scale. The results wholly confirmed what the natives had reported. When the bombs crashed on the thatched huts, Chinese spewed forth on every hand. They were so wedded to this cover that air observers noted that, after the bomb runs were completed and before the planes had left the vicinity, the surviving Chinese went right back into the half-wrecked buildings. So concentrated were their numbers that it was estimated the strength of one battalion might remain concealed within 20, or so, huts. These same findings were confirmed by Marine patrols attacking into the back country. They found minor forces operating from within works along the hilltops, in front of main bodies which had taken refuge in the villages. The air attack was credited with effectively sealing one mineshaft that was supposed to be sheltering the greater part of one CCF regiment. Eyewitness accounts both by patrols and companies in the attack and by US soldiers who were taken prisoner and later liberated, provide a substantial body of proof that CCF made systematic use of the normal man-made cover in the countryside throughout this campaign.

Whether the use of villages for daylight cover was peculiar to this one operation, and was super-induced by the effects of sub-zero temperatures on an army traveling for the most part without blankets, or heavy overcoats, and shod in tennis shoes, is a point worthy of close regard.

Certainly the loss to CCF caused by cold alone, during the long week in which its blocking groups camped on 1st Mar Div's MSR, vainly hoping to trap the Division when it attacked south, must have been terrible indeed. Hundreds of these enemy surrendered because they were no longer fit to fight; under the lash of the weather the hunters became the hunted. Many were found dead, victims of freezing, untouched by a bullet or shard. Some who surrendered were frozen through in all limbs. Others reported that they had been without food for the greater part of one week. They had kept alive by digging foxholes just barely wide enough for one man to squeeze his body into, and then like animals, had sunk themselves in these burrows, trying to conserve such warmth as their bodies would impart to the frozen ground.

Among these fighters were many who could no longer work a rifle bolt or pull a trigger. A sufficient number retained enough bodily activity, however, to persist in the main mission, until destroyed by 1st Mar Div's battalions in the sweep from ridgeline to ridgeline which permitted the advance of the motorized column through the mountain passes. By progressive fire-and-movement, 1st Mar Div eradicated these CCF over a wide belt on both sides of the MSR. The Division strong-points farther to the southward served as dustpans to the broom during this sweep, and portions of their garrisons attacked northward concurrently with the advance southward of the main column, thereby entrapping greater numbers of CCF within the corridor which they had purposed to use as a deadfall for the US force. The seemingly slow progress of this movement, which was watched with apprehension, if not alarm, by the outside world, was due to the natural difficulties of the countryside and the painstaking care with which 1st Mar Div had reorganized its resources before proceeding with the attack.

During the campaign as a whole, the temperature varied between 20° above zero and 20° below. There had been one major snowstorm with a fall approximating six inches, which built up drifts five to six feet deep in some places.

Systematic Use of Cover

As inexorable as were these conditions imposed by man and Nature on those of the enemy who thus took position in the open country, it does not follow that the use of village cover by the great body of CCF in this same vicinity was an expedient of the time and place.

Rather, the absence of any logical alternative supports the premise that the systematic use of village cover is standard procedure with CCF, and that they must refuge in the native huts in numbers which would be unthinkable to any western soldiery. They concentrate their field forces in this manner during daylight hours, using village concealment adjacent to their axis of advance and main object of attack, for the express reason that *there is no other place to hide*, except in caves or heavily forested areas. Whole armies cannot hide themselves in man-made works and escape detection by the normal means of air reconnaissance, however skilled their camouflage discipline. Nor can they dispose themselves along ridgelines and among hilltops and remain capable of reassembly within such an interval as would permit them to achieve effective concentrations against a more mobile opponent. These things are not within human possibility, and the CCF thus far have shown no super-human capabilities in its Korean operations. To deny these forces any use of village concealment would seem, therefore, to be an essential step toward the disruption and paralysis of their operations. Thrown upon the open countryside, they will lose effective mobility, in whatever season.

Lines of Advance

The mountain-plateau region above Chinghung-ni is a conifer belt and the sparse vegetation of firs, aspen and brush is thickest on the northern and western facings of the ridges except for tracts which have been reforested in recent years. CCF attacks were usually pressed along a line which took advantage of this natural cover. When CCF tactical forces were harboring in these wooded areas for any period, they sometimes cut these trees halfway up, and bent the upper portion over so as to give themselves greater concealment.

In operations against 1st Mar Div, as against 2nd Inf Div, in general the enemy came forward along the natural lines of drainage, and the paralleling tracks and paths, feeding into the US MSR. There was no stealth in the approach; they came in erect, sometimes walking, sometimes at a slow run. In repeated attacks on the same position, their initial line of advance became a beaten path, and there was little or no variation in their application of fire. Either because their lack of material things was so vast, or simply through lack of a combat discipline, they stopped to loot and pillage on occasions when their attack had been pushed within the possibility of a local success.

In the defense, their main tactic was to rely upon the effects of automatic fire from the commanding ridgelines; their skirmishers operated in close juncture to this base, and only a minority of hardy individuals would attempt to close to within effective small arms or grenade range when the US line was brought in check by fire from the heights.

In the attack, they seldom came over and down the ridges, but moved around the hill bases and through the draws. This pattern seemed to be almost invariable, except in those instances when the two sides were locked in a close fight to gain the dominating high ground.

Equally marked in this operation, as in 2nd Inf Div's operations around Kunu-ri, was CCF's preference for the night attack, which when held or repulsed, would consummate in a withdrawal just prior to dawn. Their tactics in the night attack were in no wise different than those described in the paper "CCF in the attack" except that they were not experienced in full extension because they were invariably beaten on the local ground by 1st Mar Div's perimeter forces. The attack almost invariably sought to achieve local penetration under the cover of a pinning machine gun fire. The grenade and submachine gun were the main weapons in the subsequent attempt to develop a breach. On at least six occasions these thrusts achieved an initial, partial success. This done, the enemy attempt to follow-up proved fruitless. Either further exploitation was prevented by a dam of fire lowered against the breach by 1st Mar Div's supporting weapons, or the ground was retaken and CCF driven off by the counter-attacking infantry.

Detailed study of these fire fights show five instances in which enemy personnel were either killed or wounded by the bayonet. 1st Mar Div has retained its bayonets, and in perimeter defense, bayonets were usually fixed. However, three of these killings were done by one Marine. The grenade was little used by the defender in beating back these attacks, mainly because the pins were sticking in consequence of the cold, and when troops removed their mittens to handle the grenade for any length of time, their hands became frostbitten.

Attitude of CCF

Throughout the campaign the enemy's attitude toward US wounded remained inscrutable and in major respects contradictory. For example, during the evacuations of US wounded across the frozen surface of Chosin Reservoir from the east bank to the Hagaru-ri position, CCF riflemen stood on the embankment within 100 feet or less of the rescue party. But not one shot was fired throughout two days against the wounded as they walked or crawled down the embankment and across the ice toward succor. Native North Korean agents went into huts on the east shore where US wounded were in common quarters with CCF. The latter had made no effort to feed or otherwise serve these casualties, but if they reached for food or drink for themselves, the CCF did not interfere. The native agents delivered notes to these men, in full sight of CCF, telling them what steps they were to take toward rescue. CCF did not molest the agents, nor did they attempt to stop the US wounded when they quit the shelter to comply with the instructions.

On the other hand, in repeated instances, during their attacks upon a road column, they centered their fire upon ambulances bearing the red cross marker to the extent that other vehicles moving next to these vehicles in the same convoy escaped relatively unscathed.

Organization of the US Defense Perimeter

Except for the extraordinary situation of Fox Company, 7th Marines, the organization of 1st Mar Div's defensive perimeters was based upon the battalion, as a minimum. At Yudam-ni, 7th and 5th RCT's were unified and integrated in one great perimeter enclosing their artillery, all other supporting arms, and people. One unique aspect of the defense at that point is that, despite its abnormal complexities and unremitting pressure, all command decisions were taken by the two Regimental Commanders and their S-3's, acting in council, and that unanimity of opinion and estimate, and the absence of any friction, attended this mechanism. At the other pivotal strong points along the MSR, each battalion defense was a tightly-knit "hedgehog," enclosing the artillery and airstrip, and organized to fight over 360 degrees, with the artillery usually so faced that it could fire immediately against the draws along which the enemy were most likely to advance. Combat patrols and companies in the attack, moving outward from the bases, maneuvered only within effective range of the defending artillery. Also, the operating radius of small parties in excursions beyond the perimeter was limited absolutely to that distance at which they remained within effective radio contact of the main body.

In the positioning of these perimeters, the seeming advantages of vast fields of fire were yielded in favor of that use of ground which gave the defenders assurance of maximum mutual support around the circle. Instead of going to positions which might improve the prospect for an effective kill at long range, 1st Mar Div built its defenses so as to be *certain* of stopping CCF at short range, while preserving the integrity of its own ground.

There was no over-stretching. On the contrary, the positions were contracted to the point of permitting organization of a mobile, local reserve. In the initial stage, the position at Hagaru-ri was perhaps an exception to this general rule, because of the slender numbers of the defending force, the nature of the terrain, and the necessity for enclosing the large airstrip. However, service and administrative personnel were used to plug gaps in the line and as local reserve during the emergencies arising from the CCF attack.

All positions were well dug-in, despite ground conditions which made the issue trenching tool little more than a chipping instrument, and battalion commanders personally inspected the foxholes and other installations. It is deserving of special note that in the few instances where CCF succeeded in impinging of any of these defensive positions, it was under circumstances in which the defenders had not yet completed their protective works, because of insufficient time.

Use and Effect of Wire

1st Mar Div wired-in all of its defensive works to the limit afforded by the availability of materials, which were scant. Concertinas and a few double-aprons were emplaced across the draws that seemed to afford favorable avenues of approach, and these were supplemented at some points by piled-up brush and rude abatis, though the general lack of timber in the country shortened this procedure.

Trip-wires were strung in front of the defensive lines. Trip flares were used where available.

Operations at the company level afforded a clear view of the extraordinary reaction of CCF to all wire installations. They seemed to be nonplussed upon meeting defensive wire in any form. Even when they came against trip-wire strung 18 inches above the ground, they would stop and attempt to crawl under it. This was the reaction not of the occasional individual, but of nearly all. Likewise, they would try to crawl under a concertina or double apron, rather than attempt to remove the obstacle. A line lieutenant commented: "It is as if they had some superstitious dread of wire; it will stop them every time."

Use of Illumination

There was relatively little opportunity in this operation to observe the effects of illumination behind the CCF in the night attack which would present targets in silhouette. The mortars had what should have been, numerically, a supply adequate to the testing of this technique. But the WP was a bad lot of 1944 ammunition. The excessive cold appears also to have been a factor in its deterioration. Only one WP shell out of four would fire, on the average. On the other hand, the CCF WP, which burns with a light whiter than our own, but of short duration, had almost 100 percent effectiveness.

For these reasons, and because troops tended to believe that the CCF WP were their own shells falling short, orders were soon issued at Hagaru-ri to discontinue the firing of all WP. However, in the few cases where WP was fired, and the material burned, the illuminating had a marked effect in checking the Chinese.

Mechanics of Defense

1st Mar Div used both outposts and listening posts beyond its defensive perimeters, though this practice varied from base to base, depending upon situation and the views of the local commander.

At Yudam-ni there was some use of outposts in platoon strength as far as 1,000 yards outside the perimeter.

Small listening posts were used from 200 to 300 yards beyond the front.

There were no local surprises.

Recognition of CCF usually took place at between 40 and 150 yards range.

When, during his approach, the enemy gave a hail in good English (as happened frequently), the defending line fired toward the sound of the voice.

This was done even when the speaker identified himself as a Marine, naming his unit.

Through the day and into the late afternoon, there was active patrolling along the main avenues leading into the position.

Though these patrols sought information of the enemy, their main purpose was this: 1st Mar Div held itself to be under active CCF observation at all times and it sought to impress the enemy with its own aggressiveness.

These patrols were usually in company strength, though sometimes a re-enforced platoon was used. They moved by motor or on foot, according to conditions and the purpose of the moment.

These excursions usually did not extend beyond 1500 yards, though at Yudam-ni there was active patrolling up to five miles beyond the central position. The patrols always moved within covering by their artillery. They were accompanied by an Artillery FO, and whenever possible, attended by an OY aircraft, to assist the patrols' observation and communication with home base.

1st Mar Div believed that one consequence of its extensive patrol activity was that its main bases were never harassed by small enemy groups during the day.

Getting into the back country, the patrols in numerous instances were able to get positive information about enemy concentrations and the line of an impending attack.

The perimeters usually entered the night on a 50 percent alert basis, one man resting in each two-man foxhole, with inspecting teams making the rounds to insure this being done.

The weapons were given such special care as the sub-zero weather required (see further notes on this subject).

These were the general security tactics and procedures which characterized and invigorated the defense.

To describe in full the weapons usages which kept these bases, on the whole, inviolable is not within the scope of this analysis, since it would require a blow-by-blow description of how CCF's attack was met and countered at the company level. However, a great part of this detail of action has been collected from company and platoon leaders, and provides the substance for this evaluation in brief.

The salient note in the whole record of in-fighting during the campaign is found in the promptness and strength with which all supporting weapons were brought to bear in the decisive area of engagement whenever any part of the rifle line came under pressure by direct assault.

The curtain of fire—all the mortars, the artillery, and sometimes part of the armor joining—was dropped down across the portal before CCF had time to swarm in large numbers against any wide portion of the defending front. Thereby the attack was kept canalized and the CCF assault wave was denied immediate strong support.

In this, there was nothing radical or unorthodox. The defense at all points simply exploited the full advantages of the supporting weapons, using them in varying combinations so as to achieve the maximum effect, according to the manner in which the enemy attack was developing. It was war waged "according to the book" but done with such precision and power as to reilluminate the ancient truth that weapons when correctly used will invariably bring success. The morale effects upon the defenders of these stoutly resistant small "hedgehogs" were as pronounced as upon the CCF who were beaten down by the fire. It is an old and familiar story that the rifleman feels himself pretty much alone and unhelped when at close grips with the enemy. But from riflemen who manned 1st Mar Div's front lines in the several perimeters came abundant testimony that they were so impressed with the power and flexibility of their supporting fires as to be "absolutely confident" of turning back the CCF attack. In vouching for the morale effect upon themselves of these systematized fires, they spoke as individuals who had survived an ordeal rather than as Marines putting in a plug for their own methods.

Under the system used in 1st Mar Div, the platoon and company leaders are relieved of the complex task of plotting, planning and then directing supporting fires by the heavier weapons, in preparation for, and during the course of, the fire fight. This devolves upon the SAC (Supporting Arms Center) which operates at battalion level. Essentially the SAC Coordinator is a sort of assistant S-3 in charge of the plan of fires, both in the attack and on defense. In the normal situation, he operates at the battalion OP; when in perimeter and defending all around a circle, his station is at the CP, or the S-3 tent. During the organization of a defense, he accompanies the S-3 on initial reconnaissance; this gives him opportunity to familiarize himself with the front, spot the HMG's, and take note of the approaches which must be covered by artillery and mortar fire. When the reconnaissance is completed, the front lines are plotted on a situation map. The mortar and artillery officers are then told what fires to register. The actual conduct of fire is done by their FO's; when the registrations are completed, this information is relayed to the SAC and the concentrations are plotted on an overlay to the situation map. Also, when patrols move out, the SAC keeps their positions plotted so that supporting fires can be loosed quickly. Usually, the SAC Coordinator is an infantry officer. He ties in closely to the Tactical Air Control Center so that if there are targets on which his weapons are working that would also be suitable for attack by air, coordination will be immediate and complete.

1st Mar Div's battalions attribute a great measure of the effectiveness and total organization of their supporting fires to the perfecting of SAC's operations in the course of the campaign in Korea.

The enthusiasm for the technique is general in all ranks and particularly among the line companies.

Mechanics of the Attack

The main characteristic of 1st Mar Div in the attack is the care with which it elaborates the employment and synchronization of all weapons which will assist the rifle company or battalion to win ground at minimal cost.

In the typical situation, the rifle company has temporarily been brought in check by intense automatic rifle from the high ground, and the enemy deployment* is such as to indicate that the line cannot continue its advance without taking excessive losses from fire coming at it from several directions.

---

* It has been found that CCF tends toward this practice in the setting up of hilltop positions: Not infrequently the dug-in works along the hill crests are of lesser consequence, and are intended to draw attention away from the real strength in automatic weapons which is well-concealed in the saddles between the crests.

The company then calls for mortar fire on the position, meanwhile holding its ground.

Simultaneously, or immediately following the mortar fire, artillery works over the enemy ground from which the fire has been coming, as well as the ridges beyond it.

There is an air control officer with the company.

A number of planes have been called in and are on station. It is arranged that as the final rounds of artillery fall, the planes will make their first strikes at these same positions.

The infantry bounds forward as the planes begin to attack, or—depending upon proximity to the CCF position—starts to advance at the moment of the final impact.

This is not the rare or unusual instance of coordination between 1st Mar Div's rifle components and the supporting arms, in the attack.

It is the average procedure, and during operations in the north there were relatively few deviations from it. Attack after attack, by the company, battalion or regiment, was according to this same pattern.

Clear to the average rifleman was the proof that he was being helped by every agency possible.

That this conviction gave extraordinary impetus to the infantry attack would seem to be beyond question.

The multiplying of fires, and the combining of flat trajectory, angle and vertical missiles no doubt resulted in the killing of more CCF than would have been done by any part of this combination acting singly.

However, the chief findings have to do with morale values, particularly those redounding to the benefit of the attacker.

Line companies in the attack noted that artillery fire, even when generously used, and accurately delivered upon the target area, was not a marked depressant to CCF fire except at the moment when the shells were impacting. As these fires lifted, CCF automatic weapons immediately resumed the engagement.

With the air strike, however, the shock to the morale of the defender was noticeable and immediate. The position would go silent, even though CCF had not been eliminated by the combing and strafing. From the examination of repeated instances of this character, it is even possible to hypothesize that the shock interval, in which the defender is unable to command himself as to make use of such weapons as remain available to his hand, varies between 12 and 25 minutes, seemingly according to the extent of material damage and disarrangement done the defender.

The transcendent morale value deriving from close air support is best explained in the words of one battalion commander in 1st Mar Div: "An air strike puts new zest and determination in our line in a way that no amount of artillery fire delivered before our eyes could do. The men see our pilots; they watch them come in low and take terrible chances. It makes them want to go forward again. The effect is as if they were drawn by a magnet." Statements similar to this were made by many other leaders at platoon and company level; they spoke with reference to the effects achieved in tactical situations which they proceeded to describe in utmost detail.

The data on this cooperation between ground and air, on the incidents wherein it was applied, and on the techniques which made it possible, were collected as part of the basic operational study from which this analysis-in-brief has been extracted. They are not discussed at length here because the evaluation of tactical air does not come within the scope of this study.

March Requirement

During its attack southward from Hagaru-ri, 1st Mar Div directed that every able-bodied man, other than drivers, and gunners with the vehicles, move on foot, and be ready for service as a rifleman, or his equivalent, as needed.

It was ordered that no vehicle be left which might be capable of salvage; any wrecked vehicle could be abandoned only on permission of the senior commander present.

Today, it is a main point of pride throughout this Div that this order was published and followed.

Effects of Cold

Operations by 1st Mar Div north of Chinghung-ni provided one of the best opportunities for the study of effects of extreme cold on men, weapons and other equipment under actual combat conditions, of any American battle in modern times.

A vast amount of data, covering the varying aspects of this subject, has been collected and partially collated.

It permits of some broad generalizations and considerable specification.

1st Mar Div was as well clad and equipped for cold weather fighting as any US division is likely to be under existing T/E's and issues.

Moreover, its disciplines were such as to give the individual maximum chance for survival against the cold, and to spare him abnormal privation and rigor. Tentage was taken along, and was used to the full extent permitted by the fighting situation. Troops brought in from outpost, or coming in from sustained bouts with the cold during attack beyond the defensive perimeters, were rotated through warming tents. In these tents they were enabled to dry their socks and thaw-out shoepacs. Hot coffee was served there and hot C rations, after thawing in boiling water.

The wounded were kept in warming tents. When the tents began to overflow, those with lesser injuries were rotated back to the line, and thereafter watched, lest their condition worsen.

Cases of extreme shock or exhaustion—either from the intense cold or that combined with unusual exertion—were given 24 hours rest in warming tents before being returned to duty.

Such were some of the precautions taken to maintain the health and vigor of the command against the adverse weather. The results can be summarized as follows:

1. About 20 percent of the command suffered from respiratory ailments, including everything from bad colds to pneumonia. The medical authorities considered that this figure was low in view of the conditions.

2. "Combat fatigue" cases, in the degree that the man became permanently non-duty, were so rare as not to constitute a medical problem. Of relative frequency were the "shock" cases in which the individual could return to duty after 24 hours rest.

3. The division had about 2700 non-battle casualty (NBC) cases, of which approximately 2000 were frostbite cases. Of the latter, about 95 percent were foot cases. Most of the hand cases were mild. The ear cases were found to be due in most instances to carelessness. However, in taking survey of the foot cases, General Smith, his subordinate commanders, and the Regimental Surgeons, after questioning men, platoon leaders and others, and going into the attendant circumstances, arrived at the estimate that only 20 percent of these cases came of any carelessness on the part of the individuals, and 80 percent were due to the conditions of the fight and the inadequacy of the footwear. (See subsequent note on shoepac.)

4. A high percentage of men (uncounted) was lost to the line because of acute intestinal disorders induced by the eating of half-frozen C rations. This danger became so well known to the command that the biscuit component was at a premium. In the worst stages of the fighting, men on the line ate nothing else. The criteria showed that present field rations do not supply the needs of troops on the move in combat conditions of extreme cold weather.

Shock and Fatigue

The effects of the first cold blast, when the Division was moving north, surprised some of the attending surgeons. Among troops which had been on the line for several hours and then returned to the warming tents, they noted that there was a "severe shock reaction among many of the men." It was described in the following words: "These men by the hundreds came to the aid stations in a condition similar to what you see in men under terrific mortar or artillery pounding. There was a marked tremor which was not that simply of men shivering from cold; in some cases there was a marked suppression of the respiratory rate. They responded to stimulant. In the less serious cases a shot of brandy and a little stove heat brought them back fairly quickly. While in shock, there were marked mental and physical changes in these men. Many stared into space and did not seem to understand when they were spoken to. Others sobbed for a long period, saying nothing. But over a period of days, as the units became more accustomed to the extreme temperatures, we noted the disappearance of this shock reaction."

Cold, combined with acute physical exhaustion, continued, however, radically to influence the response of the individual, presenting hitherto unexplored problems for the command. The absolute limit was reached by 1st Battalion, 7th Marines, in its nighttime attack across country to the relief of Fox Company, 7th Rgt. Its commander, Lt. Col. Davis, bears witness that in the 20-degree-below-zero weather, as his forces continued to engage CCF, he found himself almost succumbing to the desire to do nothing. The bitter cold so froze his thought that he resorted "to checking everything two or three ways" fearing that his judgments were clouded. Aware that his men had been pushed almost to their extreme physical limit, he halted them, intending to go into perimeter defense. This was near midnight. However, within a few minutes he noticed that the effects of the cold were such that his troops were "folding completely" and he decided that the best choice was to keep moving. The force toiled on through the deep snows past several more ridges. At the last hill short of Fox Company's position, the command, reaching the crest, came into ground already held by CCF. Firing began, and Col. Davis made the first moves to get his people going in the attack. Yet as his companies topped the rise, under these conditions, he saw the files successively fall flat and remain motionless, like a line of dominoes going down when impulse is given to the first one. They stayed there "paying absolutely no attention to the fire breaking around them" and they had to be vigorously shaken and otherwise manhandled by their leaders before they would rise again.

However, after winning this fight on the high ground, and resting briefly on the crest, the battalion was able again to bound forward when morning came.

The Shoepac

The shoepac is condemned by all concerned in 1st Mar Div and is blamed for the greater part of the Division's NBC losses. Among men in the line, and among commanders and medical staff, the gist of the criticism is this: During the march, and while moving in the attack, the foot perspires heavily. When movement is checked for any reason, and the line comes to rest, the perspiration freezes. Ice actually forms within the shoe next to the liner. There is then no means of protecting the foot unless socks can be changed and the shoepac dried. Under combat conditions this is impossible a great part of the time.

Weapons Under Cold

Under sub-zero conditions the performance of the M1, the machine guns, and the 75mm recoilless, was sturdy, and in general, highly satisfactory.

Praise for the latter weapon is universal among 1st Mar Div battalions. They describe it as "indispensable" for hilltop fighting and far from finding men reluctant to use this weapon because it "might give away the position," all concerned reported that it is such a valuable fighting tool, particularly against enemy emplacements, that ranks have a particular enthusiasm for it. In use against bunkers and other gun positions, it was effective up to 1200 yards. The unanimous comment on the weapon is that "we need more of the same."

In the sub-zero fighting, the 105 mm howitzer would sometimes take two minutes to move back into position, thus markedly slowing the rate of fire.

There is considerable variation in the reports on the BAR, which variation may reflect differences in methods of maintenance under cold conditions. Battalions within 1st Marines used no oil, washed the guns in gasoline to clean them of all oil, fired them periodically to keep the weapon warm, and experienced no difficulty. On the other hand, there were companies within this same Rgt which used a light coating of oil, did not fire warm-ups, and still found the weapon working well from first to last. Fox Company, 7th Marines, had its BAR's go out night after night in repeated actions, yet during daylight inspection was unable to find the source of the difficulty; care and cleaning did not help. Other units reported similar experiences. On the average, however, BAR performance was good, and the weapon retained the confidence of its users. The variations in performance, and in methods of maintenance under cold conditions (in 1st Mar Div as in 2nd Inf Div) may point up the need for further study and experiment looking to the best possible solution.

The carbine does not have the confidence of 1st Mar Div's commanders or line. The universal comment is that when the weapon was changed to include automatic features, it became "too delicate." The optimum performance by any line company in 1st Mar Div would show about 30 percent failure on the part of the carbine. Troops discarded the weapon as rapidly as they could get hold of M1's. There was also complaint about its lack of "stopping" characteristics. Junior leaders tell of putting two or three bullets into a CCF fighter at less than 50-foot range, and of seeing the target wince and still keep on coming.

In general, the fire performance by the family of mortars was highly satisfactory to 1st Mar Div's battalions, with a number of the latter expressing especial appreciation of the 4.2. They felt that they could make good use of this weapon in greater numbers, particularly if it was lightened with a view to making it more portable, while still producing the same heavy burst at shorter ranges. However, the mortars in all sizes, when subjected to high rates of fire, tended to "beat themselves to death" against the frozen ground. The seat of greatest difficulty was in the base plates which buckled from corner to corner, or cracked, or broke apart. But there was also trouble with the elevating screws which shook loose in the cold and then eroded rapidly. The data also show that firing pins broke so excessively that Ordnance Battalion had to resort to making them on the spot. The 4.2 stood up better than the lighter mortars in these respects. As to tubes, none blew up, but the armorers noted that one effect of the cold seemed to be deeper scoring by the fins, resulting in excessive muzzle flash. The most intensive use of mortars throughout the operation was by 1st Marine Rgt. The 60's, for example, fired continuously for about 14 nights. At the conclusion of operations, all mortars within this Regiment had to be replaced in whole or in part. None remained in sound operating condition.

1st Marines also resorted to washing machine guns with gasoline. The oil preservant became very heavy and slowed the action of the gun until it was warm. The HMG's were fired at 20-30 minute intervals, irrespective of situation, to make sure of operating. The antifreeze in this weapon is set to approximately 30° below, but it covers only the barrel. Barrel extensions, bolt and buffer groups are unprotected. Frost forms on the metal, and tends to freeze the gun solid; periodic firing was therefore considered necessary.

Ammunition for the 3.5 rocket launcher cracked wide open on the coldest days. It is supposed to be set for 20° below, according to those who know this subject. Personnel tried to protect it by burying it below the frost line, but the expedient did not work.

Major General Smith noted that the helicopter lost some of its hovering characteristics in the cold, thin air, and tended to land with a hard bump, dropping the last 10 feet. At least one helicopter was washed out in this manner.

Also, during the air drops, bundles tore away from their chutes before the silk could open in a high percentage of cases, perhaps 1 in 10. It is a question whether this was due to the cold in combination with altitude, or to some other condition. However, in the ammo bundles which dropped free into the perimeter at Yudam-ni, the retrievers took note that the artillery and mortar ammo dropped in wooden cases could almost invariably be salvaged, while that dropped in metal cases was destroyed beyond possibility of use.

Sources and Bibliography

Material for this book was derived, in part, from the following sources:

Asian Division, Library of Congress, Washington, D.C.

Captured Enemy Documents, National Archives, Suitland, Maryland.

Center for Military History, U.S. Army, Washington, D.C.

Foreign Broadcast Information Service Daily Reports, on microfilm at the Library of Congress: these are daily translations of Chinese, North Korean, and Russian radio broadcasts and news releases.

General Douglas A. MacArthur Memorial Archives, Norfolk, Virginia.

George C. Marshall Memorial Library, Lexington, Virginia.

History Division, Bolling Air Force Base, Washington, D.C.

History Division Headquarters, Marine Corps, Navy Yard, Washington, D.C.

Institute of Military History, U.S. Army, Carlisle Barracks, Carlisle, Pennsylvania. The Institute has three collections that were most helpful: the personal papers and records of Lt. General Edward L. Almond, Major General Charles Willoughby, and Brigadier General S. L. A. Marshall. The S. L. A Marshall collection was especially useful because it includes interviews with members of the 1st Battalion, 1st Marines, which were taken at Mason, Korea, in December 1950 shortly after the close of the Chosin Reservoir Campaign.

Personal interviews with many persons named in the text.

Official Histories of the Korean War

AUSTRALIA

O'Neil, Robert, *Australia in the Korean War, 1950–1953: Strategy and Diplomacy,* The Australia War Memorial and Australian Government Publicity Service, Canberra, 1981.

CANADA

Wood, Herbert F. *Strange Battleground,* Department of National Defense, Ottowa, 1966.

PEOPLE'S REPUBLIC OF CHINA

The Great Resist America and Aid Korea Movement, composed by the People's Republic Congress, People's Publishing Co., Peking, 1954.

REPUBLIC OF KOREA

The History of the United Nations Forces in the Korean War, vols. 1–6, The War History Compilation Committee, The Ministry of National Defense, Seoul, 1972–77.

UNITED STATES

U.S. Air Force: Futnell, Robert F., *The United States Air Force in Korea, 1950–1953,* Duell, Sloan and Pearce, New York, 1961.

U.S. Army: *The United States Army in the Korean War* (U.S. Government Printing Office)—Hermes, Walter G., *Truce Tent and Fighting Front,* 1960; Appleman, Roy E., *South to the Naktong, North to the Yalu,* 1961; Gugeler, Russell A., *Combat Actions in Korea,* 1970; Schnabel, James F., *Policy and Direction: The First Year,* 1972.

U.S. Marine Corps: *U.S. Marine Operations in Korea* (U.S. Printing Office)—Montross, Lynn, and Canzona, Capt. Nicholas A., *The Pusan Perimeter,* 1954; Montross, Lynn, and Canzona, Capt. Nicholas A., *The Inchon-Seoul Campaign,* 1957; Montross, Lynn, and Canzona, Capt. Nicholas A., *The Chosin Reservoir Campaign,* 1957; Montross, Lynn, Kuokka, Maj. Hubard D., and Hicks, Maj. Norman W., *The East Central Front,* 1962; Meid, Lt. Col. Pat, and Yingling, Maj. James W., *Operations in West Korea,* 1972.

U.S. Navy: Field, James A., Jr., *United States Naval Operations in Korea* (U.S. Government Printing Office), 1962.

Books

Beech, Keyes, *Tokyo and Points East*. Doubleday, Garden City, 1954.

Benét, Stephen Vincent, *John Brown's Body*. Holt, Rinehart and Winston, New York, 1937.

Bradley, Omar N., and Clay, Blair, *A General's Life*. Simon & Schuster, New York, 1983.

Clark, Mark W., *From the Danube to the Yalu*. Harper and Brothers, New York, 1954.

Collins, J. Lawton, *War in Peacetime*. Houghton Mifflin Company, Boston, 1969.

Davis, Burke, *The Life of Lt. General Lewis Chesty Puller*. Little, Brown & Company, Ltd., Boston, 1962.

Duncan, David, *This is War*. Harper and Brothers, New York, 1951.

Foreign Relations of the United States, 1950. Volume VII: *Korea*. United States Government Printing Office, Washington, 1976.

Geer, Andrew, *The New Breed: The Story of the United States Marines in Korea*. Harper and Brothers, New York, 1952.

Griffith, Samuel B., II, *The Chinese People's Liberation Army*. McGraw-Hill Book Company, New York, 1967.

Hammel, Eric, *Chosin. Heroic Ordeal of the Korean War*. Vanguard, New York, 1981.

Han Suyin, *The Morning Deluge—Mao Tse-tung and the Chinese Revolution 1893–1954*. Little, Brown and Company, Ltd., Boston, 1972.

Heinl, Robert Debs, Jr., Colonel, *Victory at High Tide*. J. B. Lippincott Company, Philadelphia, 1968.

Heller, Francis H., *The Korean War—A 25-Year Perspective*. edited by the Harry S. Truman Library Institute for National and International Affairs, The Regents Press of Kansas, Lawrence, 1977.

Higgins, Trumbell, *Korea and the Fall of MacArthur: A Précis in Limited War*. Oxford University Press, New York, 1960.

Joy, C. Turner, *How Communists Negotiate*. Macmillan, New York, 1955.

Klein, Donald W., and Clark, Ann B., *Biographic Dictionary of Chinese Communism, 1921–65*, Harvard University Press, Cambridge, 1971.

Leckie, Robert, *Conflict: The History of the Korean War, 1950–1953*. G. P. Putnam & Sons, New York, 1962.

Leckie, Robert, *The March to Glory*. World Publishing Company, New York, 1960.

MacArthur, Douglas A., *Reminiscences*, McGraw-Hill Book Company, New York, 1964.

Mao Tse-tung, *Talk with the American Correspondent Anna Louise Strong*, Foreign Language Press, Peking, 1961.

Mao Tse-tung, *On the Protracted War*, Foreign Language Press, Peking, 1954.

Manchester, William, *American Caesar—Douglas MacArthur, 1880–1964*, Little, Brown and Company, Ltd., Boston, 1978.

Manchester, William, *The Glory and the Dream—A Narrative History of America, 1932–1972*, Little, Brown and Company, Ltd., Boston, 1973.

Marshall, S. L. A., *Battle at Best*, Morrow, New York, 1963.

Marshall, S. L. A., *The River and the Gauntlet—Defeat of the 8th Army by Chinese Communist Forces, November 1950, in the Battle of Chongchan River, Korea*, Willis, Morrow & Company, New York, 1953.

Miller, Merle, *Plain Speaking—An Oral Biography of Harry S. Truman*, Berkley Publishing Company, New York, 1973.

Moorad, George, *Lost Peace in China*, E. P. Dutton and Company, 1949.

Moskin, J. Robert, *The U.S. Marine Corps Story*, McGraw-Hill Book Company, New York, 1977.

Rees, David, *Korea, The Limited War*, St. Martin's Press, New York, 1964.

Ridgeway, Matthew B., *The Memoirs of Matthew B. Ridgeway* (as told to Harold H. Martin), Harper and Bros., New York, 1956.

Ridgeway, Matthew B., *The Korean War*, Doubleday, Garden City, 1967.

Riggs, Robert B., *Red China's Fighting Hoards*, The Military Service Publishing Company, Harrisburg, Pa., 1951.

Santoli, Al, *To Bear Any Burden*, E. P. Dutton, Inc., New York, 1985.

Schnabel, James F., and Watson, Robert, J., *The History of the Joint Chiefs of Staff*, vol. 3: *The Korean War*, Michael Glazier, Inc., Wilmington, Delaware, n.d.

Spanier, John W., *The Truman-MacArthur Controversy and the Korean War*, Harvard University Press, Cambridge, 1959.

Sun-tzu, *The Art of War*, trans. Samuel B. Griffith, Oxford University Press, London, 1963.

Taylor, Maxwell D., *Responsibility and Response*, Harper & Row, New York, 1967.

Truman, Harry S., *Memoirs*, 2 vols., Doubleday, Garden City, 1955–56.

Truong Nhu Tang, *A Vietcong Memoir*, Harcourt Brace Jovanovich, San Diego, 1985.

Tsou, Tang, *America's Failure in China, 1941–50,* University of Chicago Press, Chicago, 1963.

Walker, Richard L., *China under Communism: The First Five Years,* Yale University Press, New Haven, 1955.

Whitney, Courtney, *MacArthur: His Rendezvous with History,* Alfred A. Knopf, New York, 1956.

Who's Who in Communist China, Union Research Institute, Hong Kong, 1966.

Willoughby, Charles, *MacArthur, 1941–1951,* McGraw Hill Book Company, New York, 1954.

Wiltz, John Edward, *The MacArthur Inquiry,* vol. 5, Chelsea House, New York, 1975.

Documents, Periodicals, and Articles

Allied Translator and Interpreter Service, "Far East Command, Enemy Documents: Korean Operations," Intelligence File, HQMC Historical and Document File Section, National Archives, Suitland, Maryland.

Allied Translator and Interpreter Section, Interrogation Reports, MacArthur Archives, Norfolk, Virginia, and National Archives, Suitland, Maryland.

Annex Baker to Division, Special Action Report, from Assistant Chief-of-Staff to Commanding General, 1st Marine Division, 15 February, 1951. HQMC Historical Branch, Washington, D.C.

Barrow, Robert A., General, "A Company, 1st Battalion, 1st Marines, 1st Marine Division (Reinforced), in Korea, 15 September-December, 1950" (unpublished).

Bradley, Omar N., General, USA Compiler, Substance of Statements Made at Wake Island Conference on October 1, 1950, Washington, Government Printing Office, 1951, MacArthur Archives, Norfolk, Virginia.

"A Brief History of the First Marines," USMC Historical Branch, Washington, D.C. 1968.

Department of State, *American Foreign Policy, 1950–1955,* Vols. I and II, Department of State, Document 6446, 1957.

DePuy, Jr., W. E., "A Re-Examination of the Chinese Decision to Enter the Korean War," J. Watson Noah Associates, Inc. (unpublished).

First Marine Division, FMF, Special Action Report, Wonsan—Hamhung—Chosin, 8th of October, 1950–15th of December, 1950, HQMC Historical, Washington, D.C.

Fleet Marine Force, Pacific, Chinese Communist Forces Tactics in

Korea, 22nd March, 1951, R&O File, HQMC Historical, Washington, D.C.

Historical Diaries, Commanding General, 1st Marine Air Wing, October-December, 1950, Command Diary (Korea), Type B Report File (Diary File), HQMC, Washington, D.C.

Historical Diaries, 1st Air Delivery Platoon, FMF, October-December, 1950, Diary File, HQMC, Historical, Washington, D.C.

Historical Diaries, Marine Air Group 12, October-December, 1950, Diary File, HQMC Historical, Washington, D.C.

Historical Diaries, Marine Air Group 33, October-December, 1950, Diary File, HQMC Historical, Washington, D.C.

Historical Diaries, VMF–212, October-December, 1950, Diary File, HQMC Historical, Washington, D.C.

Historical Diaries, VMF–214–312–323, (n) – 513, (N) – 542, Diary File, HQMC Historical, Washington, D.C.

Intelligence Summary, General Headquarters, Far East Command, Military Intelligence Section, General Staff, Norfolk, Virginia, MacArthur Archives, June 1950–March 1951.

Interview, Major Warren P. Nichols, Operations Officer, Marine Flight Squadron, 323, 30th July, 1951, HQMC Historical, Washington, D.C.

Joint Daily Situation Reports, Department of the Army, October-December 1950, Reports and Orders (1950), R&O File, HQMC Historical, Washington, D.C.

Life, June 1950–June 1951.

MacArthur, Douglas, General, U.S.A. "Eleventh Report of the Operations in Korea of United Nations Forces, 31st January, 1951," Washington, Government Printing Office, 1951.

McDonough, Gordon L., Letter to General MacArthur, September 18, 1950, MacArthur Archives, Norfolk, Virginia.

"The Marine Corps Fights for Its Life," Congressional Record, 81st Congress, 1st Session, February 9, 1949.

The Marine Corps Reserve—A History, Division of Reserve, HQMC, Washington, D.C., 1966.

Marshall, George C., "Memorandum for the Executive Secretary, National Security Council, December 13th, 1950, 'U.S. Position Regarding a Cease-Fire in Korea,'" George C. Marshall Research Library, Lexington, Virginia.

Marshall, S. L. A., Interview of "Chesty" Puller, Carlisle Barracks, Carlisle, Pennsylvania (unpublished).

Marshall, S. L. A., "CCF in the Attack, 5 January 1951, A Study Based

Upon the Operations of 2nd Infantry Division Rifle Companies in the Battle of Kunu-ri," November 1950 (unpublished).

Marshall, S. L. A., "CCF in the Attack, 27 January 1951, A Study Based on the Operations of the 1st Marine Division in the Koto-ri, Hagaru, Yudam-ni Area, 20th of November–10th of December, 1950," R&O File, Washington, D.C.

Marshall, S. L. A., Letter to Lt. Col. Nihart, January 24, 1951. Lt. Col. Cayle, USMC, Assistant Director of Marine Corps History, Washington, D.C.

"Mobilization of the Marine Corps Reserve in the Korean Conflict, 1950–1951," USMC Historical Branch, Washington, D.C.

Newsweek. June 1950–June 1951.

New York Times. June 1950–June 1951.

"Notes on the Operations of the 1st Marine Division During the First Nine Months of the Korean War, 1950–1951." Manuscript File, HQMC Historical, Washington, D.C.

Outgoing Message, Tokyo Headquarters, General MacArthur, November 9, 1950, MacArthur Archives, Norfolk, Virginia.

Outgoing Message, General Headquarters, United Nations Command, November 18, 1950, MacArthur Archives, Norfolk, Virginia.

Outgoing Message, General Headquarters, United Nations Command, December 10, 1950, MacArthur Archives, Norfolk, Virginia.

Outgoing Message, General Headquarters, United Nations Command, November 25, 1950, MacArthur Archives, Norfolk, Virginia.

Periodic Operations Reports, October-December, 1950, Correspondence File, 1st Marine Division (Korea), HQMC Historical, Washington, D.C.

Records from Division of History and Museums, Headquarters, United States Marine Corps, Washington, D.C., "Get the Marines," "The Marine Corps, and its Struggle for Survival, 1946–1947."

Reports, Messages, Journals, Correspondence, Orders, and Miscellaneous Matter, Correspondence File, 1st Marine Division (Korea), HQMC Historical, Washington, D.C.

Roanoke Times and World News. June 1950–June 1951.

Smith, Oliver P., Major General, USMC, "Chronicle of the Operations of the 1st Marine Division During the First Nine Months of the Korean War, 1950–1951," MS Manuscript File, HQMC Historical, Washington, D.C.

Smith, Oliver P., Major General, USMC, Oral History, HQMC Historical, Washington, D.C.

Time. Time Inc., June 1950–June 1951.

Terrain Handbook of Korea, U.S. Military Intelligence War Department, September, 1945, U.S. Government Printing Office, 1945, Washington, D.C.

Truman, Harry S., President, Letter to Congressman McDonough, August 29, 1950, MacArthur Archives, Norfolk, Virginia.

U.S. Congressional Record, Washington, D.C., January 1950–June 1951.

U.S. Far Eastern Command, General Headquarters, Order of Battle Information, Chinese Communist Forces in Korea, USMC, Historical, Washington, D.C.

U.S. Marine Corps Board, Marine Corps Board Study: "An Evaluation of the Influence of Marine Corps Forces on the Course of the Korean War (August 4, 1950–December 15, 1950)," 2 Vols., copy in R&O File, HQMC Historical, Washington, D.C.

U.S. News & World Report, June 1950–June 1951.

Unit Reports, October–December, 1950, Correspondence File, 1st Marine Division (Korea) HQMC Historical, Washington, D.C.

Van Fleet, James A., "The Truth About Korea," *Life*, May, 1953.

"What Price Unity?" The Defense Unification Battle, 1947–1950: The Navy, Division of History and Museums, USMC, Washington, D.C.

Wright, E. K., Brig. General, "General Headquarters, Far East Command, Outgoing Message, May, 1950: Strategic Consequences Resulting from Capture of Formosa by The Chinese Communists," MacArthur Archives, Norfolk, Virginia.